ISABEL COLEGATE is
bestselling books incl
Orlando Trilogy, *The S*
recently *Winter Journey*.

A Pelican
in the Wilderness

HERMITS,
SOLITARIES AND RECLUSES

*A man that Studies Happiness must sit alone like a
Sparrow upon the Hous Top, and like a Pelican in the Wilderness*

Thomas Traherne (1637–74)

ISABEL COLEGATE

HarperCollins*Publishers*

HarperCollins*Publishers*
77–85 Fulham Palace Road,
Hammersmith, London w6 8jb
www.**fire**and**water**.com

This paperback edition 2003

First published by HarperCollins*Publishers* 2002
3 5 7 9 8 6 4 2

A catalogue record for this book
is available from the British Library

ISBN 0-00-653188-1

Set in Postscript Linotype Minion with Bauer Bodoni display by
Rowland Phototypesetting Limited, Bury St Edmunds, Suffolk
Printed and bound in Great Britain by
Clays Ltd, St Ives plc

ACKNOWLEDGEMENTS

Writing fiction is a solitary business. Trying to tell someone about a novel in progress is like telling them a dream you have had, which I suppose is what it is. The eyes of the listener glaze over pretty soon. Writing about hermits has been agreeably different; much of this book comes from unexpected conversations and borrowed books, shared discoveries or patient explanations from busy people who know far more than I do.

I sought out Donald Allchin after hearing him talk on the radio and he was most generous with his help on the subject of contemporary Christian hermits. My daughter Emily Azis rescued me when I was in danger of disappearing beneath toppling piles of books, and for only too brief an interval in her own teaching career introduced order into my researches. I talked over aspects of the book many times with her and with Andrew McCall. I should also like to thank the Sisters of the Society of the Sacred Cross at Tymawr, particularly their librarian Sister Cara Mary, and the Tibetan Buddhist monastery of Samyeling and their Abbot Lama Yeshe. The Knight of Glin and the Irish Georgian Group welcomed us on their tour of Lebanon and Syria.

I should also like to thank Bronwen Astor, James Ayres, Tommy Bates and Jane Torday, the Duke of Beaufort, Julia Bolton Holloway, Barnaby Briggs, Joshua Briggs, Matthew Conolly, John Crook, Beth Elliot, Father Aidan Gilman, Sister Andrea de Guevel, Esther de Waal, Jill Hamilton, Sister John Francis, John Harris, Eileen Harris, Aidan Hart, Richard Hills, Father Philip Jebb, Richard Jones, John Keegan, Gerard Kilroy, Olga Lawrence, Deirdre Levi, the late Peter Levi, Sister Maximilian, Felicity Milford, Anthony Mitchell, Jeremy

Musson, Milo Parmoor, Eugene Stockton, Smansnid Svasti, Antonia Thynne, Christopher Thynne, Brigid Waddams, Christopher Woodward and Ian Wyatt. I should also like to thank for their friendly attention those hermits who wish to remain anonymous.

I am grateful to Michael Fishwick, Kate Johnson and Janet Law of HarperCollins, to Chris Carduff of Counterpoint Press in America, and to my agents Caroline Dawnay in London and Peter Matson in New York.

CONTENTS

INTRODUCTION

Autumn is a good time to see the gardens at Stourhead in Wiltshire. The trees are beautiful and the rhododendrons are not in bloom. If you walk round the lake, past the classical temple and back towards the bridge, you can turn off to your right and take the path up towards the Temple of Apollo at the top of the hill. Halfway up to your right there is a path leading to a clearing where Sir Henry Hoare, at a fairly late stage in the creation of his New Elysium, around 1770, caused a hermitage to be built, reminiscent perhaps of Arcadia rather than Elysium. He wrote to his grand-daughter Harriet:

> I am building a Hermitage above the Rock & when you are about a Quarter part up the Walk from the Rock to the Temple of Apollo you turn short to the right and so zig zag up to it and thence go under the Trees to the Temple ... It is to be lined inside and out with old Gouty nobbly oakes, the Bark on, which Mr. Groves & my neighbours are so kind to give me & Mr. Chapman a clergyman showed me one yesterday called Judge Wyndham's seat which I take to be of the Year of Our Lord 1000 & I am not quite sure it is not Anti Diluvian. I believe I shall put it in to be myself The Hermit.

In fact, it seems that the winding path which led to the Temple of Apollo actually passed through the hermitage, which formed a kind of tunnel. The whole thing was dismantled in 1814, but the Swedish landscape gardener Frederik Magnus Piper made drawings in 1779 which survive. The situation had been suggested by Charles Hamilton, who had his own hermitage at Painshill. The path was lined with oak trunks, 'with the upturned roots intertwined, which look like natural peristyles'. The oaks trunks which lined the inside of the building had their splayed roots joined at the top, as in a wigwam. There was a room to one side, furnished as a druid's cell; on the other side was a view over the whole extent of the park.

The Stourhead hermitage was one of the more eccentric, as well as one of the largest, of the retreats which sprang up in gentlemen's parks all over England in the eighteenth century. Many of them were made of wood and liable to rot, or they were concealed in dark corners of steep woodland where time and a few gentle land-slides have buried them, but enough remain to show how powerful was their appeal at the time. Some kind of game was being played here, or fairy story invented, or fruitful fantasy indulged. If it was more than simply a small step sideways into a childhood never quite lost, what was it that the hermit stood for in the play of ideas which so enchanted the eighteenth-century gentleman? Here is the classical world, the temples and groves, the measured walks, the echoes of the classical authors learned at school – and in wanders a figure quite at odds with all of it. He comes from another world. He has no possessions. He is the Green Man, personification of the ancient forest, he is Enkiddu the wild man who was the friend of Gilgamesh; at the same time he is the holy man in the desert. He is Ishmael the outcast and he is the disenchanted leader – Timon of Athens, the Emperor Charles V – he is even perhaps the ultimate reproach, the shadow over the bright clarity of the classical world, the voice in the wilderness which says blessed are the meek. Whatever he is, he has always attracted attention, sometimes awe, sometimes envy, usually respect. To our extremely gregarious species, the solitary is a challenge.

The eighteenth-century hermitage was seen as a rustic retreat for those moments when its proprietor or his guests felt like indulg-ing their melancholy or communing with nature, whose wilder aspects had recently become less terrible and more fashionable. It was also not unusual to install a hired hermit, so that when a party went walking in the woods a suitably ragged and outlandish figure would be discovered sitting there, ready to entertain or alarm the company with appropriate platitudes. Picnics were quite in order too, with servants to supply them. Romantic trysts, disguises, false friars and innocent maidens feature largely in the fiction of the time. All this was part of the game. A hermitage in a landscape played with sexual intrigue, as well as with nature and solitude, history and the idea of holiness.

The holy hermit has been there since time immemorial, somewhere up in the misty Chungsan hills of China, or wrapped in yak-skins in a cave among the Himalayan snows, or wandering through the crowds by the Ganges at Benares, or quiet in his hut in the deepest Russian forests. Until a few years ago there was an English woman living in a cave somewhere high up in Ladakh, another near Assisi; hermits are to be found in the middle of lonely Scottish moors, or for that matter at the bottom of quiet gardens in Godalming. The extent to which the solitary religious life is lived today is probably known only to the hermits' respective sustaining networks; by the nature of their calling they are unobtrusive. Nevertheless, the idea so beautifully expressed by Bellini or Dürer or any other of the many painters who have depicted St Francis in the wilderness or St Jerome in his cave, with his books before him on a rustic desk and his lion asleep at his feet, gives rise to notions of solitude, closeness to nature, a life of study and contemplation, which have an immediate appeal even to those who know that the nostalgia they feel is for a life they would never in reality choose for themselves.

The eighteenth-century antiquarian found it irresistible. The architect Sir John Soane made a 'Monk's Parlour' for an imaginary hermit in the basement of his house in Lincoln's Inn Fields. He filled it with Gothic oddments and sat there from time to time to write or muse. Most writers need solitude in order to concentrate; composers do too, though perhaps Mahler was extreme in requiring the cowbells to be muffled as he sat in his hut at the end of the garden in the Austrian Tyrol to write his Third Symphony. The poet, the philosopher, the nature lover and the seeker after

God, feel, in Wordsworth's phrase, that 'something far more deeply interfused' which the child making a raft on a pond and setting off to find an unknown island – like Richard Jefferies' Bevis in *Bevis: The Story of a Boy* – also knows, though probably does not articulate. But there is also the resentful hermit, who has eaten sour grapes and is not serene at all, who rejects the world in disgust or with a sense of failure and retreats into a distorted landscape of nightmare, tortured by malice and as often as not, the very rich having a tendency to fall into this category, counting his money.

It may be that solitude came to seem desirable for the average man or woman of sensibility in the eighteenth century only as a result of changed attitudes towards the wilderness. Rousseau's influence was enormous, all over Europe and America, though he himself said he would die of boredom if he had to be a hermit for long. In the nineteenth century the Byronic ideal – Manfred gazing over the lonely Abruzzi – and Wordsworth's attitude to nature affected more than fashionable poetic notions. The solemn John Stuart Mill in 1848 wrote about the importance of preserving places where people could be alone. 'Solitude, in the sense of being often alone, is essential to any depth of meditation or character . . . solitude in the presence of natural beauty and grandeur is the cradle of thoughts and aspirations which are not only good for the individual, but which society could ill do without.' Later on, George Macaulay Trevelyan, the historian whose passionate support was one of the founding bases of the National Trust, did not regard solitude as something for poets or contemplatives only. He thought of it as a universal need, something which from time to time refreshed the spirit of all active human beings and without which they were in danger of losing touch with the springs of their being. One can carry one's solitude with one, as many experienced hermits who have contact with the outside world know very well, and as most poets I would suppose know too, but in the modern Western world solitude is undervalued, and the need for it forgotten. To wish to be alone is thought odd, a sign of failure or neurosis; but it is in solitude that the self meets itself, or, if you like, its God, and from there that it goes out to join the communal dance. No amount of group therapy, study of interpersonal relationships, self-improvement exercises, personal training in the gym, can assuage the loneliness of those who cannot bear to be alone.

Even if we recognize our need for solitude, whether occasional or more frequent or in rare cases perpetual, even if we encourage children to let it be part of their childhood, will there still be solitary places? Who has not at one time or other in some beautiful surroundings heard, as I did once in the upper cloister at Silos in Spain, the tramp, tramp, tramp of the future on the stairs before thirty French schoolchildren with clipboards at the ready burst chattering into the silence? Car parks and visitor centres proliferate; do we save places from neglect only to destroy them by another sort of negligence? As long ago as the mid-nineteenth century, the great Staretz Macarius of Optina in Russia wrote: 'The forests which surround our monasteries must be preserved from destruction by all means in order to prevent the word "wilderness" from finally losing its meaning.' At about the same time in America, Henry David Thoreau was asserting: 'In Wildness is the preservation of the world.' How much heavier is the responsibility of hard-pressed Europe, and in particular of tiny, over-populated England.

Ruskin, who described as well as anyone the joy in nature which he nevertheless called indescribable, wrote: 'I could only feel this perfectly when I was alone; and then it would often make me shiver from head to foot with the joy and fear of it, when after being some time away from hills, I first got to the shore of a mountain river, where the brown water circled among the pebbles, or when I saw the first swell of distant land against the sunset, or the first low broken wall, covered with mountain moss.' He wrote of what he called the sanctity of nature, but it was not for him a religious sanctity. It has been so, and is, for some; for others it is only a feeling that most things can be sorted out after a long solitary walk in the country. What one might call the hermit tendency constitutes a thin but uninterrupted thread through history, a pull of the tide towards some other moon, a nostalgia for paradise or a hope of heaven. Whether for a poet or a misanthrope, a mystic or a seeker for a moment's silence, there has always been a need for a hermitage.

I live in a house on a hill, a mile or two outside the town. We look over a green valley, with a small river at the bottom. Three years ago – that is to say, a long time after we came to live here – we were able to buy the big field which surrounds us and the tangled wood which constitutes one side of a narrow valley to the east of the house. This valley has no road in it, only a footpath and a stream, and its sides are so steep that until you come upon it you would hardly know it is there. At one end the stream widens into a lake, belonging to the local water authority, and at the other end the finger of green field pushes through long abandoned fuller's earth works into the outskirts of the town.

Our newly acquired piece of land had been neglected for many years, nettles and brambles encroaching always a little further, so that the tenant farmer ploughed an ever-decreasing patch of hillside on which to grow rape or linseed. When we decided, with his agreement, to go back to grass, it seemed worth doing only if we restored the former boundaries, so an elephantine grabber arrived, which scrunched up thickets of bramble and undergrowth and nosed them into big heaps for burning. Kevin, the digger's mahout, manoeuvred with some delicacy round the edges of the field, avoiding the wildflower patch and the best of the blackberry bushes, and giving a wide berth to the island of fuller's earth which slips sandily down the hill, uncultivable and therefore having always sprouted what it liked, and sheltered what liked it, in the way of birds and rabbits and passing badgers and foxes. These of course were much put out by the depredations elsewhere of the elephant machine. Two partridges took to sitting on the wall by the house, complaining noisily, blackbirds fussed endlessly whether at the loss of their accustomed nesting places or the continuing presence of the tawny owl, and a pair of roe deer, crossing the field to their usual drinking-place, stopped and stared more in curiosity than in fear before leaping elegantly away to take cover in a clump of trees.

We left the blackthorn thickets by the edge of the wood, and planted new trees beyond them on the bare patch of ground which the adders favoured, above the old railway cutting. As far as the wood itself was concerned, the first task was more or less archaeological. We first of all established, with expert help, that it was not what is classified as 'ancient woodland', though there were a few fine old trees in it. It had been planted, apparently, as an ornamental wood, perhaps in the form of informal groves round the older trees, and there had been walks laid out in it, though now they were hard to discern. Since this planting had been done two hundred years or so ago, there had also been, as fashion dictated, an ornamental hermitage.

The restoration of a modest degree of order, though I knew it to be necessary, had at the same time rather dismayed me. I had not been a hermit in the wood but I had been a perennial trespasser; it had become, over thirty years or so, deeply familiar to me. I knew it in all seasons. Dogs in their due order of succession had accompanied me there, been rash with badgers or inefficient with rabbits; I knew which tree on the outskirts the buzzard frequented, and where beside the stream there was usually a pair of grey wagtails, and sometimes a dipper. It did not seem to matter that when the garlic overran the bluebells I frequently fell down because it was so slippery, or that certain ways through the trees became gradually increasingly hard to penetrate in the absence of any kind of path. I was wrong to be dismayed. This was not the sort of wilderness which needed to be untamed; after all, as the expert told us, it had always been artificial, a game, or a dream, or a folly.

We had always known there was a ruined tower. 'On an abrupt part of the brow which overlooks the hollow at the bottom of which a brook murmurs along a rocky channel,' we had read in a guidebook to the area, written in 1791, '[stands] . . . an elegant building called the Priory, with gothick windows and a circular embattled tower, in which is a commodious tea-room, and offices below.' Very little remains of it, and even the tower is dangerously eaten away by time, but it still just stands, and shows its pointed pinnacle above the trees quite as if the Sleeping Beauty slept beneath it. The same guidebook goes on to say: 'At a little distance from this, under a thick mass of shade, stands a rustick hermitage on the brow of the steep descent. The whole surrounding scenery is highly picturesque and romantick.' Of this building we could see no sign.

There seemed at first no sign either of the so-called 'graded walks', but the plans which had been made at the various times at which the property had changed hands did show a few dotted lines, examination of which revealed on one of them a minute semi-circle, a sort of tiny blister. It seemed hardly big enough to signify a hermitage, but something more modest might have been there, a hermit's cell perhaps, even a cave. The whole project was on a small scale, the wood about fifteen acres, no Stourhead estate; it seemed worth investigation. The place was not easy to reach, being on the steepest part of the hill and extremely slippery in wet weather. Later we made a path, or rather rediscovered one, because as soon as we stood there and looked back we could see that the bushy lime trees must once have bordered a marked descent. Then we saw the stones, lying scattered. The place is full of stones, but these were marked by the imprint of shells, the sort of stones you might gather to make a rustic hermit's cell. If it had ever been there it was certainly buried, but the damp earth on this steep hillside might well have slipped down over the years. We began to dig, with the help of Ian, a stonemason we had known ever since one day, years ago, he had come in to tell us our wall beside the road was a disgrace. When we came to the top of a fireplace we knew we were right.

The hermit's cell stands now where it was built, stone replaced on mossy stone. No new material was used, except to make the roof. The design was clearly a common one of the period; there are several illustrations with which to compare it. The roof might originally have been quite a solid affair, because there are some stone tiles lying around which might have been used, but this seemed beyond our capacities and it was more usual at the time to use thatch. In the meantime we cut poles from the nearby trees and Ian went to the Somerset levels to find withies discarded by the basket-makers and wove them in and out of the poles; it looks authentically rustic and has no pretensions to being waterproof. There is a rock outside the doorway on which the hermit probably sat to dispense wisdom to passers-by; you can hear the stream from it, and glimpse the water through the trees. One day we should clear the view; the shade is still too thick for all but the rarest summer day. But you can sit on Ian's rustic bench and think about hermits to your heart's content.

CHAPTER 1

'*Going to see the hermit,*
finding him gone . . .'

CHINA, LADAKH AND INDIA

Lao-tse — Boddhidharma —
the Chungsan mountains — Tibetan hermits —
Madame Blavatsky — a Kipling story —
Swami Abhishiktananda

> I questioned the boy under the pine trees,
> 'My master went to gather herbs,
> He is still somewhere on the mountainside
> So deep in the clouds I know not where.'

Jia Dao, 'On Looking in Vain for the Hermit'

Chinese hermits seem always to have been the most elusive. Not finding the hermit, or finding him completely silent, was no doubt part of what was to be learned from the search. The figure of the hermit is there from earliest times, a sage who rejected the materialism of society in favour of simplicity and the quest for spiritual wisdom. Hermit legends abound. The earliest known ruler of the tribes along the Yellow River lived about five thousand years ago, and is supposed to have had two hermits as his advisers; their counsel was so wise that he reigned for a hundred years. Around 2300 BC the Emperor Yao persuaded a hermit called Shun to be his heir, but when Shun in turn tried to persuade another hermit, Shan-chuan, to take on the succession, Shan-chuan refused; he disappeared into the mountains and was never heard of again.

The founder of Taosim is himself elusive. Legend has it that his name was Lao-tse and that he lived some time in the first century BC and wrote the *Tao te Ching*, which is the scripture of Taosim.

He is said to have been the keeper of the Royal Archives in the eastern Chou capital of Loyang, and to have left the court at a time of political upheaval, riding his blue ox towards the mountains. When he reached Hanku pass he was met by a certain Yin Hsi, an aged hermit. Yin Hsi had seen a purple cloud moving across the sky, and had understood this to mean that a wise man was approaching from the east. Together they travelled over 150 miles further west to Yin Hsi's hermitage and observatory, where Lao-Tse gave Yin Hsi the manuscript of the *Tao te Ching*.

Taoism, like many philosophies of solitude, seeks to follow the Way of Nature. Exposed to nature man learns what lies deepest in himself. A Taoist seeks unity with the immortal Tao, turning his back on the world of men. A Confucian is a humanitarian moralist who, rather than rejecting society, seeks to redeem it by his moderation and good manners. A Confucian might be a hermit, but he would be a scholar and a philosopher rather than a religious contemplative.

A Chinese hermit might live in a cave or a stone hut if he was high in the mountains. In less rigorous conditions he would probably have a wooden hut, thatched. He might be among pine trees; the wind in the pines sighs through many hermit poems. He was probably near plum and peach trees. Plum trees blossom during the coldest months of the year, so are particularly dear to the Chinese solitary. If he was expecting a visitor he might sweep the path in front of his hermitage and leave the gate open. He would have a bed of woven bamboo and a wood fire on which he would brew tea and cook a few vegetables which he had grown himself, or some rice which a neighbouring farmer might have given him. At daybreak and in the evening he would meditate, and perhaps chant. Whether Taoist, Confucian or Buddhist, his aim would be to attain what he understood by transcendence; he would not call it God. The Taoist might think of the P'eng, which is a great bird, so big that it has to climb 90,000 miles into the sky before it has room to turn. Contemplating the P'eng, meditating, ingesting various useful herbs, he might eventually become pure spirit, change into a crane and fly away to Penglai, where the immortals live, said to be an island somewhere in the mists off the coast of the Shantung peninsula in North China. The Confucian would sometimes think of the leopard which can change its spots, so that perfect goodness is a white leopard.

In a country as vast as China, exile was a convenient means of dealing with court officials who fell out of favour with the emperor; they would thus become hermits, however temporary. Many of them made the best of the situation by reminding themselves of the joys of country life, and writing pastoral verse, much as an ancient Roman might have done in the same situation – at least until their political fortunes revived.

Not that all banished officials enjoyed their exile. Qu Yuan, a statesman at the court of the Chu king in the third century BC, was in such despair at his expulsion from court that he drowned himself in the river Milou, north of Changsha. Rebellious students remembered him in 1989. 'Was it the indignant still-beckoning spirit of Qu Yuan from more than two thousand years ago which took you away?' wrote one of the people killed in Peking on 4 June that year.

A change of regime at court would often call the exile back, but he was sometimes reluctant to go. The poet Li Bai wrote in 701:

> They ask me why I live in the green mountains
> I smile and don't reply; my heart's at ease.
> Peach blossoms flow downstream, leaving no trace –
> And there are other earths and skies than these.

In later centuries an English exile from the seat of power might have felt much the same, though French courtiers out of favour with Louis XIV were less philosophical. The defeated Royalist gentry in seventeenth-century England took to their country estates with relief, wherever they had not been sequestered. They read Isaak Walton's *Compleat Angler* and followed his advice to 'study to be quiet'. Cromwell's General, Thomas Fairfax, lived in self-imposed exile from 1650, when he resigned the generalship of the army, until he emerged to support the restoration of Charles II in

1660. He spent most of his time improving his estates at Nun Appleton in Yorkshire, where he gave refuge to the poet Andrew Marvell.

> What wondrous life is this I lead! [wrote Marvell]
> Ripe apples drop about my head;
> The luscious clusters of the vine
> Upon my mouth do crush their wine;
> The nectarine, and curious peach,
> Into my hands themselves do reach;
> Stumbling on melons, as I pass,
> Ensnared with flowers, I fall on grass.
>
> Meanwhile the mind, from pleasures less,
> Withdraws into its happiness:
> The mind, that ocean where each kind
> Does straight its own resemblance find,
> Yet it creates, transcending these,
> Far other worlds, and other seas,
> Annihilating all that's made
> To a green thought in a green shade.

Li Bai would have felt at home.

Buddhism is supposed to have come to China from India in response to a message from the Emperor Ming ti in AD 61 asking for books and teachers. It was a rarefied phenomenon rather than a popular movement at first. For one thing the Chinese disapproved of monks, who were previously unknown in their society and who seemed to be denying the important Chinese duty of parenthood and so by implication the whole fundamental framework of filial respect. Not until Boddhidharma came to China from Conjeeveram, near Madras, in AD 520 – which makes him a contemporary of St Benedict in Italy – did Chinese Buddhism begin to develop its own character. That character was Chan (in its later Japanese development known as Zen), and there are many versions of the story of its foundation. The emperor is supposed to have asked Boddhidharma what was the first principle of Buddhism. 'Vast emptiness,' was the answer.

'Who then am I speaking to?' asked the emperor.

'I have no idea.'

All the stories demonstrate the famous shock treatment of Zen, the bringing up short of the seeker after enlightenment by a startling paradox, or sometimes a physical blow. The emperor seems not to have been receptive and showed no enthusiasm for the idea of giving up his luxurious way of life. Boddhidharma in disgust decided to go back to India, but on his way he came across a stone wall. He sat down in front of it and meditated for nine years, after which he achieved enlightenment and began to instruct his followers.

When the American Bill Porter, who had spent many years, some of them as a hermit, in Taiwan and Hong Kong, went to China in 1989 to see how much of the hermit tradition remained at that time, he was at first told that all that sort of thing had quite disappeared under the communist regime. Eventually he found his way to the Chungsan mountains, not far from Xian, where there were remote monasteries and hermits high in the hills where they had always been. The most ancient of traditions held that the shamans or magic men of earliest times had believed these mountains to be the home of the moon goddess. Hermits never specifically sought ecstatic trance, nor did they see it as their task to ascend to the sky to intercede with the spirits on behalf of their local communities, as the shamans did, but the fact that there had been shamans there before them perhaps provided a link with the mythical past.

Bill Porter wrote a book called *Road to Heaven*, in which he describes how he walked into the gorges where hermits had once lived and found their caves. He followed the steep paths to their remote stone huts. Eventually he found that although some of the hermits had been chased out of the mountains during the Cultural Revolution, some remained. In the most remote parts there were people who had lived alone in caves for many years, walking down to their nearest village only when they ran out of food. Asked which practice he followed, and whether he chanted or meditated, one of the hermits replied, 'I just pass the time.' He had always preferred quiet, he said, and loved the mountains. He chanted, and looked after the temple of a neighbouring nun when she was away. All this was high on remote and precipitous peaks, often lost in the clouds.

There must once have been hermits wherever there were high hills in China. There is a model of a Taoist temple in a small gallery on one of the upper floors of the Victoria and Albert Museum. It was acquired by the Museum of the East India Company in 1810, and is made of ivory and wood, with mother-of-pearl and semi-precious stones. It shows quite a crowded mountain with a hermit at the top of it as well as the temple on the lower slopes. There are figures in conversation here and there, some with fans; there are birds and crickets and men sweeping or looking out for approaching guests. There is a pagoda and a bridge over a river and people fishing on the banks of the river. Perhaps there are still hills like that in China. It seems unlikely that the remote regions have yielded up all their solitaries, in spite of the Chinese government's continued suspicion of religious movements. One hermit whom Bill Porter traced after much difficulty on the mountain of Huashan, at the eastern end of the Chungsan range, was with his disciple, a monk named Chou. 'Chou said that this was Master Su. I bowed and introduced myself. Without pausing, Su said I had the wrong man, that his name was Hua, as in Huashan. Then he walked off, flapping his long sleeves as if he were about to fly away.' The elusiveness remains, and is perhaps protective.

Chinese sculptures of the Buddha have a particularly remote and authoritative beauty, but the West nowadays knows more of Tibetan Buddhism. Politics have something to do with this. The Dalai Lama is seen not only as a sage but as a victim. A smaller and mysteriously spiritual country seems to be being destroyed by an enormous and powerful neighbour, whose governing ethos is materialistic. Tragedy engages the emotions, exile spreads the gospel. There have always been Western experts on Buddhism, but the growth of interest, particularly in America, seems to show that Buddhism feeds the spiritual hunger of our disorientated age by offering a religion without a God, that is to say without all the associations of home-grown institutionalized faiths. How much its Western adherents understand Buddhism, or how much they will change or adapt it, remains to be seen. In the meantime there are Western explorers, of the land and of the mind

One of the most experienced explorers must be John Crook from Bristol University who led expeditions to Zangskar and Ladakh to study village life and became fascinated by the hermits in the high Himalayas. He found that the extraordinary landscape affected him physically, so that he felt at times almost disembodied. At the same time he was impressed by the powerful spiritual presence of some of the older monks. He made further journeys to study the teachings of those he called 'the commandos of Tibetan Buddhism, the yogins'. These few monks seek to 'become Buddhas in one lifetime' rather than to progress by the slow route over many lifetimes which is the more usual goal of the Tibetan monk. In order to try to understand the techniques of meditation and mental discipline which they gradually revealed to him, Crook had to learn new ways not so much of thought as of non-thought. He spent time in cave monasteries and huts in the hills. Solitude in the mountains was part of the yogins' way of life. One of the Rinpoches, or high lamas, whom he most liked pointed out birds to him, wall-creepers, chukors, white-crested redstarts, and told him, 'If you wish to meditate choose a good place, as remote as possible, peaceful, with clean water and wild nature.' A third-century Taoist gave the same advice: 'You must be among mountains of repute, in a place without men . . .'

One of the most famous of all Buddhist hermits was the Tibetan Milarepa, who lived from 1040 to 1123. He had a wild youth, in which he was said to have practised black magic in order to revenge himself on his enemies, but when the fame of the great Buddhist teacher Marpa reached him he sought him out and asked to study with him. Marpa treated him with great severity but eventually recognized his religious vocation and taught him all he himself had learned in his many long journeys among Indian monasteries. Milarepa then lived as a hermit in remote caves in the mountains, surviving on nothing much but nettles. When people came to see him he taught them in song; *The 100,000 Songs of Milarepa* are part of Tibetan literature. A monk called Gampopa came to live with Milarepa and subsequently founded a monastery. His systemization of Milarepa's teachings became the basis of the Kagyu tradition. In the same way at about the same time, in the remote and hardly heard of West, the monk Guigo systematized the teachings of Bruno and founded the Carthusians, an order of Christian hermits.

A few years ago, there were two English women living independently of each other in Ladakh. One, whose dharma name was Padma, lived in the grounds of a Tibetan Buddhist monastery in the rock-strewn fir forest on the borders of Tibet. The other was an hour and a half's steep climb from the same monastery, in a cave 13,200 feet up in the mountains. This was Tenzin Palmo, an ordained Chinese Buddhist nun and the daughter of a fishmonger in the East End of London; her English name was Diane Perry. After twelve years of meditation in the cave she returned to the West, where she lived for some time near Assisi, and then announced her intention of raising enough money to start a Buddhist nunnery. Her avowed ambition is to be the first female Buddha, in this life or the next.

Though unusual, Tenzin Palmo was not a completely unheard of phenomenon in the East. There was a famous female hermit,

Machig Labdron, in eleventh-century Tibet. Her story parallels those of Western Christian female hermits in the Middle Ages. Her family opposed her desire to devote herself to the spiritual life because she was seen as a useful domestic worker, whose economic role was as a marriage object. When she went to live alone in a cave the abbot of the local monastery perceived her as a threat, because she was an outsider. Even when he met her and was convinced of her authenticity, he wanted her to move into a monastery and become part of the system. The yogin, male or female, like the hermit, remains an outsider, detached, to some extent mysterious, and possessed of a particular kind of authority.

The variety of Buddhist sects and meditational techniques is bewildering to a beginner and in the nineteenth century there was an attempt by certain Tibetan scholars to synthesize some of the great mass of material which existed about the different teachings and practices. This resulted in a non-sectarian movement known as Ri-me, meaning impartial. It seems possible that this movement influenced Madame Blavatsky, the founder of Theosophy, a movement whose object was to bring closer together the religious understandings of East and West.

The Theosophical movement still exists, but its heyday was in the years between 1880 and the outbreak of the First World War. It coincided with the height of the British Empire and with the fashion for table turning and Ouija boards, and it had in it elements of the exotic and the comic as well as the fraudulent and every now and then the true. Madame Blavatsky was surely a Great Woman. She could be counted an occasional hermit, because of her frequent retreats to consult her invisible 'teachers', and her noisy condemnation, when in India, of what she called the 'flap-doodle' of Simla society. In spite of her extravagances, and her salty way of expressing herself, she was one of the first to articulate what may now be thought almost a commonplace: the belief that Eastern religion has something important to offer Western religion.

Madame Blavatsky appeared in India in 1879 and seemed to have had connections both with Russia and with Tibet. The British government thought she was a spy. These were the years of the Great Game, when Russian intentions in Afghanistan were thought to be a threat to the stability of the British Empire; the mysterious travels of Kipling's Kim reflect the atmosphere of the time. Madame Blavatsky had her mysteries too. She was born in Russia in 1831, the daughter of a general with aristocratic connections. After a solitary childhood full of psychic manifestations, she was married to a much older man when she was eighteen. She ran away from him after three months, and among other things was said to have given concert tours with Clara Schumann, studied magic in Egypt with a Copt, joined the Druze sect in Lebanon, and fought with Garibaldi at Mentana in 1849, after which she was picked out of a ditch for dead, with a stiletto wound in her heart. She was sometimes vague as to the precise details of these adventures.

In 1851 she was walking in London when she saw a Rajput whom she instantly recognized from visions she had had in childhood as her Protector and Spirit Master. She subsequently spent some years trying to get into Tibet, and in the late 1860s she succeeded. Her way of transmitting her insights was often dramatic and there is no doubt that when her 'spirits' occasionally slackened in their attentions she gave them a helping hand. Having arrived at Allahabad with her American disciple Colonel Olcott, she travelled up to Simla with Mr Sinnott, the editor of the *Pioneer* newspaper of Calcutta.

Mr Sinnott, Madame Blavatsky and Alan Octavian Hume founded the Indian branch of the Theosophical Society in Simla. Hume was a man of tremendous energy and enthusiasm. Not only did he have a distinguished career in the Indian Civil Service, but it was his stirring circular letter to the graduates of Calcutta University which led to the foundation of the Indian National Congress. He was also the founder of Indian ornithology, and at the time that he met Madame Blavatsky he had a collection of many thousands of stuffed birds which had been sent to him from all over India by various agents, and which he had classified and annotated. One of the tenets of Theosophy being that the taking of life was to be shunned, he sent telegrams to all his collectors to shoot no more, and offered his whole collection to the British Museum; it is still to be seen in the Natural History Museum in South Kensington.

Madame Blavatsky was often at Rothney Castle, the house in Simla which Hume had extended with some grandeur because he hoped it would become the new Viceregal Lodge. In fact it was felt that its situation, halfway up Mount Jakko, whose steep wooded slopes rise behind those icons of the imperial age, Christ Church and the Mall, would be too inconvenient. A new building, less arduous of access, was preferred, and the ballroom at Rothney Castle, together with the extensive conservatory full of exotic plants (for Hume was a keen botanist), was at the disposal of Madame Blavatsky, who despite her scorn for those she called the 'Mrs Grundys' of Simla was prepared to swop the red flannel dressing-gown she habitually wore for a dress of black silk and demonstrate her occult powers to the assembled company. She was not an easy guest. According to Mr Sinnott, 'her dislike of alcohol in all forms amounted to a kind of mania' and 'she would vent her impatience, if anything annoyed her, by vehement tirades in a loud voice directed against Colonel Olcott'. She rose early to communicate with spirits, or to write or translate articles for magazines (she was perpetually short of money) and to deal with her extensive correspondence. For the rest of the day she talked, protesting from time to time that she was being kept from her work. She would sometimes receive a sudden call from one of her distant Masters and would hurry away to receive the message in solitude, shouting to her faithful servant Babula to see that she was not disturbed.

In her anxiety to encourage converts to the theosophical creed, Madame Blavatsky would astonish the company by finding lost rings, previously buried by Babula, or bringing out letters supposedly from her familiar spirit 'Kut Humi' but full of the American phraseology of Colonel Olcott. Simla society turned against her, and Hume himself was eventually maddened by the mixture of sense and nonsense in her conversation. He pronounced her the most marvellous liar he had ever met, though he excused her on the ground that her intention was to convert her audience to a higher faith. Nevertheless, he brought his association with Theosophy to an end, not without some bitterness on both sides.

The association between the Indian National Congress and Theosophy did continue, however. Annie Besant, who succeeded Madame Blavatsky as head of the Theosophical Society, became President of the Indian National Congress in 1918. Jiddhu Krishnamurti, her protégé, was believed by the Theosophists to be an *avatar*, or incarnation of the divine spirit, and to be destined to become the World-Teacher who would lead mankind into a new era. He courageously rejected the Christ-like status offered him, together with the whole eccentric Theosophical cosmology, and became a spiritual leader without it.

All his life Krishnamurti had periodical attacks of intense physical pain, followed by feelings of transcendence; this curious phenomenon occurs again and again in the lives of mystics and shamans, but Krishnamurti always said that the state of grace he achieved could be reached by anyone. The most important thing in his life, he said, was 'to be nothing, absolutely nothing'. In his teachings there are echoes of the nineteenth-century Ri-me Buddhism which Madame Blavatsky may have learned in Tibet.

Theosophy continued to attract followers in the earlier part of the twentieth century, particularly among poets and painters. Part of the movement became increasingly involved with spiritualism – W. B. Yeats in particular was for a time enthralled, especially when it transpired that his wife was able to do automatic writing under the influence of spirits. It was probably the more contemplative aspect which interested other artists, perhaps because of a similarity in the search for ultimate clarification of perception. A parallel might be with the present interest in Buddhism. Mondrian, for instance, was a Theosophist, as indeed was his contemporary

Kandinsky. Mondrian was more or less a recluse for much of his life, living in a small bed-sitting room near the Gare Montparnasse in Paris. There he would work meticulously on his calm geometrical paintings, whose planes of strong colour and opposing non-colour had for him a simple metaphysical accuracy. His fellow-painter Ben Nicholson visited him in the 1930s, and climbed the steep staircase to the little room where Mondrian was at work, evidently oblivious of the sound of the trains from the station and the rhythmical thumps from the dancing school next door. Nicholson wrote that the feeling of light in the little room, and the pauses and silences in Mondrian's conversation reminded him of 'those hermit's caves where lions went to have thorns taken out of their paws'.

In the Hindu tradition the fourth stage of life is the time to give away your possessions and become a holy man, or hermit.

One of Kipling's best stories concerns a certain Purun Dass, who ends a brilliant career in the Indian Civil Service as prime minister of one of the semi-independent states of north-west India. When he feels the time has come, he becomes a *Sunnyasi*, or holy man, with his begging bowl and his ochre-coloured cloak. 'He had been, as the Old Law recommends, twenty years a youth, twenty years a fighter – though he had never carried a weapon in his life – and twenty years head of a household.' He wanders towards the Himalayas, past Simla, and on towards Tibet, until he finds a deserted shrine under the shadow of the deodars, high above a broad valley. The local villagers climb the hill every day to bring him food, proud to have their own holy man. He never goes down to the village, but stays on his hillside with the monkeys and the deer and the black Himalayan bear. 'When you asked of the villagers how long their holy man had lived in Kali's shrine at the head of the pass, they answered "Always".'

The end of the story is a fine piece of drama. His closeness to the animals alerts Purun Dass to imminent catastrophe. Days of heavy rain have loosened the earth and a huge mudslide is about to submerge the village beneath. Old habits of authority resurface in the holy man. He orders the entire populace to run, in good order, taking a roll call as they go. Recognizing his innate authority, they obey without question and are saved; he dies. No one ever knows that the shrine to which the villagers make pilgrimage year after year is that of Sir Purun Dass, former prime minister of a princely state, Knight of the British Empire.

In those same Kipling days, in Simla in the 1890s, a certain Charles de Russet, ex-student of the Simla Bishop Cotton School, where he had been a keen member of the volunteer corps, was to be seen upon Mount Jakko wearing nothing but a yellow loincloth. He had become a disciple of the fakir who lived at the shrine of the monkey god. After two years he was admitted into the priesthood, and for some time wandered round Simla in his headdress of a leopard-skin, whence he was known as the 'leopard fakir', but in due course he went into reclusion at a temple further down the mountain and was seen no more. The hippies of the 1960s were not the first to find Indian gurus irresistible.

When the most famous Western hermit of modern times, the American Thomas Merton, went to India in 1968, one of the people he most wanted to meet – though he never in fact found him – was Dom Henri Le Saux, a Frenchman who had become Swami Abhishiktananda and called himself a Hindu Christian monk. Le Saux was born in Brittany in 1910, and became a monk at the monastery of St Anne de Kergonan at the age of nineteen. India seized his imagination quite early in his life. He was finally given permission by his order to go there in 1948, and he and another monk, Father Monchanin, founded an ashram at Shantivanam

near Trichinopoly in the south of India. He visited Sri Ramana
Maharshi, a Hindu sage who had settled at the foot of a mountain
called Arunachala, and began the great romance of his life. It is
possible to fall in love with a mountain; think of Cezanne. In fact,
from a certain angle, the outline of Arunachala is not unlike that
of the Montagne Sainte-Victoire, which Cezanne painted so obsess-
ively for much of his life.

Arunachala is a reddish-coloured mountain, some 100 miles
south-west of Madras. By the time Abhishiktananda went to see
Sri Ramana Maharshi, the sage was old and famous. The years of
solitude and silence in the caves of Arunachala were over and he
was surrounded by devotees; Abhishiktananda was disappointed,
and only his conversation with an Englishwoman made him resolve
to venture another visit. Miss Ethel must have been one of those
dauntless women who have appeared so often in the long story of
the English experience of India. She had been the first woman to
fly over the rainforests of South America. She had lived for some
time on the outskirts of Paris, to be near Gurdjieff, the sage whose
ferocious regime nearly killed the consumptive writer Katherine
Mansfield. At the age of fifty she had come to India and settled in
the ambience of Krishnamurti and the Theosophists, looking after
the gardens at one of their schools; she came to Arunachala for
her holidays.

Miss Ethel introduced Abhishiktananda to other disciples who
could make him see through the cult atmosphere which had grown
up around the aged sage. They told him about the days when the
Maharshi had lived in one cave or another on the side of the
mountain, retreating before the crowds of people who came to
seek his advice. His teaching was about solitude, renunciation,
spiritual reality. 'Heaven is hidden in the depth of the heart,' he
would quote from the Mahanarayana Upanishad. 'That glorious
place which is only found by those who renounce themselves.'

In fact it seems that when he first came to the mountain the
Maharshi would have known nothing of the Upanishads or any
other Hindu wisdom teachings; he came to his later understanding

of them through his own experience of solitude and contemplation and his teaching always remained simple and direct. In his boyhood he was more interested in sport than philosophy. He was seventeen when he left his father's house and went to Arunachala, whose name he had first heard only a few months earlier. He lived there for the rest of his life, at first in conditions of the utmost poverty and indeed filth, wrapped in silence and contemplation and often entirely alone for considerable stretches of time. As his fame as a holy man spread, he moved further and further away from his followers, until he settled on a part of the mountain where there was a spring, a cave and a temple in which he would meditate. Eventually, having presumably achieved illumination – knowledge of Brahman, the universal spirit, which would release him from the cycle of birth and rebirth which is implicit in the Hindu belief in reincarnation – he emerged from complete silence and when he was not meditating gave counsel and blessing to those who sought him.

A more unlikely visitor to Arunachala than the devout Abhishiktananda was the writer Somerset Maugham, at that time a sophisticated and worldly novelist enjoying his fame. He was looking for background material for a novel he wanted to write, which was to include a character who would retreat into Eastern mysticism as the only way of escape from the materialism of the West.

This was *The Razor's Edge*, which became a bestseller. Its characters now seem flimsy and sentimental, apart from the snobbish American who apes the English upper classes, a lively caricature which gave much pleasure to the London society friends of the politician and diarist Chips Channon. Nothing if not professional, Maugham read many volumes about Hindu religion before writing his novel and though when he visited the Maharshi in 1938 he did so as a sceptic, this did not apparently prevent him from believing the holy man to be a saint. He described him as 'neat, very clean and almost dapper . . . cheerful, smiling, polite; he did not give me the impression of a scholar, but rather of a sweet-natured old peasant'.

After the Maharshi's death, Swami Abhishiktananda, the French Hindu-Christian, often returned for periods of retreat to one of the many caves which were scattered over his beloved mountain. He wore a saffron loincloth. Sometimes he lived in silence, sometimes he travelled. He came to feel a great fondness for his cave, or rather his succession of caves, since he did not always return to the same one. He felt that in the caves of Arunachala he had discovered the cave of the heart. At first he often sang, but eventually he felt he had learnt from the mountain its own song, which was silence. When he was in the cave people brought him food, because that was the way of things there. In the end the mountain revealed itself to him; he saw the flame for which he had been waiting and was filled with joy, like Moses before the burning bush.

It would be wrong to suggest that Abhishiktananda's hermit life was untroubled. He had difficulty in reconciling his Hinduism with his Christianity, ardently as he wished to do so, and even caves on holy mountains are not immune from tiresome neighbours; but he had times of great happiness. He ended his days in a hut beside the Ganges at Uttarkashi in the Himalayas.

Some of the stories told of the Maharshi might have been told of hermits in any age and of any religion. He loved animals. He looked upon the stray dogs who hung around the ashram as fellow-ascetics who were atoning for their past sins, and insisted that they should be fed and housed. He was fond of a calf which wandered round the ashram at one time; he thought it was the present incarnation of an old woman who used to bring him the herbs she had gathered on the hillside. He would not allow snakes to be driven out of the caves. They were there first, he said, and should not be disturbed. He fed the squirrels and crows which came to his cave and adjudicated in the quarrels of the many monkeys, who in turn shook fruit out of the trees to assuage his thirst. When robbers came to his meditation hall, thinking that as he was so famous he must be rich, he forbade his disciples to chase them away, but retreated to another hut so that the thieves could help themselves to what little there was; when someone called the police they arrived to find the Maharshi sitting quietly, discoursing with his disciples on spiritual matters, all of them slightly battered because the thieves had thought fit to beat them about with sticks. Stories like these are told of the fourth-century Christian hermits in the Egyptian desert, and of St Seraphim, the Russian Orthodox hermit in eighteenth-century Russia. They are part of the myth of the holy hermit – which is not to say that they are not true.

The wanderer, the cave dweller and the hermit in his hut, have in common their closeness to nature; this lost harmony has always been part of what people have seen or imagined in the hermit life. The Chinese has his cranes, the Indian too many monkeys, the high mountain hermit a raven or a bear. In the Kipling story the animals come to the holy man's fireside because he does not look them in the eye; that is to say he does not assert his authority. One Victorian traveller – perhaps Kipling had heard of him – found himself at the camp fire of a holy man in northern India; becoming aware of a strong musky smell, he turned to see a leopard sitting quietly behind him in the shadows. This acceptance by the animals is something found in all hermit myths; it is part of the nostalgia for paradise which haunts those stories. Even in the wood of the ornamental hermit's cell that I know best, I do not have to be there long before the deer stop bothering about me. The biggest roebuck will pass as close as fifteen feet, picking his way unhurriedly through the shafts of misty sunlight which pierce the shade, turning a mildly curious gaze towards me, giving me time to count the six points on his antlers, admire his smooth russet coat and smile at the lackadaisical way he dangles a sprig of hazel from his mouth.

CHAPTER 2

'Cedar, and pine, and fir, and branching palm . . .'

THAILAND, RUSSIA AND SIBERIA

Ajahn Pongsak — Edward Lear on Mount Athos —
Tolstoy, Father Ambrose and Dostoevsky —
Seraphim of Sarov — Czar Alexander I —
'God's fools' — J. D. Salinger — Agafia Lykov

A Thai Buddhist who decides to become a forest monk undertakes
a pilgrimage of meditation, a forest walk called a *tudong*. Like the
wandering monks of early Celtic Christianity, he is a peripatetic
hermit. You can tell where he is by the orange cloak that he throws
over a branch of a tree when he has paused there to contemplate,
or sleep. The forest monk in Thailand has still a status not unlike
that of the hermit in ancient China. He is held to be incorruptible.
Past kings of Thailand have on several occasions brought in a
forest monk to purge corruption in a city monastery, and the close
connection with the royal family endures to this day. In the countryside his intimate knowledge of the natural workings of the forests,
on which the water supply depends, means that he is often called
upon to give advice on the maintenance of the complex systems
of weirs and canals which make it possible for several crops of rice
to be produced every season.

I once went to a valley called Mae Soi, north of Chiang Mai,
where a monk called Ajahn Pongsak was the moving force behind
a project to restore some of the forest. The whole area had been
devastated by logging, and by the depredations of the local villagers
who had been taking firewood and letting their animals graze on
land which would otherwise have returned to forest. They did not
understand that without the trees they would have no water supply.
We stayed in a hut among bamboos and scrubby woodland. Sunset

and dawn were beautiful but strangely silent; one expected more bird cries, or the howl of gibbons, but their habitat had been harmed and they had gone. All the teak in the valley had been cleared some time ago and, apart from one undisturbed patch, only young secondary woodland remained.

This one patch of old forest grew on a kind of peninsula defined by a forked stream. It had been left untouched because a malignant spirit had damaged the chainsaws of the people who had been sent to cut it down. We had to cross the stream to reach it. At the foot of the first big tree we had to leave an offering of rice sweets. We carried no cameras. The hermit spirit would have destroyed them, counting them as machines and thus detestable. It was cool under the tall trees, and the undergrowth was full of birds.

Further on we came to the huge mango tree which was the centre of the whole undertaking. It was surrounded by pots of tiny trees waiting to be planted. Further still we came to a commodious cave in which there lived a cheerful nun from Hong Kong. Not far away, beside a serious vegetable garden, there was a little straw hut, raised up on legs, into which Ajahn Pongsak could retreat when he was meditating.

Ajahn Pongsak came from a family of farmers, and had been a monk since the age of twenty. He had studied with the scholar Buddhadasa at Suan Mokkh, in the south of Thailand at Chaiya. The monastery there is in the forest, and the *vihara*, or central place where the Buddha statues are, and where the monks and nuns meet for talks and meditation, is a clearing among the tallest trees. Buddhadasa himself died a few years ago, and is said by some to be going to return one day as the Buddha of the next age.

Ajahn Pongsak wandered through the northern forests on meditation pilgrimages, and in 1964 he found his way to Wat Palad, an abandoned forest temple on Doi Suthep in Chiang Mai, where one old monk had been living alone for two years. He spent three years living there as a forest monk before beginning to teach, after which Wat Palad was revivified and expanded. Beyond Wat Palad is what remains of the original tropical forest which once covered the whole mountain. The light only intermittently penetrates the dark green canopy; there are giant mimosas, and tulip trees with great spreading roots, and orchids and lianas and poinsettias climbing high into the branches. The undergrowth is full of small birds, easier to hear than to see.

When Ajahn Pongsak went to the Mae Soi valley on his meditative walks, the people of the five local villages walked through the forest to bring him food, that being the custom. They told him that their water supply was running very low, and because he knew how the forest naturally maintained its balance he understood that the cause of the change lay in the deforestation which had been going on, not only on the floor of the valley but round the watersheds higher up in the hills. He was an enthusiastic water engineer, and extraordinarily strong. He started to build weirs and lay water pipes single-handed, and when the villagers understood what he was doing, they came to help him. They stopped grazing their cattle in what remained of the forest and started replanting native trees.

When they tried to fence the watersheds, and replant pine trees, there was trouble with the Hmong tribespeople, who had moved into these high places and were living there, growing opium and cabbages. We watched truckloads of pale green perfectly rounded cabbages bouncing down the hillside to an assured sale somewhere below. They were being grown in fields once given over to opium poppies. International aid organizations fell over each other to provide fertilizers and pesticides and every sort of inducement to entice the farmers away from the more profitable illicit crop. No one seemed to bother to look a little higher up the hill where the poppies flourished as well as ever in newly planted patches, barely concealed. The people running the drug trade around there were very frightening in those days, and probably still are, although the Thai government has recently done its best to push the whole business over the border into Burma. Pongsak himself had to be persuaded to keep out of sight for a time – though whether the threat was from drug runners or communist terrorists we never quite made out – but the Dhammanaat Foundation, which was founded to continue his work, has planted many thousands of trees, and is now able to influence government policies.

Other people have carried on what Ajahn Pongsak began but his was the original insight, and he provided the spiritual authority. His large, even formidable, presence was powerfully benign. My son worked for him for a time, and lodged with the project's brilliant benefactor and supporter, Smansnid Svasti, who turned out to have been at school with me in England in the late 1940s. We all ate hot Thai curry until the tears ran down our cheeks.

Russian hermits are associated with forests too. In Russian Ortho-dox icons the wilderness often shown in the background is the forest, not, as it was in the early Byzantine icons of St John the Baptist, the desert and the rocks. The Russian hermit tradition goes back to St Sergius of Radonezh in the fourteenth century, when the great forests of northern Russia began to be peopled by hermits, some of whom founded monasteries. St Sergius' first monastery in the forest consisted of wooden cells round a wooden refectory and a stone church; he went on to found about forty more. Byzantine monks had always tended to wander, though still in theory bound to their parent monastery which undertook to feed and support them. It was more usual for hermits to live in a group, called a *laura* or *skete*, under the supervision of a spiritual father, but ever since the Emperor Justinian had made allowances for 'those who have left the communal life for the higher calling of the life of contemplation and perfection' there had been wandering solitaries, seeking *hesychia*, or stillness, among mountains or forests, or on the rocks of the Meteora in Thessaly or the remote peninsula of Mount Athos in Macedonia.

The Russian hermit tradition comes mainly from the monasteries of Mount Athos, which had been sacred as the home of the Greek gods before Mount Olympus. According to Christian legend, the Virgin Mary landed there from Cyprus and claimed the mountain as her own garden, excluding all other females for ever. However that may be, hermits found their way there from earliest Christian times, and from the late Middle Ages onwards there have been a variety of monastic communities. Its remoteness, religious history and wild landscape have always attracted adventurous travellers. Not all reactions were favourable. Edward Lear was there in 1856, on his travels round the Mediterranean.

> However wondrous and picturesque the exterior & interior of the monasteries [he wrote in a letter to a friend] & however abundantly & exquisitely glorious & stupendous the scenery of the mountain, I would not go again to the *Agios Oros* for any money, so gloomy, so shockingly unnatural, so lonely, so lying, so unatonably odious seems to me all the atmosphere of such monkery. That half of our species which it is natural to every man to cherish & love best, ignored, prohibited and abhorred – all life spent in everlasting repetition of monotonous prayers, no sympathy with ones fellowbeans of any nation, class or age. The name of Christ on every garment and at every tongue's end, but his maxims trodden under foot. God's world and will turned upside down, maimed, & caricatured: – if this I say be Xtianity let Xtianity be rooted out as soon as possible.

He wrote to the same friend a couple of months later:

> Here my boy! Give me your eternal thanks for what I am going to suggest to you as a parliamentary motion, to be brought out & spoken on by yourself, to the ultimate benefit of society & to your own postperpetual glorification. As soon as Parliament meets, move that all Sidney Herbert's distressed needlewomen be sent out at once to Mount Athos! By this dodge all the 5000 monks young and old will be vanquished: – distressed needle-babies will ultimately awake the echoes of ancient Acte, & the whole fabric of

monkery, not to say of the Greek church will fall down
.crash & forever. N.B. Let the needlewomen be all landed
at once, 4000 at least, on the South-east side of the peninsula
& make a rush for the nearest monastery: that subdued all
the rest will speedily follow.

Fifty years ago it might have looked as though neglect, in default
of rapacious needlewomen, had achieved Lear's objective. When
the abbot of one of the monasteries died in the 1960s there were
not enough monks to carry his coffin. The average age of the
monks in the whole mountain was eighty. By 1991 it was thirty-
four.

The resurgence began in the 1970s, as the first young Greek men
began to feel the wind of consumerism blowing cold. Their
numbers were swelled after the end of communism in Russia and
Romania, but there are monks there now from New Zealand and
Peru. Simeon from Peru was born a Catholic, and travelled the
world in search, he said, of 'joy and wonder'. He spent some time
in India, but the Hindu religion did not seem to answer his need.
He met an Orthodox monk in a café in Paris, and asked him what
his habit and his beard signified. He was told that they symbolized
consecration to God and the belief that man can participate in
God, that the practice of mental prayer can bring the mind into
the heart and reach towards union with the divine, as iron plunged
into the fire can melt and be remoulded. He is a hermit now. I
heard him interviewed on the radio.

Brother Patrick is a hermit too, but he lives in England, though
his home monastery is on Mount Athos. Work being part of the
ethos of the monastery, he had to clear tables and scrub floors
when he was there, but because he had been a sculptor he was
asked to carve wood and paint icons. Loving his materials, he says
he prays with his chisel as well as with his lips. Icons are windows
to the unending worship of heaven; when he is in his chapel on
the Welsh borders he is never alone because the saints represented
in the icons with which he has covered the walls are with him

in his prayers. To him the monks of Mount Athos live between earth and heaven, and are like the angels who surround God. He heard of a visitor who asked one of the old monks what they did all day and was told, 'We have died and we are in love with everything.'

In times of general instability, especially in the thirteenth and fourteenth centuries, when a hermit had not only to run the gauntlet of his own admirers, hungry for spiritual guidance, but might run the risk of being captured by pirates and sold into slavery, monks wandered over the whole of the eastern Mediterranean. Under Peter the Great in the late seventeenth century the Church came under state control, and because it became more worldly, and indeed rich and property-owning, there was a movement, led by Paissy Velichkovsky, to return to the greater asceticism of the Desert Fathers of Egypt and Syria.

In Tolstoy's story 'Father Sergius', when the young man Kasatsky, affronted by the cynicism of the world in which his admired prince encourages his marriage to a beautiful bride only in order cynically to dispose of a former mistress of his own, chooses instead to become a monk, he does not go to any old monastery. 'The abbot of that monastery was a gentleman by birth, a learned writer and a starets, that is, he belonged to that succession of monks originating in Wallachia who each choose a director and teacher whom they implicitly obey. This Superior had been a disciple of Macarius, who was a disciple of the starets Leonid, who was a disciple of Paissy Velichkovsky.'

Both Tolstoy and Dostoevsky (though not together) visited Staretz Ambrose, who followed Staretz Macarius at Optina Pustyn (*pustyn* means desert). Optina is two miles from Kozelsk, not far from Moscow. A *staretz* was a spiritual adviser, who might be an abbot or a hermit, and was usually old, having acquired understanding and experience. The startsi would probably live in a more secluded building, more like a charterhouse, near the monastery.

Tolstoy's attitude to the Church veered between longing and disgust; longing for what the Church might know of God and disgust at what he saw as the pointlessness and superstition of much of its ritual. In the story of Father Sergius there is both the longing and the disgust, as well as a prefiguring of his final conclusion that only in the simple hearts of the poorest on earth can God be found, an over-simplification which surely does him, great landowner as he was, nothing but credit. The young man in the story wants to be a perfect monk, just as he had wanted to be a perfect courtier. A hermit's life seems braver – did not St Benedict write something to the effect that only the most courageous should go out to the combat in the desert? His fame spreads, people come to him to be healed, he retires further but still they follow. He resists a beautiful and rich woman who sets out to seduce him, and cuts off one of his fingers rather than submit to his lustful desires; but then his early fervour fades. Lesser temptations become harder to resist. He gives in to one of them. Horrified by what he has done, he flees. He goes back to see a humble hard-working woman whom he had despised in his youth, and tells her to her astonishment that her life is much better than his. When he leaves her, she knows which way he has gone only by the increasingly distant sound of the dogs barking as he passes each farm. Later she hears that he is working as a gardener somewhere in Siberia. 'Father Sergius' was made into a film called in English *Night Sun* by the Italian Taviani brothers; it is very beautiful, as well as being true to the story.

Father Ambrose, like most of the startsi, was practical in the advice he gave. Indeed, some of the most admired startsi seem more or less to have fulfilled the function of the oracle at Delphi in the times of classical Greece; people felt better for having consulted them, and their counsel was often expressed in a cliché. This gave their pronouncements an air of immemorial wisdom and enabled them, like the oracle, to hedge their bets. Dostoevsky's description in *The Brothers Karamatsov* of the scenes outside Father Zossima's cell when crowds of people are waiting to see him, desperate for counsel, must be a description of what he himself witnessed when he went to see Father Ambrose. As well as the poor and the sick, there would have been a carriage or two in which rich ladies waited behind curtained windows. Father Ambrose seems to have been endlessly patient and long-suffering, in spite of his frequent exhaustion. He wrote in 1882:

> I find myself in the midst of idle talk and bustle. The day has hardly begun . . . and they are knocking at the door and ringing the bell. One needs this and another needs that and a third needs nothing at all but sticks his nose in anyhow. And here lie piles of letters in which it is likewise written that I have forgotten this or that person. All one can do is try to achieve one's salvation as one knows best. May the Lord have mercy on us.

His advice seems to have been practical, and occasionally sharp. 'You idiot!' he wrote to a particularly egotistical correspondent. 'You always want to live by yourself. You do not understand that it is difficult but more useful to live with people. Without making any special effort you learn patience and humility and love for your neighbours; even a snake is humble in his hole, but tease him a bit and he will begin to hiss. Continue to live with your companion.'

Dostoevsky went to see Father Ambrose after the death of his son and it is supposed that Father Zossima's simple advice to the grieving mother in *The Brothers Karamatsov* – that it is right for her to weep, but that she should remember that her child is in heaven and her husband at home, needing her love – was what he himself heard from Father Ambrose. The effect of Father Zossima's death on Alyosha, and the latter's ecstasy when he dashes out of the hermit's cell, probably better express Dostoevsky's own sense of the divinity of all creation. Alyosha falls face downwards on the earth, swearing to love it until the end of the ages, 'as though threads from all these countless of God's worlds had all coincided within his soul at once, and it trembled all over, in "the contiguity with other worlds"'.

Scenes such as those outside Father Zossima's cell would also have taken place around the hermitage of St Seraphim of Sarov, when he emerged from his 'trial of silence' and made himself available to the waiting crowds who had heard of his fame.

St Seraphim is probably the most loved of hermits, not only in Russia. He was born in 1759, and at the age of twenty-eight, having become a monk at the monastery of Sarov, in the northern forest of Temnikov, withdrew to a solitary hut two hours' walk from the monastery. There he chopped wood and grew vegetables and was so cheerful that when he went to the monastery church on Sundays and feast-days the monks did not want to let him go back to his hermitage. He believed the purpose of life to be what he called 'the acquisition of the Holy Spirit', the attaining to that transfiguring light which in Russian Orthodoxy is revealed to the mystic. He said many times that despondency was to be feared more than anything. It was something with which he was not unfamiliar. At one time he was so exhausted by the number of people who came to see him that he barred the path to his retreat with branches and lay flat on his face on the ground if he saw anyone approaching. One man, with troubles so terrible that he felt he must overcome all the obstacles, found him asleep under a tree; he sat down to wait beside him, but after a time felt such deep peace and happiness that he forgot his troubles and went home, leaving the saint asleep.

Once St Seraphim was badly beaten up by brigands, and nearly died, but five months later he was back in his cell, although he was bent and walked with a stick for the rest of his life. When the abbot of his monastery died, St Seraphim took on the guidance of the nuns in the nearby convent of Divideyev; malicious tongues wagged, so that he was always careful never to spend a night under the same roof as the nuns, and would walk home to his hermitage whatever the weather. The nuns loved him and told many tales of his goodness, and of how he shared the meagre ration of bread which he brought once a week from the monastery with the animals and birds of the forest. He was seen sitting on a log, sharing his bread with a bear; one of the nuns swore she had seen the bear bringing him a wild honeycomb wrapped up in leaves. His hut was of the utmost simplicity. When he died he was found there in his usual white smock, still kneeling before the icon of the Virgin.

Czar Alexander I came to consult St Seraphim, and there is a legend that afterwards, far from dying, as was supposed, in 1825, the Czar left his throne to expiate his sins as 'Feodor Kuzmitch' a poor pilgrim. There is some evidence to support this theory; it impressed Tolstoy among others. Alexander was a restless and tormented man. He probably had a hand in his father's assassination, he was probably in love with his sister, and he was certainly overwhelmed by the political problems of his vast and backward country. He tried to introduce reforms, but then abandoned them. He tried to resist Napoleon but then became fascinated by him. They met on a raft at Tilsit in 1807, after a Russian defeat at Friedland, and more or less decided to divide the world between them. Later the enchantment faded, they quarrelled over Poland, and Napoleon invaded Russia in 1812. At the congress of the victors in Vienna, after Napoleon's defeat, Alexander's vacillations mystified his allies. Not long afterwards, at Taganrog on the Black Sea in 1825, he said he felt himself 'crushed beneath the terrible burden of a crown'. But did he die at Taganrog?

The circumstances of Alexander's death are mysterious. He was supposed to have had cholera, and no one was allowed to see him because of the danger of infection. Soon after the supposed date of his death a hermit called Feodor Kuzmitch appeared in Siberia. He was of unusually distinguished and aristocratic appearance

(Alexander was a tall man, of excellent physique), and over the next thirty years he gained a reputation for great piety and wisdom. He died near Tomsk on 1 February 1864.

When the communists came to power, they opened the graves of the Romanovs. They found what they were looking for – jewellery and other valuables to sell abroad in return for the hard currency they desperately needed. When they came to the grave of Alexander I, it was empty.

St Seraphim's asceticism did not extend to the wearing of chains, an extreme form of penance favoured by the more fanatical of the early hermits in the Syrian deserts. The 'fools for Christ', who were even more extreme, seem to have been largely a Russian phenomenon. In Tolstoy's *Childhood, Boyhood and Youth*, the fool Grisha has heavy chains beneath his cloak, and wanders in and out of the house with impunity. He is regarded with respect by the women of the household, with intermittent interest by the children, and with considerable irritation by the father of the family.

> He was so tall that to get through the door he was obliged not only to incline his head but to bend his whole body. He wore a tattered garment, something between a peasant tunic and a cassock; in his hand he carried a huge staff. As he entered the room he used the staff to strike the floor with all his might and then, wrinkling his brows and opening his mouth extremely wide, he burst into a terrible and unnatural laugh. He was blind in one eye, and the white iris of that eye darted about incessantly and imparted to his face, already ill-favoured, a still more repellent expression.

No one knows where he came from. He had been one of 'God's fools' from the age of fifteen. Later in the book the children hide in order to watch him undressing because they want to see his chains; he prays and weeps with such intensity that they creep away, ashamed. Some fools wore nothing but chains, or iron collars, walking naked through the streets of Moscow, even in winter. They were generally venerated, but the last one to be canonized was in the seventeenth century. After that they were officially considered suspect, but the tradition lingered. Dostoevsky's Prince Myshkin in *The Idiot* is hard to imagine anywhere other than in Russia.

Some of the early Irish wandering monks were not unlike the Russian 'fools', and the idea lurks behind other holy wanderers whose habits were extreme. There was an eighteenth-century saint called Benedict Joseph Labré, born in a French village not far from Boulogne. He wanted to be a monk, but first the Cistercians and then the Carthusians found him too eccentric, and so he became a perpetual pilgrim, wandering all over Europe in extreme poverty and continuous prayer, an unusual figure to find in the sceptical eighteenth century. In 1774 he settled in Rome, sleeping in the ruins of the Coliseum, and spending his days in prayer in various churches. People brought him food, but if he could find anyone poorer than himself he gave it away. He became fragile and extremely verminous, but the poor people of his locality loved him, and when he died they proclaimed him a saint, though he was not officially canonized until 1881. When Goethe visited Italy in the 1780s, he walked through Rome in the moonlight: 'The Coliseum looks especially beautiful. It is closed at night. A hermit lives in a small chapel and some beggars have made themselves at home in the crumbling vaults.' Would he have been impressed to know that the hermit was a saint?

The nineteenth-century wanderer known as the Pilgrim was not exactly one of 'God's fools' although the respect with which he was treated and the general acceptance of his apparent ability to appear in two places, if not at once, then too soon to have reached the second place by other than supernatural means, seems to speak to the same desire for holy mysteries. The Pilgrim remained anonymous, but his book *The Way of a Pilgrim* was enormously popular.

He was a peasant, who heard in church St Paul's command 'pray without ceasing', and took it literally: 'and that is how I go about now, and ceaselessly repeat the Prayer of Jesus, which is more precious and sweet to me than anything in the world. At times I do as much as 43 or 44 miles a day, and do not feel that I am walking at all. I am aware only of the fact that I am saying my prayer . . . I have become a sort of half-conscious person. I have no cares and no interests.'

The Jesus Prayer is part of Orthodox Christianity – 'Lord Jesus Christ, son of God, have mercy on me, a sinner' – and can be repeated and held in the consciousness like a kind of ground bass to all other thoughts. J. D. Salinger, who wrote the tremendously popular novel *The Catcher in the Rye*, must have come across it some time in the 1950s because his character Franny Glass becomes obsessed with it. *Franny and Zooey* was published in 1961, ten years after *The Catcher in the Rye*. In the interval Salinger apparently became interested in Hinduism, and then in Orthodox Christianity. Franny Glass is in a state of more or less nervous breakdown, disaffected from her college course and the teachers and fellow-students who seem to her phoney and pretentious. She has discovered *The Way of a Pilgrim* and tries to explain to her brother Zooey what the Jesus Prayer means, and how its continuous use is supposed to help you go down from the head to the heart so as to achieve what is meant by 'the mind in the heart'. The story drifts into sentimentality, but clearly during this time Salinger was trying to find a system of thought which would make him dislike the world less than he did. Whether he succeeded or not cannot be known, because he chose to become in effect a hermit.

The celebrity hermit, a modern phenomenon, seems to escape the tolerance, let alone respect, accorded to other species of solitary, being regarded instead with indignation and outrage. The reasoning behind this must be the thought that no one would be a writer or an actor or a musician – or indeed prominent in any way – unless their chief object was to be famous, and that therefore they should lay themselves down gladly as a sacrifice on the altar of human curiosity. As far as writers are concerned this attitude, as common among academics as among other lovers of scandal, seems to have coincided with the post-modernist theory which says that the author of a book is the least important thing about it. In spite of this, Salinger has not been allowed a peaceful seclusion. After what seems to have been an early interest in his own fame, he withdrew to a cottage in the small New Hampshire town of Cornish, just across the Connecticut river from Windsor, Vermont. There he had ninety acres, wonderful views, and at first no electricity or running water. He also had a wife at that time and seemed to want to lead a quiet family life. In 1953 a girl called Shirley Blaney asked him if she and a friend could interview him for a high-school page that came out weekly in the *Claremont Daily Eagle*. He was on friendly terms with the local schoolchildren, and accordingly agreed. The *Eagle* printed the interview on its front page as a scoop. He never gave another interview.

The English writer Ian Hamilton wrote a book about him, which Salinger tried to suppress. He applied for an injunction and had to appear in court to explain why he did not want his early letters to be published. He said he found them 'callow', and 'very painful reading'. The legal case of course gave the whole issue of his desire for solitude a great deal of publicity. Much later his daughter wrote a vengeful book describing his neuroses about health and childhood innocence. He was recently described in a newspaper as 'the most famous celebrity hermit since Howard Hughes'.

Doris Lessing wrote in *The Spectator* recently, after being the unwilling subject of an inaccurate biography: 'We are in the public domain, so the saying goes; but I would argue that our works may be, but we are not, more than we choose to be. In the present charming climate it is assumed that if a writer does not want to be done, it is evidence of a dark concealed secret; but perhaps it could be evidence of an inclination towards privacy?'

Privacy matters to some more than to others, but the public's right to know should surely be questioned more than it is. A writer's imagination is not necessarily robust; it can die.

Salinger's daughter's book feeds the idea that there is a great work to come, if only after his death. She writes of stacks of files, marked 'publish' and 'publish after revision', and of her father's agitation when anyone approaches them. But the sources of a novelist's imagination are obscure, and not infrequently they dry up. William Gerhardie, an English novelist though brought up in Russia, was well-known in the 1920s, and when he died in 1977 at the age of eighty-one it was expected that the novel on which he was said to have been working for a quarter of a century would be discovered among his papers. He had been living a hermit's life in the middle of London, not in order to avoid publicity, for those were gentler times, but as a matter of choice. The writer Olivia Manning went to see him some time in the 1960s.

> Could a writer of such quality be buried alive here today, in the heart and centre of London? I found him in his sitting-room with the curtains drawn.
>
> 'But William,' I protested. 'It is such a beautiful day!'
>
> 'Is it?' he asked eagerly, but he did not go to look for himself.
>
> The room with its purple carpet seemed at the bottom of a rock-pool, lit, as it was, by reflections from the great Louis XV mirror that once hung in the Gerhardies' Petersburg mansion. I look at a photograph of an elegant, handsome, rather arrogant young man – the brilliant sought-after author of *The Polyglots*.

In fact, though there were many cardboard boxes full of notes and fragments, there was no novel; in its long seclusion the imagination had starved to death.

The seclusion of Agafia Lykov would be very hard to break into. In 1978 some geologists looking for deposits of iron ore flew over uninhabited country near the upper reaches of the Abakan river in the Krasnoyarsk region of south central Siberia. They saw to their surprise what seemed to be a clearing in the *taiga*, the forest tundra of the Arctic regions, and signs of something that might have been a potato patch. Flying lower they were able to see what looked like a rough shelter; but nothing was shown on their detailed map. They found a landing place some ten miles away and set off to investigate. They walked through the pathless forest until at the foot of a mountain they came across what seemed to be some kind of track. They climbed for another three miles, until they reached a small clearing among the pines. There was the potato patch, and near it was a wooden hut with a thick untidy roof, made of brushwood. There was no one to be seen, but smoke was rising from the chimney. The geologists – three men and their leader, a young woman called Galina Pismenskaya – called out greetings, and waited. Eventually, with some hesitation, an old bearded man emerged, followed by a younger woman wrapped in a rough shawl, which the geologists later learned was made of birch leaves. Extremely cautious at first, they were persuaded after a few more visits to accept some bread and some salt, and gradually their answers to questions became less hesitant. It transpired that they were a family of Old Believers, who had been living there as hermits since the 1920s.

In the mid-seventeenth century, the Czar Alexei Mikhailovich and the Patriarch Nikon reformed the Orthodox prayer book. The Patriarch Nikon was a forceful character, who decided that the Russian Church should be brought back into line with the older and purer usages of Greek Orthodoxy. He ruled that religious processions should go round churches counter-clockwise, and that the faithful should say the Alleluia twice rather than three times and cross themselves with three fingers not two. New service books were introduced. Passionate resistance was aroused as it so often is in religious affairs when the liturgy is threatened. People have been prepared to die for the words in which the Word is worshipped.

The monks of Solovyetski Monastery near the Arctic Circle withstood an eight-year siege by regular troops; in 1662 the young Archpriest Avvakum was martyred for his beliefs. The schism continued. When Peter the Great became Czar he introduced special taxes for Old Believers in order to help pay for his military adventures. An Office of the Schism was instituted to seek them out. They scattered, to Turkey, Alaska, Canada and, principally, to Siberia. Small communities survive to this day. For a time they prospered in parts of Siberia, becoming farmers and leading lives of puritanical simplicity. Some kept on the move. In the earlier part of the twentieth century the search for military deserters impinged on these hidden lives; the ancient dread of being put on a list kept them moving on.

Karp Lykov, the old father of this particular family, had come from the Tuymn region. He had gradually moved his family further and further from other human habitation. The journey from the nearest settlement would have taken them at least eight weeks. They travelled by boat, but the river was fast and dangerous and at times they had to walk beside it, carrying their boat slung on poles. When they finally settled on a piece of ground which they could cultivate, they grew their own food, and used a tinder-box and flint to light the fire to cook it on. The only thing they felt the lack of was salt. There was game to be found in the *taiga*, but from September to May everything was under snow, sometimes waist-deep; there could be as much as 30 degrees of frost. When the geologists came upon them, there seemed to be only the father and his daughters Natalya and Agafia. After several visits it emerged that there were also two sons, Savin and Dmitri, who had a cabin of their own a few miles away, near the river. The family were in daily contact, and the geologists were uncertain whether temperamental differences with the old father, or perhaps the latter's fear of incest, had induced the sons to move so far away. Karp Osipovich was eighty-one at the time of their discovery, Savin fifty-four, Natalya forty-four, Dmitri thirty-eight and Agafia thirty-seven. The mother had died of hunger in 1961.

Gradually relations were established with the geologists, and also with a journalist from Moscow who came to investigate the story and when he left carried on a correspondence with Agafia. The geologists left too when the winter came. They returned in the spring, to find that Savin and Natalya had died, apparently of kidney disease. Dimitri had died of pneumonia, after getting soaked through trying to trap an elk. Later the father died too, and only Agafia remained, with her caution and consistency and her dark austere beauty. She was persuaded to visit the nearby town, but the *taiga* reclaimed her. She felt it was her home. The geologists built her a stronger wooden cabin and left her there.

CHAPTER 3

'. . . sighing once again to take part in its pleasures and allurements . . .'

NATURE AND THE AMERICAN FRONTIER

Ancient Romans and nature — Pliny's letters —
shamanism — Mircea Eliade —
trappers, explorers and mountain men in America

If to the Greeks of classical times wild nature was peopled with
gods, solitude would necessarily be risky. The sound of Pan's pipes
somewhere beyond the confines of the sacred grove would be
terrifying; at the dread hour of noon Pluto might manifest himself
and carry you off to the underworld. The oracles and temples were
crowded places; you might walk apart a little with a friend or two,
talking all the time, but only a goatherd would risk being alone,
and he would have his dog.

Marcus Aurelius recommended living in tune with nature, but
he was a Stoic; he believed that reason and self-control, as well as
a respect for the natural world, could preserve the spirit from
stress, and give it access to true freedom, which was in the mind.
The Stoic also believed in duty, that one should perform one's
function to the best of one's ability in whatever role the Judge
of the Universe allotted one. This made Stoicism an admirable
philosophy for kings and statesmen and Roman governors. In
Marcus Aurelius' case it led him not only to meditation and
religious exercises but to working sixteen hours a day on the
ordering of the Roman Empire.

In Roman times poets did feel something about the landscape
which was not necessarily anything to do with either reason or
tutelary spirits; but then the Italian landscape is the most harmonious in the world. Virgil was probably the first to find in it a
meaning beyond appearance; just as Horace was probably the first

to express the bitter-sweet conflict between the tranquillity of his Sabine farm and the bustle and gossip of the metropolis. Pliny the Younger, a successful lawyer, writing to a friend from his Tuscan villa, describes a landscape you might still see somewhere on the borders of Tuscany and Umbria.

> Figure to yourself an immense amphitheatre, such as the hand of nature could alone form. Before you lies a vast extended plain bounded by a range of mountains, whose summits are crowned with lofty and venerable woods, which supply abundance and variety of game; from hence as the mountains decline, they are adorned with under-woods . . .
> At the foot of these hills the eye is presented, wherever it turns, with one unbroken view of numberless vineyards, which are terminated below by a border, as it were, of shrubs. From thence extend meadows and fields . . . The flower-enamelled meadows produce trefoil and other kinds of herbage as fine and tender as if it were but just sprung up, being everywhere refreshed by never-failing rills . . . You would be most agreeably entertained by taking a view of the face of this country from the mountains; you would imagine that not a real, but some painted landscape lay before you, drawn with the most exquisite beauty and exactness; such an harmonious and regular variety charms the eye whichever way soever it throws itself.

Pliny was writing about a hundred years after the birth of Christ, that is to say over sixteen hundred years before Alexander Pope first used the English word 'picturesque' (in the sense of 'as if seen in a painted picture') to describe a landscape, and to initiate a whole school of landscape gardening.

Demobilized veterans from the Roman legions were customarily given pieces of land, forty acres each. There are parts of Italy where the farmhouses which crown each hill must be the successors of those Roman buildings. Most of them were probably built only two or three hundred years ago, but their simple outlines and the solid stones out of which they are built and which make them almost part of the hillside are so rational an answer to a simple requirement that they must always have been much the same. Nightingales sing day and night in June, goldfinches flash past, feeding in the cypresses, a hoopoe might nest between the stones of the house and spit at you from the dark hole if you come too near, a golden oriole whistles from the poplars by the stream. Don't believe that these places have been devoured by tourists; it hasn't happened yet. If you plant potatoes, porcupines will eat them, the walls of the terraces beneath which you find your wild asparagus will be disturbed by wild boar searching for snails. If you walk alone behind the house to the topmost terrace, where it fades into the belt of short oak trees mixed with arbutus, and sit on a rock from which the lizards have flickered away at your coming, you may hear from somewhere not far away the scrape of a hoe on dry earth or the slow footstep of your neighbour gathering wild leaves for her rabbits but you will not hear a motorway, and if you look into the farthest distance, beyond the next range of hills and then the next, you may see the sunlit towers of the ideal city. You cannot hoard all of this, but afterwards and elsewhere a certain shape of tree, or smell of herbs, can sometimes bring it back. It is the landscape which in countless works of art has stood in for that of paradise.

Ancient Greek civilization had a harsher landscape to contend with. Agriculture was more difficult on the dry, rocky, terrain. The climate was more extreme, nature less kindly, however dramatic or beautiful, the sea something to be feared as well as exploited. In ancient Greece, everything was for the *polis*, partly because it needed defending against its environment as well as against its neighbours. In the same way the American pioneering spirit was all for family and community because both needed protection, so that such early American solitaries as there were excluded themselves from the communal ethos, and were wild men or misfits rather than mystics.

Earlier still, of course, there were Native American shamans, but they were not necessarily solitary. They did not live apart from the tribe, except perhaps in some psychic sense, but they would go into isolation in the course of their initiation. Spotted at an early age as being subject to hallucinations and strange dreams, they would go through a time of sickness, mysterious pain and ecstatic seizures; after which the older masters would give them instruction. These episodes of inexplicable and extreme pain occur in other traditions. Krishnamurti suffered from them, on his way to the spiritual understanding which in time he realized did not make him an *avatar*, but which was still remarkable. There have been Christian mystics, too, who have had similar apparently inexplicable visitations. Hildegard of Bingen, in the twelfth century, had periods of agonizing pain when she felt that the marrow in her bones had dried up and her abdomen was on fire. It has been suggested that some of her symptoms – and indeed her visions – can be accounted for by a diagnosis of severe migraine, but the attack often lasted for much longer than most migraines. Some Yogic philosophies speak of a force in the base of the spine called *kundalini* or 'serpent fire' which when released, often with the utmost pain, results in episodes of clairvoyancy.

Shamans sought ecstatic trance through drumming, dancing, drugs, sensory deprivation. Their role was to ascend into the sky to intercede with the spirits. They could descend under the earth as well, and have adventures and ordeals in other worlds. Somewhere within the multitude of beliefs there is mention of 'inner light', which bears some relation to the true understanding of the mystic, but the shaman's task was on the whole rather practical, to heal, prognosticate and inculcate a satisfying awe. There was an element of spectacle, of stagecraft, and often of trickery, aimed at making imaginable another world where anything might be possible, and where the shaman's powers might achieve miracles. Native American villages might also have a hermit living not far away, somewhere in the forest in his tent of buffalo-skins, wearing a deer-skin and shoes made of bark, collecting herbs and roots useful as medicine.

The most scholarly expert on shamanism, as practised not only in North America but in Siberia and Australia and anywhere where tribal society had its medicine men and magicians, was the Romanian Mircea Eliade, who died in 1986. For the last few years of his life he taught at the University of Chicago, and because he combined academic life with literary creation and obviously had an impressive personality he was almost a cult in himself to some of his students. As a young man he had spent two years as a solitary in a cave among the pinewoods of the Himalayas, and the story of how this came about is told in two small books, both of which were reissued by the University of Chicago Press in 1994.

The first was a novel called *Bengal Nights*. It was originally published anonymously in Romania in 1933. It tells the story of a young Frenchman, Alain, who goes to work in India as a railway engineer. His immediate superior is a professor whom he comes to admire and even hold in a certain amount of awe. Alain is pleased when the professor offers to help him in his studies, and then to take him into his own house as a lodger. At the same time he is made uncomfortable by the mockery of many of his colleagues at work, who are mostly Anglo-Indians, that is to say of mixed blood, and consequently keen to show how Western they are in their attitudes and in their scorn of full-blooded Indians. Alain is very young, and this is Calcutta in the 1930s. His own attitudes are confused, so that when he finds himself falling in love with his professor's daughter he is bewildered. Sex across the racial divide seems discreditable, and love more or less out of the question. The girl is charming, and highly intelligent; they talk of art and poetry; he looks at her beautiful dark arm between the folds of her sari and thinks, she is like that all over.

In due course their youthful passions cannot be subdued; their nights of love are overheard by a jealous servant, her father berates the young man for betraying his trust and turns him out of the house. He is in despair; perhaps the father is right, perhaps the girl was playing with his feelings, perhaps the longing he feels is an aberration, a physical addiction. He runs away. Wandering in the foothills of the Himalayas, he finds an ashram where he can live in a cave in solitude and wrestle with his despair and guilt and deep unhappiness. Eventually an Australian girl appears at the ashram, a neurotic and unsuccessful seeker after self-transcendence; they make ferocious love. Alain is not so much freed from his obsession as distanced from it, or perhaps separated from it for ever. But he is not separated from what he has learned about Eastern religious thought, though he decides to go back to Europe to continue his studies there.

Bengal Nights appeared in French translation in 1950. Maitreyi Devi, however, the daughter of Eliade's professor at Calcutta University, knew nothing of it until 1972, when a friend gave it to her to read. It was, of course, her story. Her father had not been an engineer so much as a distinguished professor of Eastern philosophy, and Eliade had been his student. Otherwise the story was the same, except in one important particular. There had been warm embraces, long kisses, but according to Maitreyi's version she had not sacrificed her virginity; indeed, she came across an old book of poems in which at the height of the family drama she had written with a trembling hand, 'Mircea, Mircea, I have told my mother that you have kissed me only on the forehead.'

By now Maitreyi was a distinguished writer and lecturer, active on committees, expert on the poetry of Rabindranath Tagore, but she felt affronted, forty years later, by the thought of her impugned virtue, and decided to write her own book. *It Does Not Die* tells the story of her heartbreak, and virtual breakdown, after the young Eliade left. Why did he not come? Why did he not answer the messages she sent him? Could he not have stood in front of her father and simply said, I love your daughter? Slowly she returned to her studies. She spent some time with her family's friend, Rabindranath Tagore, at his university at Santivaram. Eventually she asked her parents to arrange a marriage for her. She went to live on a Darjeeling tea plantation, where her husband was manager. He was a kind man; they had three sons, and she interested herself in the conditions of the workers. Rabindranath Tagore came to stay, to rest and talk. As her children grew up she became involved in public life, and one day in the course of her work she went to attend a conference in Chicago.

She wrote to Eliade, and said that she would like to see him.

We have to picture her approaching the university library; would she have become quite stately by now? But she has had important positions, her charm and intelligence have been recognized. The girl she sees on the stairs would have been impressed, would have hurried obediently ahead to tell the Professor his guest was approaching. He is working at a table at the far end of the room. Does he hear her breathing, remember how she ran up and down stairs as a girl without the slightest breathlessness? 'I am here,' she says. He will not turn. She says, 'You say at the end of your book, one day I would like to look Maitreyi in the eyes again.' He groans. 'Too late.' She says, 'We are both married, I know that. My husband is a good man. You are happy with your wife. Turn, and look at me.' He will not look. She bows her head, turns to go. He groans again, grinds out between his teeth, 'One day. Beside the Ganges. I will come to you.' She seems to float down the stairs. The callow students, lives as yet unlived, instinctively give way. She is content, serene. In another life, beside the Ganges, they will be together, they will be one.

Eliade's life had many aspects. He was involved in Romanian politics before the war. His belief in the virtues of peasant life meant that at one time he was in danger of being claimed as a supporter by right-wing organizations. For a time he was unable to find an academic post and was extremely short of money. America saved him. He believed that post-colonial India was moving on to the world stage in an unprecedented manner, and that the West would be revivified, must be revivified, by learning both from Eastern religion and from traditional peasant beliefs such as he found in his own Romania. This was the belief that underlay all his many years of scholarship. Perhaps it was the sight of a smooth brown arm amid its silks which first involved his imagination as well as his intellect.

The fur-trappers who were among the first to venture into Rocky Mountain territory were far from being experts on North American shaminism; they were traders. In the middle years of the nineteenth century they pursued their trade so vigorously that they completely exterminated the beaver. Some became mountain men with Native American wives. Sometimes others joined them and small settlements arose, in which civilization had to start from scratch, in obedience to strictly practical imperatives. The frontier of settlement spread from the Mississippi river, across the prairies to the forested slopes of the Rocky Mountain range. There the trappers established themselves, and rather than make the long journey for supplies every year they sent for them from St Louis. At the time of the beaver moult, in late June, there would be a great meeting of trappers at Jackson's Hole beneath the Grand Tetons, or by the Great Salt Lake. Mountain men from all over the west would be there, as well as Mexicans from Taos and Santa Fe and French Canadian deserters from the Hudson Bay Company. Whole villages of friendly Indians would move in with their tepees. There would be a mile-long train of mules from St Louis, and some consequent scenes of debauchery and drunkenness.

In September it was back to the mountains, singly or in twos and threes, searching and trapping until the time of the beavers' hibernation, and then it was time to camp until the spring. Beaver, buffalo and Native Americans were the only neighbours. The Blackfoot were the most aggressive and the most feared, the Crow were more friendly but not invariably so. There were grizzly bears to contend with, as well as rattlesnakes, illness and starvation. In the struggle for survival men sometimes bled their horses so as to drink their blood, or cut off and ate the ears of mules or the leather thongs of moccasins. Edward Rose joined the Crow and became a ferocious leader in skirmishes with the Blackfoot. Cannibal Phil (from Philadelphia) went on one long trapping journey with an Indian and disappeared in a winter gale. After several days, when he was given up for lost, he reappeared without the Indian. As he unpacked his mule, he pulled out a black and shrivelled human leg and threw it on the ground. 'There, damn you, I won't have to gnaw on you any more.' Later, marooned by a snowstorm, he ate his squaw.

Some of these desperate characters became so used to solitude and wilderness that they could not do without it. Old Bill Williams went west as a missionary, married an Indian squaw and became a trapper. His passion for solitude and loneliness led him deep into the mountains; his skill as a trapper became famous. He became convinced that he would return in the next life as an elk in his favourite valley, and used to warn people not to go hunting elk there after his death. As he grew older he tried to give up the lonely life and bought a store in Taos. He stood it only for a week; then he threw all his stock out into the street and left for the hills.

Years later a party of trappers climbing high in the mountains found themselves in a wild canyon which opened out into a small glade, in which they decided to pitch their camp for the night. Breaking through the undergrowth to reach the glade, they found to their astonishment a single horse, weak with cold and trembling from extreme old age. One of the travellers recognized the once famous Nez Percé horse of Old Bill Williams. Searching further, they found an old camp, some charred logs and a figure seated with its back to a tree. Approaching fearfully they found the body of Old Bill Williams, frozen as hard as stone.

George Frederick Ruxton, who tells that story, was a nineteenth-century army officer who left Sandhurst at seventeen to fight in the civil wars in Spain. He joined a squadron of lancers attached to the division of General Diego Leon, and was decorated by Queen Isabella II before being gazetted to a commission in the 89th regiment and sent to Canada. There he found his expeditions into the wilds so fascinating that he resigned his commission to become an explorer, supporting himself to some extent by the articles he wrote for *Blackwood's Magazine*.

Although liable to an accusation of barbarism, I must confess that the very happiest moments of my life have been spent in the wilderness of the Far West; and I never recall, but with pleasure, the remembrance of my solitary camp in the Bayou Salade, with no friend near me more faithful than my rifle, and no companions more sociable than my good horse and mules, or the attendant cayute which nightly serenaded us. With a plentiful supply of dry pine-logs on the fire, and its cheerful blaze streaming far up into the sky, illuminating the valley far and near, and exhibiting the animals, with well-filled bellies, standing contentedly at rest over their picket-fire, I would sit cross-legged, enjoying the genial warmth, and, pipe in mouth, watch the blue smoke as it curled upwards, building castles in its vapoury wreaths, and, in the fantastic shapes it assumed, peopling the solitude with figures of those far away. Scarcely, however, did I ever wish to change such hours of freedom for all the luxuries of civilised life; and, unnatural and extraordinary as it may appear, yet such is the fascination of the life of the mountain hunter, that I believe not one instance could be adduced of even the most polished and civilised of men, who had once tasted the sweets of its attendant liberty, and freedom from every worldly care, not regretting the moment when he exchanged it for the monotonous life of the settlements, nor sighing and sighing again once more to partake of its pleasures and allurements.

There have probably always been successors of those early mountain men in the remoter parts of America's great expanse, most of them known only to a few neighbours from local settlements. Earl Parrot lived for many years in the 1930s and 40s in a log dugout just above the rim of Impassable Canyon near the Middle Fork of the Salmon river in Idaho. He did a little prospecting for gold, grew vegetables and occasionally hunted deer. He would make the seventy-mile trip to the nearest settlement once a year to buy matches, salt, tea and bullets. His cabin could be reached only by climbing a ladder up a wall of rock and following a two-mile trail, with occasional wooden ladders up the steepest of the cliffs, almost as far as the rim of the canyon.

There was a nearby valley with a stream in it which provided water for the solitary's garden; he kept it fenced with poles against the deer, and grew corn, beans, potatoes, sweet potatoes, cabbage, beets, carrots, peppers, cucumbers, raspberries, strawberrries, watermelons, peaches and apricots. He kept seeds from the best of each crop for the succeeding year, and dried and stored most of the produce, keeping the corn and beans in split and hollowed pine logs, whose edges he smoothed so that they fitted exactly. His cabin was small but neat, his bed was made of poles covered by a bear-skin, he had sheep- and goat-skins for warmth and a kid's hide for a pillow. In the winter it was too cold to do much but sleep. As the years went by, adventurers took to trekking out to see him; he tried to discourage them by telling them he kept five rattlesnakes. In the end he became ill and had to be taken to the nearest town; he died in a nursing home there at the age of seventy-five in August 1945.

Further north in Idaho, William Moreland, known as the Ridgerunner, was last seen in 1964. He had eluded the forest rangers for many years, surviving in the woods in all weathers, occasionally stealing food, candles or clothing from the rangers' cabins; from time to time they caught up with him and he served a brief prison sentence for burglary. The last time they caught him, a judge decided he must be mad and sent him to the county asylum. He escaped. By now he was well known, and anyone who met him was inclined to help him.

'I came back to see if these mountains were as beautiful as I remember them,' he told a Forest Service worker who met him on the trail. 'I'm not going to stay.'

A year later a man sawing logs saw him pass, and asked him where he was going.

'I'm leaving.'

'I thought these mountains were your home.'

'They were, but there's too many people here now. I'm leaving for good.'

No one ever saw or heard of him again. Neither Idaho nor Kentucky has a record of his death.

There will always be people hiding from the law, or each other, or themselves, but there may well be other solitaries in the vast wilds of America, not just those who have grouped themselves together in a joint rejection of society as usually constituted, like the Vietnam veterans who went to live in the woods of Oregon – or the less agreeable extreme individualists who reject government authority and live in armed enclaves known to the general public only when violence erupts – but individuals obeying nothing more than their own strong inclination for solitude. I heard of one living in the Catskills, where adventurous hikers are surprised to see elegant dresses, usually white or gold, on hangers on trees miles from anywhere; their owner, who has a name like an English duchess, offers no explanations and keeps to her tent.

The American wilderness is true wilderness, a place where the landscape is untamed. Perhaps it is addictive; it is certainly dangerous. Alaska, for instance – Jack London's 'savage, frozen-hearted Northland Wild' – has accounted for quite a number of insufficiently prepared adventurers, looking for a test, or an escape, or something they vaguely called 'reality'. In April 1992 the body of Chris McCandless was found by a party of hunters in an abandoned bus in the wilderness north of Mount McKinley. The bus had been left to rust just off the Stampede Trail, an unfinished road which followed the route first taken in the 1930s by a miner called Earl Pilgrim, who had made some antimony claims many miles further along. In 1961 an attempt was made to turn the trail into a road, and when the scheme was abandoned two years later one of the buses in which workers had lived was left behind as a shelter for hunters or trappers. Hard to reach, because a fierce river intervenes, the bus was usually visited at some time during the moose-hunting season by those few hunters who knew the way. McCandless did not know the way, and had no map; it seemed he had been determined to walk into terra incognita, taking with him only a bag of rice.

The McCandless family was prosperous and successful. The boy had been brought up in the expectation that he too would do well in the world. He was bright, enterprising, opinionated and self-centred. Rebellious feelings towards his parents' generation were reinforced by unwelcome discoveries about his father's first marriage. He read Tolstoy and Jack London, gave away his possessions and began to wander. He survived long treks in the Mojave desert on the borders of Mexico, travelled up the West Coast, paddled a canoe down the Colorado river to the Gulf of California and into Mexico, moved around the south-west, the Grand Canyon, the Oregon coast, and back to Arizona. On his way the people he came across, who fed him or gave him a few months work, mostly came to like him. One man in his eighties wanted to adopt him, and after the boy left for Alaska the old man followed his typically didactic advice and took to his way of life, moving into an old van near a patch of cottonwood in the Californian desert, hoping each day for the boy's return.

A journalist called Jon Krakauer became intrigued by McCandless' story and determined to reconstruct the events leading up to his death. He came to the conclusion that McCandless probably died as a result of eating the poisonous seed pods of the wild potato, whose roots he had been eating without harm. The seeds are apparently poisonous only at a certain time of the year, and none of the books McCandless had studied warn of the danger. The effect of the poison is to prevent the body from processing any other food properly, in other words it leads to death by starvation. The book Krakauer wrote became a memorial to a young man who was not entirely feckless, who if he had survived might have felt that in testing himself so rigorously against the wilderness he had won his independence from his family, and who among his books had left a copy of Pasternak's *Doctor Zhivago* with a passage marked HAPPINESS ONLY REAL WHEN SHARED. He might have intended to come back and give the human race another chance. He might also – as his last diaries seem to indicate – have found that the life of the solitary hunter-gatherer offers only limited possibilities for high thoughts, most of the time being spent, of necessity, either hunting or gathering. Jon Krakauer's book, *Into the Wild*, became a bestseller, perhaps because families all over America thought of their rebellious sons and felt a frisson of fear.

CHAPTER 4

'. . . then would I wander far off, and remain in the wilderness . . .'

THE EGYPTIAN DESERT

St Antony — Syria — St Simeon —
Julia Butterfly Hill — St Jerome —
the Wife of Bath — Deir Mar Musa

St Antony is the prototype of all Christian hermits, Abba Antony
to all his successors. He suffered temptations, was beaten up by
demons, and reasoned with the wild asses until they desisted from
eating his vegetables. He emerged from years of solitude, like a
Boddhisattva who has achieved enlightenment, and gave counsel
to his fellow-hermits and an example to the world. His temptations
are terrifyingly depicted by Hieronymus Bosch and feverishly
described by Flaubert. The thought of him has authenticated a
thousand retreats into the wilderness, a thousand flights from the
world.

He went out into the Egyptian desert in 270 AD. The idea of the
desert as a place of encounter with God already existed in religious
tradition. The Old Testament prophets had wandered there. Elijah
had been brought bread by a raven and Moses had heard God's
voice speaking to him from within a burning bush. John the Baptist,
crying in the wilderness, had foretold the coming of the Messiah.
Jesus himself had gone there to overcome temptation after his
baptism. Pre-Christian sects such as the Essenes had withdrawn in
the same way, seeking emptiness and space. In the third century,
when the Roman Empire was in decline and its periphery became
increasingly lawless, there were other reasons for taking to the
desert. It might have been to escape the tax collector, or an angry
neighbour reclaiming a debt, or a violent father or a shrewish wife,
or if you were a woman an unwelcome suitor (in which case you

would probably be disguised as a man – there are several cases of hermits whose sex was discovered only after their deaths); or you might have been an outcast, or a leper or a lunatic. There were also intermittent but sometimes ferocious persecutions of Jews and Christians until 313, when religious liberty throughout the empire was proclaimed in the time of Constantine by the Edict of Milan. When Christianity became the official religion of the Roman Empire its followers were deprived of their martyrs' crowns; but the red martyrdom of blood could be replaced by the white martyrdom of the desert for those devotees who wanted to distance themselves from the newly fashionable, and increasingly rich, established Church. All these things meant that the desert, vast though it was, was not entirely unpeopled.

Antony was twenty, the orphaned son of moderately prosperous Christians, when he heard the Gospel read in church, 'If thou wilt be perfect, go and sell all that thou hast and give to the poor, and come and follow Me.' According to his biographer Athanasius, Bishop of Alexandria, who knew him, he arranged that his sister should be looked after by a 'community of virgins'; this is interesting, because monasticism had not yet come into being, so there must have been autonomous 'convents' of consecrated women, presumably outside the institutional Church. Having given away all his possessions, St Antony went to live among some tombs close to his village, near an old man who was already leading a solitary life. In his first years he had to struggle for self-discipline, suffering and then overcoming the attacks from demons for which he is famous. He went further into the desert, into an abandoned fort at Pispir, on the east bank of the Nile, fifty miles south of Memphis. There he lived alone for twenty years, after which some of the people who had come to see him and been refused admission forced their way into his retreat. They were astonished to find him not only sane but apparently healthy and happy.

Followers began to gather round him, and he no longer refused to speak to them but advised them as to their way of life, and sometimes gathered them together in order to preach to them.

After a time there were hundreds of hermits living nearby in huts or cells, and crowds would come out from the towns and villages to seek his counsel. Eventually he retreated a hundred miles or so to a cave on Mount Kolzim, which he called his Inner Mountain, 'a place he fell in love with as soon as he saw it'. A mile and a half west of his cave, twenty-two miles west of the Gulf of Suez and south-west of Zafaranah, there now stands a Coptic monastery known as St Antony's Monastery.

It is difficult to be certain how the early Christian hermits felt about the actual desert in which they lived their daily lives, as opposed to the metaphysical one which they had chosen for spiritual reasons. Some seem to have feared it, others to have emphasized its harshness and desolation in order to magnify their own powers of endurance. Some came to love it because of what they had learned from it. St Antony said, 'A monk out of his cell is a fish out of water . . .' He was said to have gone for a walk every evening before sunset to enjoy the austere beauty of the desert landscape. His disciple St Hilarion, another recluse who had to retreat from his own fame, moving from Egypt to Sicily and Dalmatia and finally to Cyprus, went in his old age to visit Antony's Inner Mountain. St Jerome describes the occasion in his life of Hilarion.

> There is a tall and rocky mountain, about a mile in circumference, that produces water at its foot, some of which is absorbed by the sand while some flows down to the lower area, gradually forming a stream. Above this stream grow innumerable palm trees which make the place very pleasant and comfortable. Here you might have seen the old man Hilarion rushing from one place to another with the blessed Antony's disciples. 'Here,' they said, 'he used to sing psalms; here he used to pray. Here he would work and here he would rest when he was tired. He planted these vines and bushes himself. The little garden he made with his own hands. He worked very hard to construct this pond to irrigate his

garden. This is the hoe he used for many years to dig the ground.'

St Jerome, who spent little more than two years in the desert and disliked it, claimed that there had been a hermit earlier than St Antony, and his life of St Paul the First Hermit is one of the most touching of the many stories told and retold about the Desert Fathers. When Antony was ninety and Paul a hundred and thirteen, Antony came to understand that somewhere in the desert there was a better monk than he, and that he should make haste to find him. So he set out, walking with a stick, across the desert, through the burning noonday heat. Directed on his journey by a centaur, who gave him some dates, and a dwarfish faun, he saw on the dawn of the third day a she-wolf, panting with thirst, who seemed to vanish into the foot of the mountain. Following her he came upon the entrance to a cave, which opened out into a space open to the sky, with an ancient palm tree growing by a spring of clear water. There he found Paul, and the two old men sat down together to talk and pray. A raven brought them a loaf of bread, which they shared, and they drank from the spring. Then Paul asked Antony to go back to his cell and fetch the cloak which Athanasius the bishop had given him, because he was dying and would like to be buried in it; he did not want Antony to have to see him die. So Antony went to fetch the cloak, three days' journey to his cell and three days back, and when he returned Paul was dead. He wrapped the body in the cloak and carried it outside, but he had no spade to dig a grave. In his anguish he prayed for death, but then two lions came running from the inner desert and, after roaring their sorrow by the body of the dead man, they went a little way away and dug a grave with their paws. Antony blessed them, and buried Paul in the grave. Representations of this story, some of them from the very earliest years of the spread of Christianity, are to be found in places as far apart as Greece and Scotland.

The flight to the desert which Antony initiated lasted at least until the end of the fourth century, and coincided with the collapse of the Roman Empire. Many of the hermit settlements were very large, great spreading encampments of solitary individuals, a huge silent protest against what was happening in the society they had left behind.

At the centre of each settlement would be a church, a bakery, and probably some accommodation for guests. These might be seeking spiritual guidance ('give me a word that I may live') but they might equally be merely curious; hermits and hermitages have always attracted sight-seers. A hermit has to have a means of subsistence, and the inhabitants of these settlements would often have agents in the nearby villages who would collect the baskets, mats, ropes or linen which they made, and take them to the local markets to sell so as to provide basic food and clothing. The hermit would grow his own vegetables if he could find enough water. The truffles which still grow in the barren desert in the winter months are said to be the original manna from heaven.

The settlements reached further and further into the desert, from Pispir to Nitria, and from Nitria nine miles further on to Cellia, where there was space enough for the cells to be so far apart that none was in sight of the other. There the hermits only came together once a week in the church. If one was missing, others would go to see if he was ill; otherwise they never disturbed each other. Even so there were some who went even further, to Scete, a day and a night's journey into the desert; there some of the zealots strove to outdo each other in penance. Macarius made a tunnel from his cell to a cave, so that he could retreat secretly if anyone came to see him; Moses the Ethiopian stood up all night for six years, rather than sleep. Sometimes the hermits quarrelled among themselves as to matters of belief, and some of them moved west, into Italy and Gaul, where the climate, so much gentler in every way than the harshness of the desert, reduced the fire of the extreme ascetic.

The hermits were not always looked upon with approval by the institutionalized Church, nor indeed by government officials. They could appear a potential force for disorder, as when during the Aryan controversy they suddenly thronged the streets of Alexandria, walking in from the desert, emaciated, hairy and wild-eyed.

In the meantime a form of monasticism had emerged, led by Pachomius, who had been a soldier and perhaps felt that the growing crowds of those who had turned their backs on the disintegrating Roman Empire needed some regulation. He founded several communities in the Nile valley at Tabenna, and gave them a written rule. He probably had about seven thousand men and women in various congregations under his rule. In the second half of the fourth century St Basil the Great advocated the coenobitic, or group, life over the solitary. He clearly felt that an uncontrolled hermit could too easily become an aimless wanderer, some kind of early hippie.

St Antony did not advise his followers to push themselves to extremes of asceticism, nor did he himself succumb to the lure of fame, perhaps the holy man's most subtle temptation. Before his death, at the age of over a hundred, he asked to be buried where no one would find his grave, because he did not want it to be made into a shrine. Not all the early hermits were as selfless. Nor did they all attain the serenity of his last years. Some of them were probably of doubtful sanity, especially in Syria.

I have been to Syria, one of the most beautiful and ancient and fascinating countries in the world, and in my short visit I seemed to see in Syrian eyes a certain willingness to go along with the unlikely which was wholly beguiling. A longer stay would of course have taught me more but, as it was, this idea of a people well disposed towards any kind of oddity – despite the fact that they were living at that time in a police state, which meant that many things had to be left unsaid – harmonized with the fact that in early Christian times the Syrian hermits were infinitely the most eccentric. It also made hiring a four-wheeled drive vehicle to go into the desert a negotiation so tortuous and conversationally exhausting as to stand comparison only with a similar encounter many years ago in Ireland, before that country hit its present economic success and lost its whimsical inefficiency.

Hermits who went up on to the tops of pillars were known as stylites, and those few who lived up trees were dendrites. St Simeon, a Syrian, was the most famous of the stylites. His pillar became a place of pilgrimage, and the church which was built round it some time between 476 and 491 was the largest in the world before Justinian built St Sophia in Constantinople in 537. It is now a huge and splendid ruin, in style halfway between the classical and the Romanesque. The hill on which it stands smells of herbs, and there are flocks of goldfinches, as there so often seem to be around sacred ruins. The area was prosperous in the Roman period, and deserted after the seventh century. By then the Arab invasions had put an end to trade with Europe; olives and wine were no longer sent to Constantinople and Rome. During the Ottoman period Bedouin tribes wandered over the increasingly desiccated landscape with their herds. Now that agriculture is beginning to return, some of the villagers still store rainwater in sixth-century cisterns. The deserted villages are known as the 'Dead Cities'; they were hardly cities but their architecture was sophisticated; there were hundreds of churches, convents and villas.

In Refadah, one of the villages at the foot of the hill of St Simeon, two peasant families have settled in the ruins of a villa which must once have been imposing; it has two towers and a portico overlooking an interior courtyard. One fine-looking man told us he had five cows and two horses and was content. The horses were well-built stocky animals, one of them a bright chestnut; they were not at all like the Arab horses we saw elsewhere in Syria. An old man bringing home firewood pointed towards the sky with every indication of being pleased with providence; the woman and small child who were with him passed us with eyes averted. There was a ruined tower outside the village, with a lavatory built out from the top floor. Recluses often lived in towers, sometimes with a disciple on the ground floor to attend to their needs, but the archaeologists seemed to think that this one had been a watchtower.

Edward Gibbon, the historian of the decline and fall of the Roman Empire, who thought little anyway of the Christians of that time, reserved his utmost scorn for the Syrian hermits.

> The aspect of a genuine anachoret was horrid and disgusting. They were sunk under the painful weight of crosses and chains; and their emaciated limbs were confined by collars, bracelets, gauntlets, and greaves of massy and rigid iron. All superfluous encumbrance of dress they contemptuously cast away; and some savage saints of both sexes have been admired, whose naked bodies were only covered by their long hair . . . The most perfect Hermits are supposed to have passed many days without food, many nights without sleep, and many years without speaking; and glorious was the *man* (I abuse that name) who contrived any cell, or seat, of a peculiar construction, which might expose him, in the most inconvenient posture, to the inclemency of the seasons.

St Simeon's seat was certainly of peculiar construction but he did speak. He lived on the top of a pillar for about thirty-six years, and shouted cheerfully to the crowds below him. 'Welcome, man of God!' he would yell. But for women there was no welcome; he would not allow them to see him. Even a female cat who wandered inadvertently into his presence was said to have been immediately struck dead. He was born about 386 AD in the town of Sis, not far from Adana in modern Turkey, the child of moderately prosperous peasants. He joined a group of recluses near Sis for two years and then moved to a mountain monastery, where he spent ten years in ever stricter self-denial. Then he was asked to leave for fear that other monks might follow his example and do themselves injury. He settled instead in the village of Telanissus, on the southern slope of the mountain where he was to spend the rest of his life. At first he lived in a small monastery, in a tiny cell, frequently fasting for forty days at a time. Then he went up the mountain and lived in a small fenced circle, where he tied himself to a chain ten yards long until the Bishop of Antioch told him his enthusiasm was excessive. His fame spread and people came to see him from all over the Middle East and Europe. He built himself a pillar about three feet high to escape their attentions, and as the crowds grew so he went higher and higher until he was nearly sixty feet high. You can still see the solid base of the pillar with a worn piece of stone a few feet high upon it, which is all that remains. The diameter of the original pillar was three and a half feet, and on top of it was a wooden balustrade, enclosing a space of about forty-three square feet. Seekers for advice could, with the saint's permission, climb a ladder and speak to him in relative privacy. There was a lavatory, consisting of an earthenware pipe extending from the top of the pillar to a pit at the base. The top of the pillar was protected from the sun and the rain by a canopy of palm branches. During the last three years of his life St Simeon removed the canopy.

He seems to have provided a more or less continuous show. He remained standing from sunrise to sunset, shouting sermons; he was famous for the number of genuflections he could do; an observer counted up to 1,244 before giving up. The crowd would cheer him on. In the interval between performances he would arbitrate judiciously in local disputes over property or cattle. When he died the Bishop of Antioch had to send six hundred soldiers to remove his coffin, so anxious was the local population to keep it.

In 460 the recluse Daniel, who had known St Simeon, went up

on to a pillar on the western side of the Bosphorus, where the emperor was in the habit of consulting him on many important matters. Stylites were not unusual in that part of the world for many years thereafter. They were not all such performers as St Simeon. Some of the remoter ones went up on to their pillars in silence after years of contemplative practice, feeling that they were mounting their place of crucifixion.

It should perhaps be remembered that St Simeon Stylites, though he might have called himself a hermit, was not even pretending to be a complete recluse. He was more of an evangelist than a solitary. He wanted to attract attention to his cause, and he succeeded. The closest parallel in our own time is probably not a stylite so much as a dendrite. Julia Butterfly Hill climbed 180 feet up a giant redwood high on a hill in one of the last ancient redwood forests in the world on 10 December 1997. The tree was a thousand years old, the forest was in Humboldt County, California. A logging company was clear-cutting, destroying hundreds of trees and causing dangerous mud slides. Two years later, after surviving loneliness and storms, a siege by security guards and endless negotiations and legal battles, she came down to earth. The logging company had admitted defeat, and agreed to leave the tree standing. Julia Butterfly Hill – briefly as famous in her own society as St Simeon Stylites in his – became a national heroine.

St Jerome was born at Stridon in Dalmatia, the son of Christian parents who sent him to Rome to be educated. Always ascetic, he became increasingly obsessed by his own sinfulness. About 372, when he was twenty-seven, he went on pilgrimage to the East and Jerusalem, taking his books with him. At Antioch he stayed with Evagrius, an influential priest. There he learned Greek, and became aware of the austerities of the Eastern anchorites. He had a dream in which Christ told him he was a Ciceronian and not a Christian.

He swore, 'Lord, if ever again I possess worldly books, if ever again I read them, I shall have denied you.' Humanist scholars have found the implications of this awkward ever since. He became a hermit in the Syrian desert, somewhere between Antioch and Palmyra, in about 374 and he stayed there for two or three years. He seems to have brought his books with him (though presumably not Cicero), and to have carried on with his scholarly translations, often helped by young monks who acted as scribes.

Perhaps in later life Jerome exaggerated his suffering: 'Oh how often, when I was living in the sun-scorched solitude of the desert, which offers monks a savage hospitality, how often I imagined myself back among the pleasures of Rome!' He was tormented by visions of Roman dancing girls. He would have agreed with Job when he said of the Devil, 'His power is in the loins, his strength in the navel', loins and navel being Job's delicate way of referring to the male and female genitals. Jerome seems to have hated women, though he had numbers of devoted female followers, usually well born. He also hated various rival scholars, and he certainly detested the Syrian anchorites who were his neighbours in the desert. They were mostly simple peasants, speaking only Syriac, sometimes living in holes in the ground, filthy and hairy, wearing nothing but goat-skins, and often hung around with heavy chains; Jerome would have agreed with Gibbon.

He learned Hebrew in the desert; he said it took his mind off sex. He was the first Latin Christian to do this, and was said to have had his teeth filed so that he could make the necessary sibilant sounds. 'After the subtlety of Quintilian, the flowing eloquence of Cicero, the dignified prose of Fronto, the smooth grace of Pliny, I set myself to learn an alphabet and strove to pronounce hissing, breath-demanding words.' So began the work which culminated in his translation of the Bible into Latin; known as the Vulgate, it became the standard Bible of the West.

St Jerome left the desert with relief, apparently much resented by his despised neighbours, who thought him an intellectual snob and friend of grandees. Back in Rome, his reputation as a scholar grew and he was much consulted by Pope Damasus. Certain well-born women had at this time formed themselves into small religious communities, following an ascetic way of life; two of these, Paula and her daughter Eustochium, became particularly close to St Jerome. In due course, Jerome set up a monastery and Paula a convent, in Bethlehem. When Paula and Eustochium died in 404 and 418 respectively, Jerome grieved for them deeply. After the sack of Rome by the barbarians in 410, refugees flooded the Middle East and wandering bands of tribesmen caused unease; the settled world of the Roman Empire was finally crumbling; the number of hermits in the desert increased, some of them trying by their excesses to pre-empt the pains of Hell. St Jerome the scholar worked on at his books until his death in 420.

As time passed, Jerome's legend grew in response to demand from the pious. The story arose of how St Augustine had been sitting at his desk to write to Jerome when heavenly light and fragrance filled the room; it was the moment of Jerome's death. Paintings multiplied. In the mid-fourteenth century a professor of law at Bologna named Giovanni d'Andrea took over the legend, dedicating a chapel in the cathedral at Bologna and paying for a priest to serve it, encouraging others to do similar things, and laying down that Jerome should always be painted with his cardinal's hat beside him and a lion at his feet. In fact the College of Cardinals was not instituted until the end of the eleventh century; Jerome was somehow posthumously elevated because it seemed appropriate.

The lion, however, seems less appropriate. The irascible saint does not strike one as likely to be naturally kind, whether to man or beast. It was probably St Gerasimus who took the thorn out of the lion's paw. He was a hermit in the desert near the Dead Sea around 450 and later instituted a *laura* or group of hermits in separate cells near the river Jordan. His story (and the lion) come in John Moschus' *Spiritual Meadow*, a collection of stories about the monks and hermits in the desert written in the early sixth century.

For a time there were Jeronomite monasteries in Italy and especially in Spain. They were ascetic and anti-intellectual – the penitent Jerome rather than the scholar. The Emperor Charles V ended his days as a hermit in one of them. After 1600 the eremitic life lost its hold, and the Italian Jeronomites more or less disappeared while the Spanish went in for liturgical splendour rather than austerity. Jerome remained supreme as the scholar who gave the world the Vulgate and stood for the authority of the Church, monasticism and celibacy. He appears in an enormous number of paintings – the National Gallery in London alone has thirty representations of him in its collection.

Chaucer's Wife of Bath thought nothing of St Jerome. Catching her fifth husband Jankin laughing at the book he was reading she 'rent out of his book a leef/For which he smoot me so that I was deef', which seems a rather violent reaction until one remembers how valuable a book would have been at the time. What chiefly infuriated her was that the book was anti-feminist: 'This book of wikked wives,' she calls it. Of St Jerome's contribution she says

> And eek ther was somtime a clerk at Rome,
> A cardinal, that highte Seint Jerome,
> That made a book again Jovinian

Jovinian had denied that virginity was a higher state than marriage and abstinence better than thankful eating. St Jerome replied with a diatribe upon the dangers of marriage and the appalling moral frailty of women, as evidenced by their frivolity, vanity, duplicity, avariciousness, wantonness and so on. The Wife of Bath in her splendid riposte displays abundantly all the weaknesses he mentions, while leaving the reader in no doubt that she has Chaucer's support. The fact remains that the strength of St Jerome's feelings against women left a nasty little heritage somewhere in part of the Christian world; and yet it seems he truly loved Paula and Eustochium. Perhaps it was only when they aroused his own lust that he hated them. It is reported of Paula that she seldom washed.

The Syrian desert, where St Jerome went, is of the North African variety, rather like the northern parts of Morocco, stony and occasionally mountainous. We drove a little way into it, in search of Deir Mar Musa, where we had been told there were some hermits. We had hired a four-wheel drive vehicle in Damascus, but the driver, though friendly, was not in sympathy with our project. Asking the way in the small town of Nebek he seemed to choose only those bystanders who looked unlikely to know the way to the next street, until we spotted someone who must have

been the local philosopher and man of letters, and who described the way at some length and added, 'You will meet Father Paolo. He is no ordinary man. He has two doctor's certificates.' Then he said, 'You will have to walk. If you go to a historic place it is good to walk.' We agreed, hoping all the same for moderation. Ali the driver struck boldly across the expanse of sand and small stones.

Nebek disappeared from sight behind us. Before long a considerable rocky escarpment rose before us. Ali expressed doubts, but at the foot of it we could see some kind of temporary building with workmen mixing cement beside it, and urged him on. Soon it became clear that what appeared at first sight to be no more than a cleft in the rock was in fact a building made of the same stone; it looked like something one might expect to see in Tibet or Ladakh. We started to walk up the steep path; Ali, with relief, settled down for a sleep.

It was not very far, but it was steep and hot. On the way we met a pale young man coming down. We asked for Father Paolo. 'Go and see,' he said. A long line of rope carried a bucket of cement slowly up to a flat rock some little way away from the monastery where building work was in progress; there was no sound except its creaking, and the whistle of a bird somewhere down in the shade where perhaps there was water. A bearded young man shouted a welcome from above, standing beside a donkey and a mule. As we reached the top of the path a monk appeared, of similar appearance, laughed at the idea that he might be Father Paolo, and introduced himself as Tony. He indicated a low door through which we went, stooping, into what seemed to be a cave. It opened out on to a wide terrace, part of which was covered with rugs and shaded by a loose canopy. Father Paolo had been cataloguing the library; he emerged from another low door, a big man, possibly formidable but welcoming. His face did not express the joyful holiness of the monk Tony but rather a certain large-hearted determination; he is a trained Jesuit and he has a plan.

The monastery was probably built about 560 AD; the small church contains some extraordinary frescoes. The Syriac Orthodox monks who built it probably came from Palestine after the Council of Chalcedon and perhaps after some Byzantine persecution. They would have lived as a small group, or *laura*, using the caves as hermitages and collecting rainwater; they had no well. Moses, or Musa, is an Ethiopian saint. Possibly Moses the Egyptian, the son of the king of Ethiopia, first went to Palestine and then to Mar

Musa. The monastery may also at one time have been a Roman look-out post; the caravans from further east would have passed within its view. In the fifteenth century there was new life; émigrés arrived from Lebanon (again, possibly from Ethiopia). They came within the see of the bishop of south Syria, whose diocese included Homs, Damascus and Lebanon. In 1831 they became Catholic; the present foundation also is within the Syrian Catholic Church. Eventually the conditions of the monks' life, so much more ascetic even than the lives of the surrounding Bedouin, became too harsh to be borne, and as time went on vocations to Mar Musa faded away; the place was abandoned except as an occasional refuge for outlaws and bandits.

Paolo dell'Oglio was born in 1954 and has been a Jesuit since 1975. In 1977 he studied Arabic in Lebanon. In the early 1980s Syria was politically unstable. There were Israeli invasions and a long-drawn-out economic crisis. In 1981 and 1982 Muslim fundamentalism was growing, centred in Hama; it was rumoured that the president was ill and that his brother was pushing for power. In 1982 President Assad ordered a crackdown on Hama; thousands of people were killed. In 1982 after ten days of prayer at Mar Musa, Father Paolo founded the *laura*; he now intends to move towards a coenobitic way of life. The building we saw some little way away is for a community of nuns; there is also a hermitage being built for a nun. When we were there there were four monks and two nuns; they did not come from previous religious orders. Tony came from Djoun in Lebanon and had had a religious experience at Mar Musa, Freddy, a Swiss monk we met later, hoped to become a monk of Mar Musa. For five years a Little Brother of Jesus (of the order which grew up after the death of the French hermit Charles de Foucauld) lived in the hermitage at the top of the hill behind the monastery. Half an hour further into the desert there is another small foundation, closer to the Bedouin, who like it and visit it.

We asked if the community lived according to an existing Rule; it became clear that Father Paolo had his own ideas. He spoke of three elements as underlying what he was trying to do. First he wanted the community to live an experience inspired by ancient traditions. The idea of the monastery in the desert, he said, was familiar also to Muslims. Second, he believed in manual work, not just in conformity with St Benedict's precept *'ora et labora'* but because he wanted to achieve harmony, not only with nature, but with the local community and in the end with Islam. So there were goats, local housing projects, an arrangement with an agricultural institute working on plants which could survive in the desert and co-exist with goats. His third principle was hospitality, from which we were benefiting in the form of mint tea brought to us by the monk Tony.

It was when he spoke of the inter-religious dimension of Mar Musa that the extent of Father Paolo's ambition became clear. His inspiration, he said, was the work of Masignon, the friend and follower of Charles de Foucauld. He also spoke of a Sufi named Halaj who lived in Baghdad in the early years of the twentieth century. Father Paolo is a much-travelled man; he has been to Albania and Egypt, and by bus through Turkey and Iran to Pakistan. He talks of opening a prayer hall in Ispahan, and a new monastic community at Dalwal, near an old semi-abandoned school of the Capuchins high in the hills between Islamabad and Lahore. He talks of the Christian minority providing a leaven in the bread of Islam. He mentions Malawi, the South Philippines. There is not the slightest glint of madness in his eyes, only intelligence, competence and that steady determination. He speaks with admiration of some Carmelite nuns in the Philippines who have been twice kidnapped; he would not, one suddenly thinks reject martyrdom should the need arise. It is just possible that the need might arise; part of the fascination of that part of the world has always been its danger, and it is not yet quite clear what will happen now that President Assad, that man of iron, is dead. If fanaticism should take over, those who work for the reconciliation of Christian and Muslim are unlikely to be popular. Much, after all, has come from the blood of the martyrs. Including, of course, for the martyr himself, eternal glory.

Father Paolo went to pick some tomatoes, and Tony led us into the church. Three-aisled, in spite of its small size, its dark interior glows with the colours of the frescoes on the walls, strong depictions of saints and angels, even a stylite on a pillar, dark-rimmed eyes and rows of haloes, hierarchies of the blessed draped in stiff robes, some devils, some damned, a dove, a horse. The floor is covered with rugs; this is where the community comes twice a day for prayers or for silence or to celebrate the eucharist.

Down another small stair, a low door opened into another cave-room, where the monk Freddy and a girl assistant were seated at the computer. Tony teased them when the printer seemed not to be working, but Freddy smiled at it affectionately and it came to life, disgorging the English Newsletter.

The pale young man was coming up the path as we went down. He smiled as we congratulated him on the beauty of his habitation, but his English was not good; he might have been Eastern European, or Russian. On the floor of the desert little white-rumped desert wheatears scurried between the stones. Our driver woke. 'Damascus?' he said hopefully. Damascus.

CHAPTER 5

'The act of departure is the bravest and most beautiful of all . . .'

THE LURE OF DESERT PLACES

Charles de Foucauld —
Isabelle Eberhardt — Lady Hester Stanhope —
the Epic of Gilgamesh

Above Deir Mar Musa, looking out over an even vaster view of the stony desert, was the little hermitage in which a follower of Charles de Foucauld had lived until just before our visit.

At the time of Charles de Foucauld's death in 1916, he had no followers at all. He was murdered by brigands in 1916 in the Algerian desert. He first went to North Africa in 1881, a fat French cavalry officer with good connections and a certain lazy charm. When he died he was a solitary ascetic priest, who divided his time between the oasis of Tamanrasset and a tiny observatory on the plateau of Assekrem, among the bare black rocks of the Hoggar mountains, about 8,000 feet above sea level in the remotest part of the Sahara.

At the beginning of 1881 Foucauld was living on half-pay in Evian-les-Bains. His colonel had taken exception to the fact that when his regiment had been ordered to North Africa Foucauld had sent his current mistress, the charming Mimi, on ahead to rent an agreeable house. Mimi was effusively welcomed as the Vicomtesse de Foucauld by the sous-préfet at Bone – which in St Augustine's day was known as Hippo – but when the colonel arrived he unceremoniously ordered Foucauld to send her home. Foucauld objected, on the ground that as a free French citizen Mimi had a right to live wherever she liked. As a result he was placed on the non-active list – in other words, effectively retired at the age of twenty-three. He had probably been saved from earlier disgrace only by the reputation of his grandfather, a respected colonel of engineers who had brought him up since the age of six, both his parents having died in their forties. The spoilt boy had been an idle student at St Cyr military school, and when he progressed to the cavalry school at Saumur his bad behaviour became famous among his contemporaries. He gambled, ate and drank too much, consorted with women of the town, and was often in trouble with his superiors; someone claimed to have seen him looking out of a window from behind a fan, elaborately made up and dressed as a woman. He hardly ever turned up at early-morning exercise, having made friends with the doctor, who had given him exemption on health grounds. Surprisingly, perhaps, he was widely liked.

It seems that a life of idleness in Evian with Mimi soon began to pall. When he heard that his regiment was to be part of an expedition to Tunisia, he hurried to the War Office and asked for reinstatement. The authorities allowed him to retain his rank but assigned him to another regiment, sending him not to Tunis but to Oran where a certain Bu-Amana was preaching a holy war.

This was the period about which John Buchan wrote in *Greenmantle*, and Pierre Loti in his desert stories. Not much later T. E. Lawrence began his romance with the desert when he came as an undergraduate to make his first surveys of the Crusader castles. Somewhere not very far away Isabelle Eberhardt was making her wild solitary forays into the Sahara. All this coincided with what was regarded at the time as the high adventure of colonialism. Foucauld believed in the *mission civilisatrice*, the destiny of France as governor and guide of the peoples of Algeria; he never foresaw self-government for them. From their military outposts the French explored the far reaches of the Sahara. Foucauld might well have been among them had he not been, first of all, too impatient, and then diverted by what he never doubted was a higher call. As it was, the desert transformed him as soon as he arrived there. Filled with new energy, he became a hard-working army officer and an inexhaustible traveller. When the campaign was over he applied for extended leave to explore the southern Algerian desert. When this was refused, he resigned his commission and decided on a more adventurous expedition.

Morocco was at that time more or less a closed country to Europeans, hardly mapped. The Sultan of Fez ruled about a fifth of the country; elsewhere, independent tribes had their own leaders. Foucauld spent two years in Algiers, finding out all he could about Morocco, and learning Arabic and Hebrew. When he had made his preparations he went into Morocco disguised as a Jewish rabbi, taking as guide Mordekai-Abi-Serur, a rabbi who had been his Hebrew tutor. For about a year, from June 1883, he wandered all over the country. Because Jews were despised, they were not usually suspected of being spies or thought worthy of being robbed. Foucauld was robbed all the same. On one occasion everything was taken except his mapping materials and his notes, which the thieves thought of no interest.

At the end of his travels, Foucauld arrived at the French Algerian frontier with no money at all, having had to sell his mules. A hotel manager whom he asked for food turned him away with indignation, spurning as a forgery the card which proclaimed him to be the Vicomte Charles Eugene de Foucauld; fortunately an astonished army officer recognized the bare-footed traveller through his rags, and welcomed him enthusiastically. The book he wrote about his travels won him a gold medal from the Paris Geographical Society.

Foucauld had been struck by the piety of the Arabs and Jews he had met on his travels, and he began to return to his childhood Catholicism. The Abbé Huvelin of St Augustine's Church in Paris became his great influence; they remained in touch until the Abbé's death in 1910. Foucauld went on a pilgrimage to the Holy land, and then he applied for admission to the Trappist monastery at Our Lady of the Snows, 3,000 feet high in the hills about Viviers. He knew this monastery had a small daughter house at Akbes in Syria, and before long he was transferred there.

He had always been impatient. Life in the monastery was not

hard enough, the poverty not sufficiently abject. He began to suggest that there should be little groups of poor hermits living among infidels in the poorest places, preaching the Gospel only by their lives. Abbé Huvelin restrained him, but eventually helped him to leave the Cistercian Order and set off once again for the Holy Land.

The Abbé had said, 'You should be at the gates of a monastery, not in the monastery itself.' Accordingly Foucauld found himself a wooden hut in the garden of the convent of Poor Clares in Nazareth. He lived there with a few books, and worked as a general handyman for the nuns. He wore a smock held in by a leather belt with a large rosary hanging from it, and a woollen cap wrapped round by a cloth so that it looked like a turban. When the nuns understood what kind of man he was, they urged him to become a priest. This he did, back at Notre Dame des Neiges, on 9 June 1901.

He had not lost his urge to get back to the desert. The following autumn he arrived at Beni-Abbès, an oasis and garrison town, with permission to live as a hermit. Soldiers helped him build his hermitage: he always felt it part of his vocation to minister to such of their kind who needed him, or were ill, or wounded, or dying, and he never in fact severed his relationship with the French army. He made two more journeys into the Sahara with old army friends, but then he settled in the Hoggar mountains, whose harsh, dramatic landscape answered his need for the extreme. From then on he divided his time between Tamanrasset and his other hermitage in the tableland at Asekrem twenty-eight miles away, with occasional short visits to France.

He wrote of Asekrem: 'The view is more beautiful than can be expressed or imagined . . . From my window I can look out over the mountains and watch the sun rise behind them. I am above them all . . . At least every other day there is a big wind that makes you think you are at the seaside.' He worked on his Tuareg–French dictionary. He always hoped to find a companion with whom he could celebrate mass, and who might become his successor, but he never succeeded. The abbot of Our Lady of the Snows had written, 'the austerities that he practises and that he intends, too, to make his companions practise, are such that I believe would cause a novice to collapse in a very short time. Moreover, the extreme recollection that he expects of his disciples is such that I am afraid he would send them out of their minds before they died of excess of austerity.'

When war broke out in 1914 Foucauld thought of offering his services as a military chaplain or a stretcher-bearer but was told that his duty lay in the desert. The military authorities gave him ammunition in case the Tuareg chief Musa ag-Amastana and his people needed to take refuge. Senussi tribesmen from the Italian colony of Tripolitania across the Algerian frontier were making raids over the border. Foucauld moved his hermitage nearer to the village, and made a large enclosure which could provide a refuge for the villagers if necessary. On 1 December 1916, the hermitage was surrounded, not by Senussi but by a wandering band of robbers. Foucauld was held with a pistol to his head. Unfortunately two soldiers passing on their way to their camp called in and were shot by the thieves. In a panic the man holding Foucauld shot him through the head.

When news reached the nearby camp, Captain de la Roche, the commanding officer, went with a soldier and a sergeant to see what had happened. They made a rough tomb of stones and put a wooden cross over it. Captain de la Roche collected some books and the letters Foucauld had been writing; he found in the sand a small monstrance with the sacred Host still in it. He wiped it clean, wrapped it in a linen cloth and put it in his satchel; then he rode off on his camel.

Loving his solitude, Foucauld had nevertheless prayed for companions, who never came. He had foreseen that if the Muslim hold on the peoples of North Africa could not be weakened they would one day rise against the Christian French. He had dreamed of peopling the Sahara with small groups of hermits who would convert the Muslims by their example. In fact at Beni-Abbès he had baptized one old blind woman, and a three-year-old child. At Tamanrasset there were no converts at all. His failure was so complete as to amount to a kind of triumph.

Foucauld had composed Rules for Little Brothers and Sisters, though there had been none in his lifetime. In 1933, seventeen years after his death and in obedience to his Rule, René Voillaume and four other priests settled at El Abiodh Sidi Cheik on the edge of the Sahara. The Little Sisters of the Sacred Heart were founded at Montpellier in the same year. Both orders spread, mostly following Foucauld's ideal of living among the poorest, often in towns, and labouring with them at whatever their labour might be. In the course of time his example brought other posthumous disciples. In Morocco, André Poissonier was inspired by his example to become Father Charles-André, a hermit and doctor at Tazert, fifty-four miles from Marrakesh, where he lived from 1931 to 1938. Another Franciscan, Fr Abel Fauc, carried on his work after his death.

General Lyautey, the conqueror of Morocco, admired and twice visited Charles de Foucauld, whose *Reconnaissance au Maroc* he had used as a guide in his campaign of 1912. More surprisingly perhaps, he also admired Isabelle Eberhardt, who went to the desert first of all to look for the murderers of the Duc de Vallombrosa, and then in pursuit of sensation, terror, solitude and finally death.

Half-French, half-Russian, loudly and affectedly Slav in her emotional outbursts and swings of mood, harsh-voiced, small and sallow, frequently drunk or drugged, sexually promiscuous and scornful of conventional morality, she dressed as a man and liked to sit and smoke and drink with soldiers or tribesmen from the deep Sahara. She was married to an Arab. She scandalized the army wives. She maddened authorities of all kinds. As General Lyautey recognized, she was highly intelligent and knew the Arab world intimately.

Born in Geneva in 1877, she was the illegitimate child of a Jewish mother, who at that time was still married to the Russian general who was the father of her other four children. Isabelle's father had been the children's tutor; her mother had run away with him. This tutor, Trophimowsky, was an Armenian ex-priest, huge, handsome and bearded, possessed of ferocious views on almost every subject, regarded in respectable Geneva as a probable member of a Nihilist terrorist gang, and perpetually surrounded by an atmosphere of high drama and emotional extremes. Two of the general's children later committed suicide, including the youngest brother with whom Isabelle was in love. She and her mother escaped to North Africa to start a new life. They arrived in Bone in May 1897. In no time at all Isabelle was speaking perfect Arabic, and had become a Muslim. She began writing stories. When her mother died she bought a horse, dressed as an Arab man, and galloped off alone into the Sahara.

'Now I am a nomad,' she wrote. 'With no other homeland than Islam, with no family, no one in whom to confide, alone, for ever the proud and darkly sweet solitude of my own heart.'

The need for money brought her back, but the solitary dash into the desert became an often repeated feature of her short life. In Paris she met the widow of an old companion-in-arms of Charles de Foucauld, the Duc de Vallombrosa, who had been mysteriously murdered somewhere near Tripoli on an expedition to Timbuktu; she undertook to find his assassins. She never did, but the commission enabled her to return to the desert.

The rest of her life is a story of excess. She had many Arab lovers and married one. She rode all over the desert, alone or with the nomads, she yearned for spiritual development and had long earnest talks with religious leaders, sometimes going into retreat with them; she drank, smoked hashish, made herself ill, and rode off into the desert again. In the course of her wanderings she came to know and understand a great deal about the life of the Arabs, and about their religion, of which it was said she had an instinctive understanding. Her happiest times were probably alone in the desert, in a state of spiritual exaltation. She was said to have become a member of the powerful Qadriya Sufi brotherhood, which was opposed to the extension of French influence. General Lyautey respected her knowledge of the desert and its inhabitants, and hoped that she might help him to win the trust of the Arab leaders. He gave her a military pass, so that she could carry messages for him. But by now, even stronger than the desert, the final attraction was death.

'Who knows?' she wrote. 'Perhaps I shall soon let myself slip into it, voluptuously and without the slightest worry. With time I have learnt not to look for anything in life but the ecstasy offered by oblivion.'

In October 1904 she was drowned in a flash flood in the little village of Ain Sefra, not far from the Moroccan border. Lyautey ordered her burial in the Muslim cemetery, and chose the marble stone with her Arabic name, Si Mahmoud.

Lady Hester Stanhope, granddaughter of the great Lord Chatham and niece of William Pitt the Younger, was another intrepid traveller who occasionally exasperated her companions. She went to Palmyra in 1813, when it was almost inaccessible to Europeans, and ended her days as a notoriously eccentric recluse not far from Sidon in Lebanon. Her father, a vigorous supporter of the French Revolution, seems to have been similarly eccentric and even more autocratic. Most of his family found it impossible to live with him for any length of time. Her mother died and he married again, producing half-brothers of whom Lady Hester was fond. She went to live with her grandmother, Lady Chatham, at Burton Pynsent in Somerset, from where she did her best to rescue her half-brothers from the strange household of their mutual father.

She had a tremendous admiration for her uncle, William Pitt, and for three years lived with him as his hostess and general support. He was always kind to her, and awarded her a government pension, later the subject of much contention, when his successor Palmerston declined to continue it. She had a fondness for, and perhaps even an understanding with, Sir John Moore who, when dying in the arms of her brother James at Corunna, went so far as to say, 'Give my regards to your sister, Stanhope.'

After Pitt's death and the burial of Sir John Moore, Lady Hester retired for a time to a cottage near Aberhonddu in Wales. Her sense of adventure soon reasserting itself, she began her travels in the East, taking with her her own doctor, whose diaries tell of their adventures and the sometimes hard-tried esteem in which he held his imperious patient. After a notorious affair with a travelling English grandee a good deal younger than herself, she ended her days at Djoun not far from Sidon, in Lebanon, and was more or less a recluse for about fifteen years. She became famous, and was visited by the French poet Lamartine and by Alexander Kinglake, a young law student who in the autumn of 1834 decided to interrupt his studies and travel, rather more adventurously than most young men of his time, in the Near East. He was a cheerful fellow, perfectly content with his country, his class and his lack of introspection. 'If I had my way,' he once wrote, 'I would write in every church, chapel and cathedral only one line: Important if True.'

Lady Hester Stanhope was a childhood friend of Kinglake's mother and by the time he called on her was advanced in years and eccentricity. She was thought a great princess in Syria, and her autocratic behaviour seemed to bear this out. In order to reach Palmyra, a place of fable and mystery, supposedly inaccessible to foreigners, she had had to repulse an army of angry Bedouins. Kinglake relates:

> [S]he stood up in her stirrups, withdrew the yashmack that veiled the terrors of her countenance – waved her arms slowly and disdainfully, and cried out with a loud voice

'Avaunt!' The horsemen recoiled from her glance, but not in terror. The threatening yells of the assailants were suddenly changed for loud shouts of joy and admiration at the bravery of the stately Englishwoman, and festive gunshots were fired on all sides around her honoured head . . . Lady Hester related this story with great spirit; and I recollect that she put up her yashmack for a moment, in order to give me a better idea of the effect which she produced by suddenly revealing the awfulness of her countenance.

At the time of Kinglake's visit, she had huge debts and lived in almost complete seclusion, apart from a few attendants. Some Albanian soldiers had taken refuge from the ferocious Ibrahim Pasha in the vast half-ruined convent where she lived; her reputation as a great prophetess protected them. Her own interest by now was almost entirely in the occult, though she interrupted herself occasionally to ask for London gossip or to do cruel imitations of Lord Byron. Mostly, though, she 'talked to me long and earnestly on the subject of Religion, announcing that the Messiah was yet to come. She strived to impress me with the vanity and falseness of all European creeds, as well as with a sense of her own spiritual greatness. Throughout her conversation upon these high topics, she carefully insinuated, without actually asserting, her heavenly rank.'

Increasingly involved in financial chaos, robbed by local bandits, she struggled on in ever-advancing delusion until she died in 1839. Her burial was witnessed by the British consul at Beirut and an American missionary, Mr Thomson: 'It was evening when they arrived, and a profound silence was over all the palace; no-one met them; they lighted their own lamps in the outer court, and passed unquestioned through court and gallery, until they came to where *she* lay. A corpse was the only inhabitant of the palace, and the isolation from her kind which she had sought so long was indeed complete.'

The two men carried her out to the garden at midnight, and buried her in a vault which already contained the bones of a

Frenchman who had died years before and been buried there at Lady Hester's command. The situation, under an olive tree overlooking the view from the mountain, was a favourite one of hers. On a square block of stone, approached by three steps, was written, 'Lady Hester Lucy Stanhope. Born 12 March, 1776. Died 23rd June, 1839'. Her tomb was destroyed during the recent civil war. Rumour has it that her remains were held to ransom by the militia. However that may be, they now rest in the grounds of the summer residence of the British Ambassador at Abey in the Chouf mountains. Whether or not anyone counted the bones to see whether the Frenchman was there too is not known.

High on the limestone tableland of Lebanon, such of the ancient cedars as remain are now protected. You pay to see them, and may buy a seedling in a lump of clay to take home and plant in your garden to give shade to your great-grandchildren. The cedars once covered huge areas of the mountain range; Solomon's temple was made from their wood. Long before Solomon, in the mythical times of which the Epic of Gilgamesh tells, there must have been cedar forests in Assyria too, as there still are in the Taurus mountains of Turkey. In the ancient Epic of Gilgamesh, the giant of the cedars wielded power over a huge domain, until he was challenged by the hero Gilgamesh and his companion Enkidu.

You could say that Enkidu was once a kind of hermit. He lived apart from what we call the world, until rumours of his existence sent men to seek him out. He is the hermit as wild man. He hints at Adam before the Fall, or the world before the division between man and beast became established.

The Epic of Gilgamesh dates from the third millennium. The clay tablets on which it was preserved were only discovered in the nineteenth century, when excavations in Iraq revealed the remains of the libraries of the Assyrian Kings. Hundreds of cuneiform tablets were found which had been buried since 612 BC in the ruins of ancient Nineveh. Some of them have still not been deciphered. The Epic tells the story of the heroic Gilgamesh, who exhausts his people by his energy so that they look for a companion for him, 'To be as like him as his own reflection, his second self, stormy heart for stormy heart. Let them contend together and leave Uruk in quiet.' Rumours begin to spread of a wild man who has been seen in the hills. He is strong and hairy and fleet of foot; he ranges over the hills with the wild animals and eats grass. One evening a hunter sees him drinking at the river with the animals, and tells the people of Uruk, that he is indeed a man and not a satyr. They decide that he would be a fit companion for Gilgamesh, but he is wary and impossible to approach. Eventually a beautiful harlot from the city is persuaded to walk to and fro on the near side of the river. When he approaches she lets fall her garments; Enkidu swims the river and is seduced. When he returns to the animals they reject him.

The hunters take Enkiddu to Gilgamesh. After a trial of strength they become companions, and undertake a quest into the mountains to destroy the giant of the cedars. Their adventures come to an end only when Enkiddu becomes ill, and dies. Long before Achilles grieved for Patroclus or David wept for Jonathan, Gilgamesh laments the loss of his beloved companion.

Gilgamesh then wanders far in search of the secret of immortality. Failing to find it, he returns home humbled, with only the consolation that the strong walls which he caused to be built for his city will be his memorial. Like all great myths, the Epic of Gilgamesh affirms what you bring to it. There are many interpretations, as well as many different versions, but it may be just possible to imagine that behind the unkempt figure paid by some dilettante to sit in an artificial grotto and allow his nails to grow there might lurk the high heroic wild man who ran with the gazelles through the cedar forests of ancient Assyria.

CHAPTER 6

'A clear pool to wash away sins . . .'

CELTIC SOLITARIES

*Francis Kilvert and the Solitary of Llanbedr —
St Issui — Pennant Menangell —
Irish wandering hermits — the Skelligs — Bardsey —
Bach on Iona — St Columba —
the Buddhists at Samyeling*

The idea of the hermit's life – simplicity, devotion, closeness to nature – lurks somewhere on the periphery of most people's consciousness, a way glimpsed, oddly familiar, not taken. It is like one of those tracks you sometimes see as you drive along a country road, a path leading up a hill and disappearing into a wood, almost painfully inviting, so that you long to stop the car and follow it, and perhaps you take your foot off the accelerator for a couple of seconds, no more. Most of us wouldn't like it if we did walk up the hill, we'd become bored, depressed, uncomfortable, take to drink. But the idea is still there: the path we didn't take.

The Celtic countries are full of such paths, little lanes running with rain leading to holy wells, hillsides where a few stones mark the site of a solitary's last home, tracks over muddy fields and through streams to hermitages even now in use, half buried or still lovingly maintained shrines to obscure saints, Issui, Menangell, Ita, Illtud.

The tradition did not die; such is the lie of the land that the solitary has a place in it. Francis Kilvert, the diarist, visited one near Llanbedr when he was a curate at Clyro in Radnorshire in 1872. He walked up the hill behind a farm where you may still walk, and with his friend Tom Williams of Lowes took the track across the side of the hill until he came to a little cwm 'closed at the end on both sides by the steep hillsides but open to the South, and the sun and the great valley of the Wye and the distant blue mountains'. The little green cwm is still there, and so is the view of the valley and the mountains, and the upper and lower springs which join their streams just as Kilvert described them, but there are only a few stones left on the grassy platform where the Solitary's cabin stood.

> It was built of rough dry stone without mortar and the thatch was thin and broken. At one end of the cabin a little garden had been enclosed and fenced in from the waste. There was one other house in sight where the cwm lay open to the west . . . Not a soul was stirring or in sight on the hill or in the valley, and the green cwm was perfectly silent and apparently deserted. As we turned the corner of the little grey hut and came in sight of the closed door we gave up all hope of seeing the Solitary and believed that our pilgrimage had been in vain. Then what was my relief when I knocked upon the door to hear a strange deep voice from within saying 'Ho! Ho!' There was a slight stir within and then the cabin door opened and a strange figure came out. The figure of a man rather below the middle height, about 60 years of age, his head covered with a luxuriant growth of light brown or chestnut hair and his face made remarkable by a mild thoughtful melancholy blue eye and red moustache and white beard. The hermit was dressed in a seedy faded greasy suit of black, a dress coat and a large untidy cravat that had once been white, lashed round his neck with a loose knot and flying ends. Upon his feet he wore broken low shoes and in his hand he carried a tall hat. There was something in the whole appearance of the Solitary singularly dilapidated and forlorn and he had a distant absent look and a preoccupied air as if the soul were entirely unconscious of the rags in which the body was clothed . . . [he] came forward and greeted us with the most perfect courtesy and the natural simplicity of the highest breeding.

Kilvert was astonished by the interior of the house: 'a wild confusion of litter and rubbish almost choking and filling up all available space . . . In heaps and piles upon the floor were old books, large bibles, commentaries, old fashioned religious disputations, C.M.S. Reports and odd books of all sorts, Luther on the Galatians, etc. . . . In this cabin thus lives the Solitary of Llanbedr, the Rev. John Price, Master of Arts of Cambridge University and Vicar of Llanbedr Painscastle.'

Kilvert helped him to load some peat on to a cart as fuel for his fire, and the Solitary explained the system of shorthand which he had invented in his solitude and had had published in Manchester and London. Then they walked together down to the nearest farm so that the Solitary could show his visitors the way through the lanes to the church.

> The people who met him touched their hats to his reverence with great respect. They recognized him as a very holy man and if the solitary had lived a thousand years ago he would have been revered as a hermit and perhaps canonized as a saint . . . The last I saw of him was that he was leaning on the gate looking after us. Then I saw him no more. He had gone back I suppose to his grey hut in the green cwm.

Later news was unfortunate. The Solitary fell into his fire one day, perhaps after over-indulging in the 'black mixture which he called I suppose port', which he had pressed upon Kilvert, and 'before he could recover himself his stomach, bowels and thighs were dreadfully burnt, and he has had to stay away from Church for three Sundays. Yet he will let neither doctor nor nurse come near him. The poor solitary. He used to visit Sarah Bryan kindly and assiduously when she lay a-dying and was a great and lasting comfort to her. She died very happy.' Perhaps he did too, for he recovered from his burns and died in 1895 at the age of eighty-five. He is buried in the graveyard of Llanbedr church.

It was raining when I went to Patricio, which is not far from Llanbedr. All down the steep hill the water ran in silvery runnels, on the road and in the grass beneath the trees, and the stream beside the hermit's holy well had overflowed its banks. The well may have been a place of pilgrimage before Christian times, but St Issui built his cell beside it and preached Christianity, until a passing traveller to whom he had given hospitality ungratefully bludgeoned him to death. Early in the eleventh century a pilgrim was cured of leprosy by the water of the well and left a hatful of gold to build a church on the hill above, where it still is, much altered because the ground periodically shows a tendency to slide downhill. What may have been the old chapel seems to have been made into a cell for a hermit or an anchorite. There is a small square window above the altar through which the enclosed one might see the mass being celebrated at the altar in the main church. The little building on the path to the lych-gate was where the priest could stable his pony and leave his outer clothes to dry in front of the fire while he conducted the service. By the time I had climbed the hill the wide view which opens out beyond the church towards the river Usk was lit by late-afternoon sunlight through the thinning rainclouds.

The hermit of Pennant Menangell was a young woman, who is said to have lived there in the seventh century. Pennant Menangell is more remote than Patricio, and further north, not far from Welshpool, in Powys. According to legend, Menangell was an Irish princess who had taken refuge in Pennant to escape the marriage which her father had arranged for her. She was discovered one day by a certain Prince Brychwel. He was hunting in the woods when a hare ran into a bramble thicket. Pursuing it with his dogs, he came upon Menangell in prayer, with the hare 'lying boldly and fearlessly under the hem or fold of her garments, its face towards the dogs'.

Brychwel urged on his hounds, but they fled, whimpering, with their tails between their legs. Brychwell ordered his huntsman to blow his horn, but no sound would come. Eventually he asked

Menangell who she was and when he heard her story and that her
intention was to remain a holy virgin until her dying day he gave
her the land as a perpetual asylum and swore that no hare should
ever be killed there. She remained there for thirty-seven years and
the hares lived with her in safety. After her death the place became,
and remains, a place of pilgrimage. The rare twelfth-century stone
shrine, which was destroyed in the sixteenth century, has recently
been most carefully restored and the apse behind it rebuilt. There
is a small centre for cancer healing a little way down the valley,
but when I went there the church, open and welcoming, was alone
in its round churchyard and its beautiful circle of hills.

The Celtic monastic tradition differed from that of the rest of
Europe because there were fewer cities and centres of habitation.
Monasteries became centres themselves and sometimes gathered
round them lay-people who had nowhere else to go. Monks wandered more, and hermits had less commitment to stability. Some
of the very earliest were not unlike the holy fools of Russian tradition. The Irish wandering hermit was on continuous penitential
peregrination. He communed with nature and consorted with
lepers and outcasts, and though he lived alone and avoided normal
human contact his advice was often sought and his pronouncements, weird or to the point, taken seriously, because of his status
as an outsider. His tendency to excess was rather like that of the
Syrians. He might spend long periods of prayer standing in cold
water to quench the flames of lust, like Oengus who 'used to chant
his psalms thus, while he was at Disert Iegusso, to wit, fifty in the
river with a withy round his neck and tied to the tree, fifty under
the tree, and fifty in his cell'.

Christianity came to the Celts first in Ireland. Ireland had never
been part of the Roman Empire. It remained a tribal society, with
a strong tradition of respect for learning. Society was rural,

hierarchical, family-based. There was no tradition of urban life or culture. A king ruled a tribe, a high-king over him. Early monasteries were more like fortified villages or farms, a collection of small rough huts within the surrounding wall with a church or sometimes a tall thin round tower into which people, cattle and such other belongings as could be accommodated, could shelter in the event of a raid by a hostile tribe. Monasteries were often founded by local powerful families, with a member of the family as the abbot. There were sometimes smaller daughter houses not far away. The organization of the Celtic Church was not diocesan, as was the Latin way, but monastic. Hospitality was a duty and the monks took vows of poverty, chastity and obedience, but did not have to take a vow of stability – as they still do not in the Eastern Church today. Monks wandered, not so much to proselytize as to find places more and more remote from the temptations of the world. In the fifth and sixth centuries they sailed and rowed in small open boats made of cowhides stretched over light wickerwork frames, often setting off without knowing where they were going. Some reached an island called Papos, off the south coast of Iceland, where the foundations of their stone huts can still be seen. When Vikings appeared on the coast of Iceland in the ninth century, the monks set off again, rowing west, towards Greenland.

Partly because pilgrimage was a feature of Celtic religion, and partly no doubt because of the solitary beauty of many of the places which came to be thought of as holy, hermit legends are not forgotten. Any rock or islet may have harboured a saint, as the Skelligs did off the coast of Ireland, or Bardsey off the coast of Wales, where 20,000 saints are supposed to be buried. Lindisfarne sheltered St Cuthbert, Iona was the site of St Columba's landing from Ireland. Pilgrimages were suppressed at the Reformation, as being all part of Romish superstition. Some have come back in recent years, restoring ancient holy places to their former prestige.

Bardsey, as well as its 20,000 saints, has several other characteristics appropriate to a holy island. It is very difficult to get to, for one thing. Its name in Welsh means Island of Currents and the crossing can be dangerous. Its back, or higher part, is turned to the mainland and its arms – two low peninsulas – stretch out towards the west, where no land is to be seen. So in the old days you went there to die – or to be a hermit, until you died – and you turned your back on the world to face the setting sun. You also hoped, when the time came, for an easy access to paradise, being in such good company.

The island now belongs to a trust, which rents the land to three farmers who keep sheep and small Welsh black cattle. Manx shearwaters breed there, coming in to nest in their burrows under cover of darkness in order to avoid greedy gulls or peregrines, and when the breeding season is over they fly thousands of miles to spend the rest of the year at sea, in the South Atlantic. There is no electricity on the island and only well water or rainwater. There are remains of a thirteenth-century Augustinian abbey, where in the twelfth century there would have been five or six hundred monks; but there were only seven permanent inhabitants recorded in the year 1000, and there were seven recorded in 2000 also. There has been a succession of Anglican nuns living there as hermits since the 1960s. One was there for about thirty years. The latest moved there in August 2000.

Local saints abound in Celtic countries, as place-names in Cornwall, or Ireland, or Brittany reveal. Some of them were hermits, seeking solitude in remote places.

> My heart stirs quietly now to think
> Of a small hut that no one visits
> In which I will travel to death in silence

Some went much further than the small hut in the woods, and sought the dangerous edges of the world. Skellig Michael, an inhospitable rock ten miles or so off the tip of the Kerry coast in Ireland, is covered with the beehive cells of the hermits of former times. Such is the perilous position of the furthest of the hermitages, high on the steep rock, facing the Atlantic, that the imagination fails. They were not as we are, these particular saintly obsessives. Not for them the comforts of which other Irish hermits wrote,

> Leeks from the garden, poultry, game,
> Salmon and trout and bees.

They were at the outermost limits, face to face with infinity.

The hermits who went into the Egyptian desert when the persecution of Christians had come to an end, and who were thereby deprived of the opportunity for the red martyrdom of death, had spoken of the white martyrdom of solitude. The Irish Christians seem to have introduced the idea of the green martyrdom. The seventh-century *Cambrai Homily* calls it

> Precious in the eyes of God:
> The white martyrdom of exile
> The green martyrdom of the hermit
> The red martyrdom of sacrifice.

On Skellig Michael they probably sought all three.

On the mainland not far from the Skelligs, on the Dingle peninsula, Gallarus Oratory sits on the marshy grass among low stone walls. Mount Brandon rises 3,000 feet behind it and the sea lies away towards the west. Built of dry stones in the same manner as the smaller beehive huts, its simplicity is timeless, its history unremarked. Some say it was built in the seventh century, others say the twelfth. A pilgrims' way, known as the Saints Road, passes nearby on its way to the summit of the mountain where honour is traditionally paid to Saint Brendan.

The journeyings of the Irish monks all over Europe carried the classical learning their skilful scribes had preserved to places which in the turmoil of the barbarian invasions had forgotten it. St Columbanus, St Columba's younger contemporary, started several monasteries in France, and in the north-west of Italy he founded the great monastery of Bobbio, where St Francis of Assisi came, six hundred years later. Some say the insistence on simplicity and love of the natural world which are associated with the Italian saint were absorbed by him from the Irish tradition.

I have been to Farne Island, off the coast of Northumberland, in very heavy rain. Leaning over the cliff behind St Cuthbert's chapel the smell of fish was overpowering; there must have been at least fifty cormorants perched up and down the cliff below. The island's desolation is beautiful, even in the rain, even with the cormorants.

It rained on Iona too, but not on the evening we arrived. We landed in perfect weather, the sea silkily blue and quiet, the sky clear and the air as sweet and soft as we remembered it. It was in the morning that it rained. We set off all the same to find the hermit's cell, marked as such on the map. The kind young man in the shop had suggested that we should go round the hill, because it was less likely that we would get lost. The hill was steep and boggy, he said, and there was no path. If we went round we could walk on the flat ground beside the sea before turning up into the rocks. We might get lost there too, but it was easier walking.

Following his directions we came to the white shell beaches of the Bay at the Back of the Ocean, where there were oyster-catchers, a single sandpiper, and a few eider ducks sitting motionless on the glassy sea. Past the first rocky outcrop we turned inland and crossed the uneven sheep-grazed turf towards the higher ridges. The rain had turned into a gentle drizzle. The rocks receded before us, repetitive shapes of grey in the still grey air whose soft touch was damp on our faces. Here a tiny stream, there a patch of swamp, with bog cotton growing in it and sea pinks at the edge. We climbed, the sea behind us. A solitary walker said, yes, she had been to the hermit's cell once, it was over there somewhere, beyond the next ridge, or the one after that, a little to the left perhaps, and higher up. We began to flag, separated to widen the search, lost each other, added our faint cries to the crying sheep, despaired.

I sat on a tussock and two minuscule rock pipit chicks floundered helplessly in a ditch at my feet. Removing myself hurriedly to a nearby rock, I watched the parent bird, beak full of food, hopping and chirping a foot or so above them, failing to find them. The other parent bird chirped in agitation from the rocks. Time passed. The chicks presumably drowned. Should I have lifted them out on to a rock where the parent could see them or would I only have made matters worse? Wasteful nature cared not at all, and I was lost, and this was the desert.

If it was St Columba, or one of the twelve monks who came with him from Ireland to Iona in 565, who had made the cell among these grey rocks, on this yellowish turf sprinkled with tiny flowers, among the rock pipits and the white-rumped wheatears, it would have answered his need for self-abnegation as perfectly as the sands of the Sahara did for St Antony or the northern forest of Temnikov for St Seraphim of Sarov. It was nowhere, bathed in the pure light of nothing. Each rock differed only subtly from each other rock, each swampy patch could have been the one I had walked through ten minutes before. There were crows, but far away on a higher ridge; they did not have the look of crows that bring bread to hermits. The sea was out of sight, guarded by rocky distance, the pearly clouds concealed the sun. One might dissolve into the soft atmosphere; the seasons would change, cyclical rather than progressive; only one's bones, showing through the flesh, would mark the physical journey towards the stark skeleton whitening among the stones.

We struggled on, of course, and in the end we stumbled upon a small circle of stones and convinced ourselves that this was the place. Then we limped back and were revived by soup and walked quite easily along to the abbey to be amazed by sound. Sir John Eliot Gardiner, the Monteverdi Choir and the English Baroque Soloists were on their Bach Cantata Millennium Pilgrimage and had come to Iona for the day of Bach's death. To be more accurate it was the day before his death; they were giving the concert that afternoon as well as on the following morning because so few people could be fitted into the abbey. The logistics defied the imagination. All their instruments and equipment had had to be transported from the mainland to the island of Mull and from Mull across the sea to Iona. Three days earlier they had been in Mühlhausen, two days later they were to be in Anspach. Tickets for the concert were free, because Iona is a holy island.

The cantatas they sang for Bach's death day were among his most sublime, being on the themes of death, fear, faith and holy joy. The last chorale was sung outside the abbey, in front of the west door. Afterwards, in the low evening sunlight, incongruous on this remote northern island, a tall man in a frock coat stood smiling and bowing, a neat group of superlative musicians looking slightly shy behind him. Together with the audience scattered around the grassy mount in the churchyard we acclaimed them, thinking of St Columba, thinking of Johann Sebastian Bach, thinking of our mysterious species' extraordinary need for something to praise, something to glorify.

St Columba, or St Columcille as he is known in Ireland, set off with twelve monks for Iona in 565. It seems he had no idea of being a missionary. There had been some kind of quarrel, possibly over a question of copyright. It seems the saint may have copied a particularly beautiful psalter without the permission of the bishop to whom it belonged. The local king forced him to return the copy to the owner of the original, but later St Columba, himself the son of a princely family, defeated the king in battle and won back the psalter. But as a monk who had taken up arms, he had to be exiled, in penance.

He had already founded monasteries in Ireland and he continued his work among the Irish who had settled in western Scotland, his reputation for peace-making and holiness spreading wherever he went. It is said that when at last he was weakened by age, St Columba was resting on a rock when the old white horse which brought the milk every morning to the monks of Iona came and laid his head upon his breast. The horse wept and foamed copiously, but the saint would not allow the monks to lead him away until he had given the affectionate beast his blessing; and the next day St Columba died.

There is another Holy Island in Scotland, a very small one, off the coast of Arran. It has remains of monastic buildings from the seventh century, but it belongs now to Tibetan Buddhists. There is a cave, with a spring nearby, which is said to be where St Molaise, also known as Laserian, lived as a hermit. He died in 639, having also founded a monastery at Inishmurray in County Sligo. He went in for severe penitential practices and was said to have infected himself with thirty diseases at once in expiation of his sins. The Buddhists have made some buildings at the other end of the island into a centre for solitary retreats, some of which can be short and some the traditional three year, three month and three-day retreat of Tibetan tradition.

Their home monastery is Samyeling, which is not far from Lockerbie in Dumfriesshire. There is a huge Buddhist temple there, surprising among the Forestry Commission plantations of conifers, beside the busy little Scottish river Esk. The temple has been there since 1967, the year Dr Akong Tulku Rinpoche arrived from Tibet. He is still there, and Lama Yeshe, his brother, is Abbot and Retreat Master. We spent a night at the monastery, in a small house which had been the only building there in 1967. Its sparseness had something more Western than Eastern about it; it felt more like a hostel for the homeless than a place of spiritual renewal. There were notices stating that no responsibility could be taken for drug and alcohol abusers or the mentally ill. Mild admonitions about keeping the place clean and tidy were also pinned up here and there and it was some time before we understood that in some sense, these were in fact obeyed. Near the hostel a huge stupa was being built. New buildings were gradually spreading all around, and there was a new retreat centre a little way away; the place, in a certain chaotic kind of way which is completely within its own nature, was flourishing. I talked to a man who had been there several times and had now decided to stay, hoping in the end to become a monk. He said the lack of organization was somehow fundamental, that things happened in spite of it: ten people would concern themselves with planting one cabbage, no one would water the carrots – and yet in the end there were enough vegetables. What he wanted to do was to introduce some structure without losing the way-wardness; the West, he said, had something to contribute.

When I asked Lama Yeshe whether he thought the present popularity of Buddhism in the West would change the religion, he said that was not possible; Mind was Mind, and there was no way in which it could be changed. His calm presence was reinforced by his evident well-being, reminding one how the author of the *Cloud of Unknowing* had said that true contemplation would make the adept pleasing to behold. His smile was delightful and a little remote. He had beautiful feet. Mind was the same as Soul, he said, and meditation was the same as contemplation. I was not sure that all Buddhists, or all Christians, would agree; but Lama Yeshe himself was clearly a contemplative and not enormously concerned with definitions. He had spent twelve years in solitary retreat and had done two *bardo* retreats, during which he had been in total darkness and silence for weeks at a time. For this, he said, you have to be very strong, to defeat the hallucinations.

According to Lama Yeshe, most people in the West cannot endure solitude. There is so much to come out, he said, so much pain, so much anger. He encourages them to come in groups only, with two experienced solitaries, a monk and a nun, to guide them through chanting, meditation, silence and some time spent alone in their own rooms. The tradition exists in Christianity, he said, but has been lost; Christianity has become dry. He finds Europeans very intelligent and well educated; in the East the mass of the Buddhist population is not attentive to its religion, it would be wrong to think otherwise. Materialism is taking over the East also. He had heard of Christian missionaries there and suggested optimistically and perhaps not quite seriously that East and West might revivify each other's religions. He was not at all concerned that Buddhism might be becoming too fashionable and too much linked to Hollywood film stars. Nothing could change the nature of the ultimate reality. Or, he added, the importance of Buddhism to Tibetan exiles.

There are forty monks and eighteen nuns at Samyeling. Visiting lamas who come to conduct retreats or courses include some of the most experienced in the world. In the temple, bright with gold, a lama and two young monks chanted, while a congregation of about twenty westerners sat on chairs or cross-legged on cushions; those on cushions joined in the chanting, those on chairs did not. In between the chanting there were periods of silence, which were peaceful and conducive to contemplation. From time to time the lama made a few faint hums of a companionable sort. The woman next to me fell into a deep sleep.

CHAPTER 7

*'. . . going forth well-
armed . . .'*

HERMIT RELIGIOUS ORDERS

Cave hermits — the hermit of Dinton —
regicides in Judges' Cave — San Baudelio —
St Benedict — St Martin of Tours — Conques —
Eve Lavallière — Camaldoli — St Bruno in Calabria —
the Order of St Paul the First Hermit

The first hermitage must have been a cave. The first hermits lived in cave country, the mountains of China and India, the rock-strewn deserts of North Africa. Caves have a perennial fascination, being ways into the earth itself, easily imagined as gateways to the underworld. The Hindu Christian monk Abhishiktananda loved the caves on the mountain Arunachala, where he felt his mediations had led him into the cave of his own heart. He wrote of one of them:

> The cave was narrow, but high enough for one to be able to stand upright. On the left there was a cavity; facing the entrance was a rock about three feet high which later became my favourite seat. At the back of the cave on the right side was an opening which gave onto a sort of corridor, and at the end of the corridor was another cave where there was a spring of water in the rainy season, which was reached through a very narrow hole.

If there is a hermit in all of us, perhaps there is also a cave-dweller. The early hermits in the Egyptian desert were of course ascetics, but they could have made themselves quite comfortable in their caves, in that dry air, had they allowed themselves to do so. In the nature of things, they cannot all have been saints. A young neophyte was once visiting one of the old men, and became so engrossed in their conversation that darkness fell before he noticed it, and he had a long way to walk back home. The old hermit told him to sleep in the outer cave, and gave him a goat-skin for covering. The desert night was bitterly cold and in the morning the shivering young man was amazed to see the hermit apparently unaffected. How could this be, he asked him.

'A lion came, and slept beside me, and kept me warm.'

Of course. But the hermit might also have had a plentiful supply of skins in his sheltered inner cave. He might have had a fire in there, an oil-lamp to see by, honey and lentils to eat, a secret spring of water.

A cave commends itself to a hermit because of its simplicity. Nothing needs to be added to it; it is the most basic kind of shelter. Human instinct, however, tends to attach meaning to the habitual home, often leading to affection. Would the strictest asceticism require the hermit to move on before he found too mundane a satisfaction in his own dwelling?

A traveller walking recently in Nepal was given shelter for the night by a Tibetan Buddhist in his cave. There was a blizzard blowing at the time, and beneath his orange silk the hermit was wrapped up in layers of yak-skin. He had a kerosene stove for making tea, and once a week his wife from the village, an hour and a half's walk away, brought him a supply of food. He spent his time reading from scrolls and chanting mantras. He gave the travellers seeds and oil to eat and put silk threads round their necks before assuming a silk hat in order to bless them for the rest of their journey; they were going higher up the mountain and would be knee-deep in snow. Between October and early April the hermit was always surrounded by snow. He told them with the utmost cheerfulness that he was seventy years old, and had been living in his cave for thirty years. Whatever else he loved and however unlikely it might seem, it was clear that he was very fond of his cave.

Such English hermits as lived in caves would have had an easier time. There was one in the sandstone hillside near Bridgnorth in

Shropshire, and another at Warkworth in Northumberland, where you walk down a grassy bank from the church and take a boat across the river Coquet and then climb up to a hermitage so picturesque you think it must come from some eighteenth-century landscape artist's imagination. In fact, a tiny fourteenth-century chapel sits above the dark hall and kitchen where the hermit lived and was paid to pray for the salvation of his patrons. In the fifteenth century Thomas Barker, who was appointed for life by the fourth Earl of Northumberland, received a yearly stipend of £3.33p.

Where there were no caves, a hermit had to build a hut. It was the idea of the hut which afforded so much pleasure to the ingenious eighteenth-century builder of rustic hermitages. The cave became the grotto, to his way of thinking. The grotto had classical associations, being the cave of the sibyl or the haunt of the river god. Where there was a natural cave, an improving landowner might even remove it, as seems to have happened at Carden Park in Cheshire, where a cave was apparently smoothed out of the way in the interests of a larger view.

In the seventeenth century there was one hermit, apparently interested in solitude for its own sake and without any particular religious intent, who did seem to appreciate the comforts of a cave, despite some apparent damp. Thomas Bushell was one of Francis Bacon's attendants, and when Bacon died in 1726 he retired to some land he had in Oxfordshire, where he had a cave dug out of the hillside for himself, and there spent most of his time.

'He did not encumber himself with his wife,' noted John Aubrey. 'But here enjoyed himself in this paradise . . . When the queen mother came to Oxon to the king, she either brought (as I thinke) or somebody gave her an entire mummie from Egypt, a great raritie, which her majesty gave to Mr. Bushell, but I beleeve long ere this time the dampnesse of the place has spoyled it with mouldiness.'

Not very long after this, John Bigg, a clerk to Simon Mayne, one of the judges who signed Charles I's death warrant, became a hermit when his master was imprisoned in the Tower of London on the restoration of the monarchy. He retired into a cave in the grounds of Dinton Hall, Mayne's country house, and lived there for thirty-six years. He mended his clothes out of odd pieces of leather which people gave him and which he nailed on to the original garment until it became a patchwork of leather pieces. According to Aubrey:

> His garments were fastened together, so that he put them all on or off at once. He mended his shoes in the same way by fastening fresh pieces of leather or cloth over the decayed parts, until they became of more than tenfold thickness, composed of above a thousand different pieces. Round his waist he wore a girdle and suspended from it he usually had three bottles, one of which he kept for ale, one for small beer and the other for milk.

One of his shoes is preserved in the Ashmolean Museum in Oxford. He was famous enough to have a pub in the nearby village of Ford called after him, the Dinton Hermit.

Simon Mayne died in the Tower, but seven of the other regicides were excluded from the general pardon in the Act of Indemnity and some of them were hanged, drawn and quartered. Two – William Goffe and Edward Whalley – made their escape before Charles II was proclaimed king, and arrived in Boston in July 1660. It was not until months later that the governor understood who they were, and that there was a price on their heads. Goffe and Whalley went into hiding, but in fact the governor, though he made a show of looking for them, was unwilling to hand them over to certain death. They made their way through Connecticut and were hidden by a clergyman in New Haven until they moved on into the woods, and then into a cave, known even now as Judges' Cave. It is among a jumble of rocks in the middle of a national park, and could have afforded only a very basic sort of shelter, but the two regicides, deeply devout to the end and convinced of their eventual vindication, survived the hardships and died many years later, without ever returning to their native land.

Whalley, who was the father-in-law of Goffe, died in Hadley, Massachusetts, where they had moved and were living concealed in the house of the Revd John Russell. In 1676, during the wars between the settlers and the Native Americans, Hadley came under attack. Although the settlers were greatly outnumbered, at the turning point of the battle a white-haired stranger appeared and took command, to such effect that the Native Americans were quickly routed. The stranger disappeared and was never seen again. The villagers thought he was an angel, but he could have been the Puritan General Goffe, fighting his last battle.

The grotto did not always lose its association with the hermit. Some extraordinary baroque sculptures in Czechoslovakia include representations of the hermits Onufrius and Garinus, apparently crawling out of the natural sandstone rocks. They are the work of Matthias Bernard Braun (1684–1738) who was commissioned by Count Sporck to embellish a part of the woodland of his immense estate by making a series of allegorical sculptures of the vices and virtues. Whether the count felt guilty because his father, a soldier, had amassed a great fortune during the Thirty Years' War, or whether his apparently morbid imagination was a feature of the baroque taste of his time and his intention was simply to beautify Bohemia, the resulting works are astonishing, though now in poor repair. There was also a chapel, a hermitage of St Antony, a hospital and a spa. The count's bedroom was so arranged that he could look across the valley to his own mausoleum; he was said to sleep every night in a coffin.

In the Middle Ages, Count Sporck could probably have endowed a hermit to pray for his soul. Hermits were familiar features of the medieval landscape. All over Europe there are signs of their habitations, legends of their lives, chapels built where once they prayed. Most of the hermitages were built long after the time of the hermit they commemorate, whose cave or hut, or simply the rumour of his or her erstwhile presence, is subsumed in the later symbol of a holy place. Some of the buildings are very simple, some complex. The hermitage of San Baudelio at Berlanga di Duero in Spain is an extraordinary example of Mozarab architecture. It must be still as remote as it ever was, on a hill in Aragon, five miles from the village.

Berlanga had some fine medieval walls, in good condition. We climbed up the hill to see them on an evening of early spring sunlight. The distance was so deceptively clear that a big flock of sheep among the still bare poplar trees below looked for a moment like an approaching army. There was a black redstart grinding out its little song from somewhere in the walls and huge holes in the ground exposed unsuspected dungeons dangerously far below. We stayed in a small hotel which was full of building workers; they appeared to be making a new square or football pitch below the castle. They were as hungry as we were and when at last the single barman opened the door into the dining-room we all unceremoniously crowded in, to be served at incredible speed and with an air of understandable desperation by the same barman, the only member of the hotel staff we ever saw, so perhaps he had done the cooking as well.

The hermitage is a few miles away from the village, amid bare hills, a small square building with the relics of an ancient graveyard beside it and a thin plantation of wind-blown pines beyond. It was completely silent except for the singing of the larks and a few twitters from the finches in the bedraggled pines. A strangely striated table mountain opposite, with the snow-capped sierra beyond, gave the landscape a bleak Spanish grandeur. Eventually a small white car appeared below and began the curving approach. It was the custodian, radio at full volume, so that between jingles we could hear that Nato was bombing the Serbs and the vice-president of Paraguay had been assassinated. When he unlocked the door of the hermitage we could see the vaulted interior, and the central cylindrical pillar from which the vaults seem to spring like the branches of a palm tree. San Baudelio himself would have seen none of this because it was not built until the eleventh century; he had been there in the fifth, and his small cave is still to be seen in a dark corner. The walls of the church were once covered with beautiful twelfth-century frescoes. They were removed in 1926 by an American, and taken to the Metropolitan Museum in New York, which still owns them, though some are on permanent loan to the Prado. You can see only their shadows now. The hermit was fond of animals so the painters gave him hunting dogs and hares, an elephant with a howdah, an elongated monkey, a big-footed camel. There were falconers, with an almost Persian look about them, and a soldier in a wine-coloured tunic carrying a round green shield. Only their shades dimly disport themselves where once they were resplendent.

Outside the hermitage a tiny firecrest hung upside down on a wind-blown pine branch. In the central square of the village there is a plaque to commemorate Fray Tomas di Berlango, eminent naturalist and discoverer of the Galapagos Islands.

News of the hermits of the East had come to Western Europe through John Cassian, a Romanian monk who had studied monasticism in Egypt. He came to the West from Constantinople in the early fifth century and founded two monasteries near Marseilles, one for men and one for women. The extremes of the Syrians were not thought appropriate for the gentler West. One hermit did set himself up on a pillar in 585, at Carignan in the Ardennes, but he was firmly told by his bishop to come down, and his pillar was destroyed in his absence.

Meanwhile, the Franks were advancing through Roman Gaul. Whenever barbarians encroach there are probably quiet corners where the old ways continue, out of the limelight, pushed to the margins. Some quiet estates in the less-frequented areas of Burgundy, Touraine and Aquitaine unobtrusively kept up Gallo-Roman ways, though occasionally, such was the temper of the times, a young heir might become a recluse and disappear into the forests of the Jura or Le Perche. Sometimes his mother would carry on the estate, looking after the cultivation of the vines and olives, and sometimes he himself might return and found a religious house, which she would support.

St Benedict is the patriarch of Western monasticism. He was born in 480, and left his studies in Rome to live alone at Subiaco in the Abruzzi hills, fifty miles or so from Rome. At first his cave was known only to one monk, who brought him food, but his fame spread and he was asked to become abbot of a local monastery. The monks regretted their choice, finding his precepts too stern, and tried to poison him. A helpful crow carried away the poisoned bread, and St Benedict went on to found the monastery of Monte Cassino and to formulate his Rule, on which most subsequent monastic life is based.

St Benedict's Rule makes provision for 'those who, not in the first fervour of religious life, but after long probation in the monastery, have learnt by the help and experience of many to fight against the devil; and going forth well armed from the ranks of their brethren to the single-handed combat of the desert, are able, without the support of others, to fight by the strength of their own arm, God helping them, against the vices of the flesh and their evil thoughts'.

Subsequent Christian hermits, mistrusted as they sometimes were by their institutional superiors and vulnerable to outside scepticism or mockery, found in this provision their authentication.

St Martin of Tours, who was a soldier in the Roman army before he left it to become a hermit, had almost as great an influence as St Benedict on the more northern part of Europe. He was stationed in Amiens when he gave half his cloak to a beggar and then saw Christ wearing it in a vision. He left the army about the middle of the fourth century, and became a hermit on an island off the Italian coast, and then in a small community of hermits near Poitiers. He was made Bishop of Tours because of his great holiness, and in spite of criticisms of his 'dirty clothes and unkempt hair'. He continued to live the life of a hermit as far as possible in the monastery he founded outside Tours. He was a patron of churches in Britain from earliest times; his feast-day is on the eleventh of November, which is why he is often represented with a goose, November being the time that migrating geese arrive from the north. If there is fine weather in early November it is known as St Martin's Summer.

The idea that the hermit was holier than other monks persisted. One medieval hermit, Pietro de Maroni, was felt to be so particularly holy that he was made pope at the age of eighty-four, much to his distress. He was so miserable that he was allowed to retire four years later and return to the hermit life, in which he continued until he died.

Medieval Western hermits would not necessarily have been monks going forth from their monasteries. They sometimes simply appeared, and were given authenticity by grace of a local bishop. Attempts to regulate the hermit life were not always successful, certainly until a thirteenth-century pope ordained that all hermits who did not belong to any recognized rule should become members of the Augustinian order.

The ninth-century hermit Dadon appeared beside a spring in a remote valley in the Aveyron, and settled there among the chestnut woods and the wild rock-strewn hills. Nothing much is known of him, except that other hermits came to join him, and he in due course withdrew to a hermitage further down the river where you may still see his small church and the plaque which records its restoration in 1975 by a local boy who made good in California. The community Dadon had founded grew and the abbey church of Conques was built there in the eleventh century; his spring still flows just below the small square in front of the church.

As the pilgrimage to the tomb of the apostle James at Compostella became the most important of European pilgrimages, Conques became one of the stages on the route. By the eleventh century there were crowds of pilgrims to accommodate. There are still crowds of pilgrims, though most of them are tourists now, and it is as well to go out of the holiday season if you can. Even so, if you stay until most of the tourists have gone, there is an evening calm in which you can take in the unexpected height of the plain Romanesque columns inside the church, a consequence of the constricted space on which it is built; the height is like a phrase in music whose final arch of sound you had failed to anticipate, a shock of delight beyond your expectations. The hermit Dadon is among the detailed carvings on the tympanum over the doors, between St Peter and Odolric the second abbot. He has plenty of hair, neatly parted in the middle, and a fine moustache and beard, a short cloak, a solid stick and big useful hands.

The writer Prosper Merimée, author of *Carmen*, which Bizet made into an opera, and *Colomba*, which one day someone will realize should be made into a film, was the first Inspector of Historical Monuments in France. He went to Conques in 1837, accompanied by Stendhal, and was horrified to find the abbey church almost in ruins. It had already been in decline when the revolution of 1789 abolished the chapter of canons who had been responsible for maintaining it and the council of the tiny town of Conques was quite unable to stand the expense of repair. An early conservationist, Merimée threw himself into the task, only just in time. Fortunately he found that the abbey's treasure, its extraordinary collection of jewelled vases and reliquaries, had been preserved through all its vicissitudes by the ingenuity of the inhabitants, who during the revolution had concealed them in a variety of stables and chestnut-drying sheds, returning them intact when the danger was over.

Not far from Conques, St Tarsice, apparently the granddaughter of Kind Clothilde the First, lived in a 'desert' near Rodez in the early seventh century. Female recluses seem to have abounded in France, saints Trojecia, Bertilie, Berth, Ulphe, Delphina, Colette, predecessors all – for a feature of the hermit life is its perpetual recrudescence – of Eve Lavallière. In 1917, under the influence of a holy man named Charles Henrion, Eve Lavallière, a well-known actress, gave up everything to retire to Thuillières, a village in the Vosges. There she lived a life of simple devotion, accompanied only by her dresser, Leona, who had worked for her in her years of success in Paris, and who had fortunately been converted at the same time.

The eleventh and twelfth centuries saw a new kind of hermit movement. The hermit whose only desire was to live alone with God still went his own way, but there was also a movement of protest from within existing monastic life. As monasteries became part of the established order, they inevitably changed. For one thing they became considerable property owners. As they became richer, not only did they tend to make life more comfortable for themselves but they became politically significant. The moral authority which the support of a powerful abbot could give to a feudal grandee was worth any amount of useful endowments. The movement away from such worldliness towards a new sort of semi-eremitical way of life led to such foundations as the Camaldolesi and the Carthusians and in due course the Cistercians who, for all the fierce asceticism of their founder St Bernard of Clairvaux, eventually became among the richest and most powerful of all.

The new hermits were looking for more than personal enlightenment. They wanted to make new communities, and it was the community that was to be solitary – that is to say, cut off from the world – rather than the individual. Success brought problems of organization, which led to new institutions, though often only after the deaths of the founders, whose personalities were usually powerful enough to hold things together without a systematic structure. Once a way of life became institutionalized, it was liable to assume just those characteristics which the founders had rejected in the powerful Benedictine foundations they had left: wealth and power, large property holdings, abbots absent on affairs of state. Sometimes a member of one of the new communities would seek further solitude and withdraw, alone or with one or two others. There were rivalries and disagreements between different orders, there were misunderstandings with popes and bishops, there were doubts about how to admit, or whether to admit, women – even children, for sometimes whole families came to join the hermits – but the steady gaze backwards towards the Egyptian desert, and the belief that solitude in wild surroundings would clarify the mind and cleanse the heart, meant that, unlike most utopian communities of any affiliation, many of these movements endured.

Camaldoli is high in the Apennines. Its woods, which the monks maintained and which have now become part of the national park of the Casentino, are so steep that the sun falls through the descending crests of the trees in beautiful shafts of light unknown in the forbidding forests which surround the nearby less mountainous monastery of Vallombrosa. Romuald of Ravenna, who founded the order of the Camaldolesi in the late tenth century, was said to have been horrified when his father killed a man in a quarrel about property, and so retired to the monastery of St Apollinaire in Classe, near Ravenna. Later he became a hermit and instructed other hermits in the ascetic way of life, but he seems to have been a restless man and travelled widely. He came to the woods of Camaldoli late in life and founded a hermitage high in the hills; two hundred feet below it he reorganized an ancient pilgrims' refuge, which became a guest house and later a monastery. Both the monastery and the hermitage flourish today; in the summer of 1999 seventeen out of the twenty-one hermits' cells were occupied.

The places to which the hermits went to find their 'desert' or wilderness or solitude always held a great importance for them. Outsiders may have seen them only as remote and harsh, but the hermits themselves often grew to love them, not just because of the fierceness of the landscape but also because they developed a closeness to the natural rhythms of the seasons in the starkness of such surroundings.

St Bruno, founder of the Carthusians, went with six friends into the bleak mountains of Haute Savoie in 1084. 'Only those who have experienced it can know what heavenly joy and benefit the silence and solitude of the desert can bring to those who love it,' he wrote.

Later he was called to Rome to become a counsellor to Pope Urban II, but in 1093 he persuaded the pope to let him return to the hermit life. He wrote to a friend:

> I am living in the wilderness of Calabria, far removed from habitation. There are some brethren with me, some of whom are very well educated, and they keep constant watch for their Lord, so as to open to him at once when he knocks. I could never even begin to tell you how charming and pleasant it is. The temperatures are mild, the air healthy; a broad valley, a delight to the eye, reaches from one mountain peak to the other along their whole length. It is quite filled with fields and meadows that boast all manner of sweet-smelling herbs and flowers. The impact of these gently undulating hills all around with their folded valleys in between through which flow a variety of brooks and streams is quite indescribable. And for good measure, we ourselves have an abundance of lush gardens that boast every kind of fruit tree.

Bruno had not intended to found an order. That was really accomplished by Guigues de Saint-Romain, the fifth prior of the Grande Chartreuse, who was a brilliant organizer. St Bruno lived from 1032 to 1101. Remote in hardly imagined Tibet, the Buddhist hermit Milarepa lived from 1040 to 1123. His disciple Gampopa performed the same function as Gigues; he systematized the holy founder's teachings after his death. It is a pattern which recurs: Jesus was followed by St Paul. To say that Bruno and Milarepa were roughly contemporary is not to suggest that the European and the Tibetan, separated by much more than geographical distance, would have been anything other than astonished had they come face to face. But the solitary voyage of the practised mind into the void is probably of all quests the one which varies least with time and place.

The first Carthusians came to England in 1178 at the invitation of Henry II, who patronized several new monasteries in an attempt to expiate his guilt over the murder of Thomas Becket. They settled at Witham in Somerset, then at Hatherop in Gloucestershire, and then back in Somerset at Hinton Charterhouse. Not until after the Black Death in 1348 did other Charterhouses follow, it being considered that the harder the lives of the monks the more efficacious might be their prayers. At Mount Grace in Yorkshire, which is now a ruin, you can see a restored Carthusian cell. There is a herb garden, too, much as it might have been. The place is beautiful, on the edge of the North Yorkshire moors, not far from Rievaulx Abbey, perhaps the best situated of all the ruined abbeys in England. The cell is simple but not particularly small; upstairs there is a large light room for the monk to work in, weaving or reading or copying. Carthusian monks live as hermits, maintaining a measure of community life only for protection and for reasons of practical economy. The monk's life is spent alone in his cell, praying at specified times, meditating and working, perhaps cultivating his small garden. Lay brothers bring food to the hatch built for that purpose.

A more forbidding image of the Carthusian life may be seen at St Hugh's Charterhouse at Parkminster in East Sussex, an immense building designed originally to house all the refugee monks from mid-nineteenth-century France. The life there is lived today in the same way as it was in medieval France, in surroundings of intimidating gloom, austere and solitary except for the weekly walk which the entire community takes together. Not everyone who goes there stays the course – 'We take sick people and make them sicker,' said one – but there are some who want no other life, and find the weekly conversational walk the only hardship, much preferring the customary silence.

Medieval hermits lived as solitaries but did not necessarily stay in the same place; anchorites were enclosed in cells from which they did not move, speaking only to those who came to their windows, or their personal attendants. Hermits often mixed with people, and sometimes preached to them. They might also keep bridges, lighthouses or city gates. Some of them were experts in herbal medicine. Some might even have been looking for nothing more than a room, however meagre, of their own, a rare luxury for many in those times. Not all were under the aegis of any particular religious foundation or bishop, and some were probably fugitives of one sort or another. Langland in *Piers Ploughman* is scornful of 'grete lobies and longe that loth were to wynke clothede hem in copies to be knowe from othere and made hem-selve eremytes hure eise to have' (great long lubbers who hated work and were got up in clerical gowns to distinguish them from laymen and paraded themselves as hermits for the sake of an easy life).

Most of the simple hermits of the later middle ages took an oath to live under the Rule of St Paul the First Hermit, which prescribed for them a few prayers and a life of hard manual labour. They were not allowed to beg, but people were encouraged to give them alms. They were a most economical form of that prestigious branch of the French civil service now known as the *Ponts et Chaussées*, where many of the elite of the educational system start their careers in public life, overseeing bridges and thoroughfares.

CHAPTER 8

'... no beast but one kat...'

MEDIEVAL ANCHORITES

Eve of Wilton — Christina of Markyate —
the Ancrene Riwle —
Robert of Knaresborough — Godric of Finchale —
Guthlac and his sister Pega — ex-soldiers

In Anglo-Saxon times a great abbess, such as Hilda of Whitby, was a powerful figure, ruling over both monks and nuns. Norman culture was more exclusively masculine, and after the Conquest monasteries increasingly became for men only, making it harder for women to find a retreat from the world.

The religious life was often the only way of escape from a fiercely male-dominated world. A woman deciding to become a hermit might want to dedicate her life to God, but she might also want to escape an unwelcome marriage, or simply get away from home. In the tenth and eleventh centuries women were hated and feared as much as at any time in history. As always during such periods, there are instances of gentleness breaking through and love being allowed in, but generally speaking – and particularly among the ecclesiastical authorities – women were to be seen as dangerous, probably in league with the Devil, and above all overwhelmingly lustful. The Church, asserting ever more control over people's lives, alerted the faithful to what they might expect from any woman who escaped the domination of her husband. She was likely to bewitch, or even poison, them by her culinary arts, she would certainly seduce their friends, servants, and even their animals, in pursuit of her depraved pleasures, and she was liable to introduce them to all sorts of forbidden knowledge. She was, it had to be remembered, Eve's daughter.

Sometimes consecration as a holy virgin was the only way for a woman to avoid an enforced marriage. Under the control of their fathers, docile daughters could do a lot for their families by an advantageous match. A local bishop might be an ally of the father, and a determined woman might have to rely on the support of a male hermit or priest. Often she would fly to such a one in her distress, and live near him. The associations this gave rise to were various, and in some cases very close. Speculation arose at the time, and has continued ever since. There is even a word – syneisaktism – to describe a monk and a nun living together without carnal knowledge of each other. Common sense leads one to suppose that sometimes they did and sometimes they didn't.

Eve of Wilton was given as a seven-year-old child to Wilton Abbey by her Danish father and Lothringen mother. As a friend of her parents and an occasional chaplain at Wilton, Goscelin of St Bertin, a Flemish monk who had come to England as part of the court of Bishop Hermann of Ramsbury shortly before the Conquest, took an interest in Eve as she grew up. He travelled around during the last two decades of the eleventh century collecting stories of Anglo-Saxon saints and abbesses whom he felt had been under-rated by the self-confident Normans, and as he travelled he corresponded with Eve. In 1080 she suddenly left for France, with one companion, and from her mid-twenties to her mid-forties she lived a life of extreme austerity at Saint-Laurent de Tertre in Angers, near other eremitic men and women. Goscelin, twenty years her senior, would appear to have been heart-broken. 'Oh dearest light of my soul,' he wrote, 'Behold, while I write, the raging sorrow cannot be ignored.' Had he advised her on the purification of the passions, and when she learnt too well found he had forgotten how once he had transformed his own?

Eve clearly inspired deep devotion. She seems to have moved to St Eutrope near the priory of Levière, where she 'lived for a long time with the companionship of Hervey', a monk of Vendôme who had left his monastery to become an anchorite. Again there was speculation, but the Abbot of Vendôme wrote to them, 'Who is perfect in love, let them not fear.' A poet, Hilary, wrote, 'This love is not in the world but in Christ,' and praised 'the wondrous love of such a man and such a woman, which all approve and discover without reproach'. When she died, Hervey was left 'dejected with a great desolation'.

Christina of Markyate went as a child to St Albans Abbey with her parents, merchants from Huntingdon. She was so inspired that she took a vow of virginity in her teens. She was a pretty girl and her parents had hoped for a splendid marriage. Their only hope was to persuade her to break her vow, because she could not become a nun unless she was a virgin. When she remained obdurate a helpful bishop did his best to rape her. When she escaped him by hiding in a cupboard, her parents introduced a certain Burthred into her bedroom and tried to get her drunk. They did succeed in making her go through some form of marriage ceremony, but she apparently suggested to the hapless Burthred on their wedding night that they should live chastely together until in due course each would go into a religious order. This plan failing to appeal to Burthred, she was helped to escape by a solitary called Eadwin. Disguised as a man, she fled the marital home on a horse and for six years lived secretly, two years with the anchoress Alfwen and four with a relative of Eadwin, the hermit Roger.

Roger built Christina a tiny cell next to his, and eventually a small community of other women gathered round her. In spite of an episode of severe temptation when a monk fell in love with her, and probably she with him, she eventually became a respected holy woman attached to the diocese of St Albans, her counsel widely sought. She was of Anglo-Saxon descent, as were most of her associates, some of whom spoke no French. She would have had a particular position, detached but not a foreigner, in touch with the local community through a whole network of gossip. She may have become as valued a counsellor, even sometimes an adjudicator, as St Simeon Stylites had been, up there on his pillar.

The various medieval books of rules for women leading the solitary life seem mostly to have been written for a particular hermit, or perhaps group of hermits, and there is a certain fond concern, even fussiness, in them. A 'presbyter' called Grimlaic wrote a rule in the early tenth century, and later Ailred the Abbot of Rievaulx wrote a guide for his sister, which he clearly intended to have a general application as well. The most famous rule is probably the *Ancrene Riwle* (Rule for Anchoresses) written in Middle English in the early thirteenth century by an anonymous priest or monk, possibly an Augustinian canon, for the guidance of three sisters; like Ailred's, this rule was also meant for general use.

The actual practice of any hermit or anchoress would of course have varied according to the advice of the local bishop or parish priest and the individual disposition of the recluse, but in general she was supposed to have a means of subsistence, though some were endowed by a patron or had money of their own. They were supposed to work as well as pray, whether copying manuscripts, making church vestments or clothes for the poor (or themselves), compiling dictionaries, or tending their gardens. Idleness was to be dreaded, sloth being well-known to lead to despondency. The *Ancrene Riwle* has precise instructions as to prayer, food, work, rest, repetition of ritual, 'falling to the earth if it be a workday, bowing somewhat downward if it be a holiday. The anchoress is to say or sing the night office, matins, prime, none, and compline . . . Your shoes should be large and warm. By variation of activities, idleness is to be routed.'

It was understood that an anchoress was to be thought of as having taken the part of Mary, in the biblical story of the two sisters, Martha the active one and Mary the contemplative. 'My dear Sisters, ye shall have no beast but one kat. Ancre that hath cattle seemeth better housewife than Ancre – as Martha was.'

Sometimes bishops became worried about ageing anchorites. Archbishop Wickwane of York writes to the Vicar of Blyth in Nottinghamshire to take care of Lady Joan, a solitary 'languishing miserably in her cell', unable to keep up the 'lawful occupations in which at times she used to engage for the sake of a livelihood'. Did the vicar not know of her existence, or did he know only too well and had he been hoping not to have to take responsibility for a difficult old woman?

Most medieval anchoresses would have had a servant. Julian of Norwich had two. The *Ancrene Riwle* sets out in some detail what the servant's duties should be, and how she should comport herself so as not to bring ill repute upon her mistress. More than one of these servants took the place of their mistress on the latter's death.

'Solitude' often seems to have referred to the spiritual life rather than the material one. Grimlaic wrote: 'This especially should be aimed at by Solitaries: the presence of not less than two or three Solitaries together – yet thrust into individual cells, so that they can speak to one another through a window and the one be able to stir the other to God's work . . . More prayers can be got through by two rather than by one.'

We hear of a spiritual adviser spending some time 'dwelling with an Anchoret, this woman's confessor'. Visitors would come to seek counsel. Margery Kempe, a religious woman of the fourteenth century who seems to have caused a certain amount of alarm, or perhaps tedium, by her excessive enthusiasm and frequent bouts of uncontrollable weeping, would consult her 'principal ghostly Father the Anchoret of the Preaching Fairs in Lynne', and she was allowed by the ever-forbearing Mother Julian to spend 'many days' at her anchorage in the graveyard of the church of St Julian in Norwich 'communing in the love of our Lord Jesus Christ'. The rules for anchorites were always much stricter than for hermits. The author of the *Ancrene Riwle* was distinctly uneasy about guests, even suggesting that if a friend of an anchoress calls it might be better to 'cause her maid – as in her stead – to give her friend good cheer; and she shall have leave to open her window once or twice, and to make signs toward her of good cheer' (a tactic unlikely to reassure the friend, one might have thought). He wrote disapprovingly: 'Some Ancre make their board with their guests without. That is too much friendship; because, of all Orders, that is most against the Order of Ancre – who is all dead to the world.' Nevertheless, visits did take place. In Sir Thomas Malory's *Morte d'Arthur* for instance, Sir Perceval visits an anchoress whom he only later discovers to be his aunt, and who in her anchorage gives him 'all the cheer that she might make him'.

The thing that most seems to alarm the author of the *Ancrene Riwle* is the danger of time wasted in idle tittle-tattle:

> Nowadays you will hardly find a Recluse before whose window there sits not a garrulous or babbling old woman – occupying her with fables, giving a food of rumours or

detraction, describing the form, face, or habits of this or
that monk or clerk or man of any Order whatever. Seductively
does she bring in the lasciviousness of girls, depict the freedom of widows able to do what they like, the astuteness
of wives in taking their fill of pleasure and in cajoling their
husbands – her face distorted meanwhile with laughter and
jeers, o'er limbs and flesh the sweet poison spreading.

Certainly, things must have occasionally got out of control. At
Whalley in Lancashire, where there had been several anchorites
and recluses on the property of a Cistercian abbey, it seems that
several of them had left without permission to live on their own
elsewhere and the servants had been 'misgovernyd and gotten with
chyld withyn the seyd plase halowyd – to the grete displeasuance
hurt and disclander of the abbeye aforeseyd'.

To Malory, writing in the fifteenth century, the hermit seems
to have been a familiar figure, more familiar probably than Sir
Perceval's aunt, the anchoress. The hermit's knowledge of herbs
made him sought after as a medicine man, 'a good man and a
great leech', as King Arthur finds when he is wounded in a joust
with the 'big man of might', Pellinor. 'So the hermit searched all
his wounds and gave him good salves; so the king was there three
days, and then were his wounds well amended that he might ride
and go, and so departed.'

After Arthur's disappearance on the barge, Sir Bedivere finds
his way to a hermit, who somewhat surprisingly seems to be the
Archbishop of Canterbury. He is tending a new grave. Sir Bedivere
asks whose it is and the hermit tells him how 'this night at midnight
there came a number of ladies and brought a dead corpse and
prayed me to bury him; and here they offered an hundred tapers
and they gave me an hundred besants. Alas, said Sir Bedivere, that
was my lord King Arthur that here lieth buried in this chapel.
Then Sir Bedivere swooned; and when he awoke he prayed the
hermit he might abide with him still there to live with fasting and
prayers.' And there indeed he remained, until he died.

*   *   *

The rules for the enclosure of an anchorite or anchoress were strict. When in 1402 Dom Robert Cherde, a monk of Ford Abbey in Dorset, wished to be enclosed in a building in the churchyard of the nearby parish church of Crewkerne, he had to appear before the Bishop of Bath and Wells, show him his letters of discharge from the Abbot of Ford and back his application with sworn witness statements as to his character. The bishop then wrote to the relevant clergy:

> We have found Dom Robert of laudable life and honest conversation – constant, fit, and suitable for the solitary life. And accordingly – after previous reception, from the same Dom Robert, of a bodily oath touching the faithful maintenance of chastity and other observances due – We have admitted his supplication aforesaid as consonant with reason; and we decree that Dom Robert be introduced into the said house – according to the manner, form, and custom usually practised in such [cases] – and that he be shut up in the same perpetually, without any egress whatever, as justice counsels.

The splendid church of St Bartholomew still stands, but the hermit's cell, and another one, apparently for an anchoress, which once existed somewhere nearer to the west end of the church, have disappeared.

Many of the hermits did disappear without trace, but others left legends, which tradition has modified over the years. Robert of Knaresborough, in Yorkshire, who was born about 1160, is known to have spent some months in a Cistercian monastery in Northumberland, because his brother was a monk there, but he soon retired to a cave on the banks of the river Nidd, and thereafter followed his own way. He could well have been part of the myth of Robin Hood or a character out of Scott's *Ivanhoe*. He shared his cave with a knight who was hiding from justice, but who returned to the world on the death of the king. Robert retreated further into the wood and was protected by a woman of some standing who allowed him shelter near the little chapel of St Hilda. One day thieves broke in and destroyed his cell and he moved on again.

By now people had begun to hear of him, and they came to ask for his counsel. His former associates had been outlaws, poachers or other casual forest wanderers, and though he was used to giving them advice or help he felt himself unworthy to be taken seriously as a teacher or spiritual guide by the rest of the world, and so he fled before the increasing crowd of visitors. He tried to return to a monastery, with some Cluniac monks, but was scandalized at what seemed to him to be their easy way of life, his own being ascetic in the extreme. Not unnaturally the monks encouraged him to return to the woods, but there the local lord accused him of harbouring criminals, and destroyed his hermitage, so he went back to his original cave near St Giles's Chapel on the Nidd. His persecutor made another attempt to eject him, but was fortunately deterred by a timely vision and instead endowed the hermit with a good piece of land and promised him his protection. There Robert lived for many years, in harmony with man and beast, impressed by no grandees. King John himself came to visit him, but Robert, in true hermit fashion, gave him short shrift.

These medieval hermits have a robust English air about them. An eighteenth-century landscape designer, with his fashionable interest in antiquarianism, would doubtless have welcomed one into his woods, though he would have had to forgo the hope of much in the way of deference.

Godric of Finchale was born about 1069 in Norfolk and was a pedlar in Lincolnshire, with a market stall in Lindsey. With a group of others he built a trading vessel and was for sixteen years a merchant venturer (or possibly smuggler) on the east coast and across to Brittany, Flanders and Denmark. He always called in at Lindisfarne or Farne Island where he heard tales of the great and holy St Cuthbert, who had died four hundred years before. He went on several pilgrimages to Rome and Jerusalem, then, having made a success of his business, sold what he had and became a wandering hermit, sometimes living in the woods on roots and berries, until he met an old hermit called Aelric, and lived with him for two years until Aelric died. Then he became door-keeper at the church of St Giles in Durham, where he learnt the psalms. The Bishop of Durham gave him some land at Finchale, and he settled on the beautiful site now occupied by Finchale Priory. His mother, brother and sister came to see him. The mother and brother settled nearby. The sister became a hermit too; Godric built her a hut near his own.

Godric and his sister both wrote hymns which are still sung. In the winter he brought rabbits and field-mice into his hut to warm them. A hunted stag took refuge in his hermitage, but when a whole herd of deer came to eat his newly planted orchard he drove them away with a big stick; he was a practical man, like most hermits. He trained his cow to take itself to pasture and come and find him when it needed milking; this was to the great comfort and relief of his young nephew who was supposed to look after the cow but found it boring, the way young nephews will. Godric was said to have been only just over five feet tall and to have had 'a broad forehead, sparkling grey eyes, and bushy eyebrows which almost met. His face was oval, his nose long, his beard thick. He was strong and agile, and in spite of his small stature his appearance was very venerable.'

An earlier Lincolnshire hermit was Guthlac, a soldier in the late seventh century. He gave up the military life after about ten years and went into a monastery at Repton where there were both monks and nuns, presided over by the abbess Aelfrith, but before long he went as a hermit to a site at Crowland accessible only by boat. He had a sister who was an anchoress at Peakirk; Pega was her name.

Nowadays an ex-soldier is unlikely to think of becoming a hermit, and yet according to a recent newspaper article 25 per cent of London street-dwellers are former soldiers. They have learned to conceal their weaker feelings, and sometimes they take to drink without the ritualized male life of the army to support them. The rules they lived by, even their courage, even their medals, seem to mean nothing in the outside peacetime world, where military discipline is a joke and the chain of command obscure. An ex-Guards officer with three tours of duty in Belfast behind him took an office job, and when he asked a junior girl to get him a cup of coffee he was told, 'F*** off and get it yourself.' It was never like that in the officer's mess.

There were other forlorn former soldiers in the 1920s, haunted by memories of the Western Front. According to Richard Cobb, in an article in the *TLS* in December 1981:

> In and around Tunbridge Wells, in the mid-Twenties, there were still five fixed hermits: one, a kilted Scot (who had nothing on under his kilt), camped on the Common; schoolboys were warned against him, but he was quite harmless. Another, before 1914 a keen cricketer, lived in a tent near the Hawkenbury Corner (on ground now occupied by the Ministry of Pensions); he still maintained the rather bedraggled uniform of his pre-war enthusiasms, wearing a very old pair of white trousers that were going green and grey, rotting tennis shoes, and an unidentifiable blazer, and he carried his spartan shopping from the store in Hawkenbury in an old cricket-bag designed for pads. He talked to himself, rather loudly, about pre-war county matches. He was said to be shell-shocked. There was a third living in an elaborate wooden structure, in the woods between Tunbridge Wells and Speldhurst. A fourth actually lived in a cave, conforming to eighteenth century requirements, in the Happy Valley, beyond Rusthall church. During the same period, there were two permanent hermits on Port Meadow, north of Oxford. The hermit's life, like chicken-farming, seems to have provided one of the refuges from the human wreckage caused by the first World War.

There is another odd parallel between the soldier's life and the hermit's. It stems from St Benedict's words about the 'single-handed combat of the desert', and it has led some writers to refer to hermits as 'commandos' or 'terrorists for God'. This thirst for glory might be a temptation worse than St Jerome's dancing girls or Flaubert's Queen of Sheba. It contributed to the downfall of Tolstoy's Father Sergius, who wanted to be the bravest hermit of all, and it occurs over and over again in the advice given by spiritual guides to ascetics. In the same way, those in charge of training the SAS say that the man who is unnecessarily courageous is a menace. One can't help noticing that some of the old hermits were terrible exhibitionists. The SAS expert would say it's all in the training; perhaps the spiritual adviser would say the same. The verse which adorns the column at the SAS headquarters on which the names of those who have died are written, reveals not only the boyish heroism of its founders, but if you add the second verse it points the parallel.

> We are the pilgrims master, we shall go
> Always a little further. It may be
> Beyond that last blue mountain
> Across that angry or that glimmering sea.

This is the verse quoted on the column. It was a favourite of Sir Fitzroy Maclean, one of the founders of the SAS. In fact, there should be no full stop at the end of it. It carries on into the next verse, which concludes the sentence:

> White on a throne or silent in a cave
> There dwells a prophet who can understand
> Why men were born: but surely we are brave
> Who take the Golden Journey to Samarkand.

It is by James Elroy Flecker, a poet not much remembered now.

CHAPTER 9

'I could be bounded in
a nutshell . . .'

MYSTICS AND HERMITAGES

*Richard Rolle — The Cloud of Unknowing —
Walter Hilton — Julian of Norwich —
Shakespeare and Catholicism — the Emperor Charles V —
Gaudí — the hermitages of Monserrat —
Philip Thicknesse — Mrs Pobjoy*

Richard Rolle was a hermit in the early part of the fourteenth
century. He fled to solitude at eighteen, leaving his studies at
Oxford and tearing up some dresses of his sister's to make a hermit's cloak, to which he added an old hood of his father's. He
seems never to have lost his youthful romanticism, nor his scorn
for worldly priests and pedants. He is almost imaginable as a
rebellious young idealist of our own time, but there was no New
Age softness about the discipline with which he strove to live the
religious life.

He lived in troubled times. There was famine and plague all
over Europe. Thousands died in the Black Death of 1348; whole
populations were disrupted by the Hundred Years' War; the Papacy
was acrimoniously split between Rome and Avignon.

This time the flight to the desert seems to have been rather a
flight of the mind to God. Mystics of powerful intensity emerged
in Germany and Flanders, France and Italy. England produced
four, Richard Rolle, Walter Hilton, the anonymous author of *The
Cloud of Unknowing* and Mother Julian of Norwich. Their works,
produced largely outside the boundaries of the established Church,
are a remarkable expression of that intense longing for God which
is at the heart of the religious contemplative life; they are not so
much attempts to describe the indescribable as guides for other

travellers on that particular spiritual journey. They have been used as such ever since they were written.

Richard Rolle's sister told him he was mad. She had hurried to meet him in the woods, obediently taking her white dress and her grey dress and her father's old rainhood. Perhaps she hoped to assist at a romantic elopement, instead of which he put the white dress on himself, tore the sleeves off the grey dress and put it on top and added the hood. He was furious with her for not taking him seriously and ran back into the woods in a rage. Soon afterwards he was noticed in church by two brothers he had known at Oxford, whose father was the local landowner. Whether or not this meeting was entirely coincidental is not clear, but the father, John Dalton, equipped Rolle with more suitable hermit clothes, allowed him to live in a simple shelter in his woods, and supplied his daily needs for some time.

'Great liking I had in wilderness to sit, that I far from noise sweetlier might sing, and with quickness of heart likingest praising I might feel; the which doubtless of his gift I have taken, Whom above all thing wonderfully I have loved.' When religious fervour overtook him he sang loudly. He wrote poetry, struggled to purge and refine his soul, spoke unamiably of women, and wandered a good deal in Yorkshire, ending near a convent of Cistercian nuns at Hampole in Yorkshire, where he is buried. His attitude to women must have softened with the years for his book *The Form of Living* was written for another recluse, Margaret Kirkby, and he was said to have been kindly in his spiritual advice to the Cistercian nuns. He died in 1349, perhaps from the plague. Margaret Kirkby, though she had taken a vow never to leave her hermitage, came to his funeral.

Richard Rolle was criticized at the time – and since – for the exuberance of his faith, but T. S. Eliot read him. When, in *Little Gidding*, Eliot wrote, 'We only live, only suspire, consumed by either fire or fire,' it is hard to believe that he did not have at the back of his mind Richard Rolle's *Fire of Love*. He had been reading the fourteenth-century mystics. His friend and correspondent John

Hayward was obviously less familiar with them, for he queried the quotation from Julian of Norwich:

> Sin is Behovely, but
> All shall be well, and
> All manner of thing shall be well

Eliot answered:

> I forgot in my previous letter to give an explanation which bears on your query of behovely. This line and the two which follow and which occur twice later constitute a quotation from Juliana of Norwich. The beautiful line the presence of which puzzles you toward the end of page 11 comes out of *The Cloud of Unknowing*. My purpose was this: there is so much 17th century in the poem that I was afraid of a certain Bonnie Dundee period effect and I wanted to check this and at the same time give greater historical depth to the poem by allusions to the other great period, i.e. the 14th century. Juliana and *The Cloud of Unknowing* represent pretty well the two mystical extremes or, one might say, the male and female of this literature.

Perhaps a memory of Richard Rolle's ardour forced itself into the poem too.

The line from *The Cloud of Unknowing* which Eliot quotes is, 'With the drawing of this Love and the voice of this Calling'. The author of *The Cloud of Unknowing* was probably a priest living somewhere in the east Midlands. He wrote his book for the instruction of a young person beginning a life devoted to contemplative prayer, and though he meant it to be useful for other people he was anxious that the book should not fall into the hands of people who would not understand it. His God is a transcendent God who cannot be known. 'By love he can be caught and held, but by thinking never.' The Buddhist and the Sufi are not far away. This is the apophatic path, the way of negation, the God known by what he is not, oneness with whom means oneness with nature, awareness of whom awakens compassion in the enlightened and love of the whole of creation in the saint; it is the God occasionally vaguely apprehended by the average anxious agnostic.

Walter Hilton died in 1395. He seems to have been a hermit at some stage, and to have felt that he did not have the true vocation for it. He was probably an Augustinian canon at Thurgarton in Nottinghamshire and his book *The Scale of Perfection*, which was popular in his lifetime, was again written for a young solitary, a woman this time.

The mystic is often looked on with suspicion by the established Church, whose hierarchy he or she bypasses in making a direct approach to God. Women in particular were likely to arouse this suspicion; perhaps they still are. Like St Teresa of Avila two centuries later, Julian of Norwich was sometimes in danger of persecution, and even death. St Teresa was careful to keep a number of priests in her confidence and on her side, and in the same way Mother Julian was always anxious to show how her revelations were within the orthodox faith of the Church and meant by God for all Christians. If this makes her look sometimes almost too cautious, it is important to remember that she was in actual danger at the time. By the time she wrote the second of her two accounts of her visions, there were laws, strictly enforced, against women preachers, and there was persecution of the Lollards and the followers of John Wycliffe, who were taken to be heretics.

In her thirties Mother Julian became very ill and nearly died. In the course of her illness she experienced sixteen 'shewings' or revelations which she spent the rest of her life thinking about and trying to explain, to herself and to other Christians. She became an anchorite at St Julian's church in Norwich, hence the name she adopted. She claimed to have very little education, although there seems to be evidence in her writings that she was aware of the work of other mystics. The efflorescence of writings of this type in the early fourteenth century is probably not entirely coincidental; it is quite possible that there was a network of communication between like-minded people. Norwich was the second largest city in England at the time and certainly had trading links with those parts of the Low Countries and Germany in which Meister Eckhart, Hildegarde of Bingen, and the Dominicans of the time were writing. A certain Adam Easton, who was a Norwich man, became a cardinal in Rome, and was certainly known to Mother Julian.

Very little is known about Julian of Norwich. The emphasis in her work on the physical suffering of Christ is symptomatic of her time, when devotion to the corporeality of Christ had reached a new intensity, exemplified by the increasingly realistic representations of the crucifixion in art, but nothing is known about her own illness, except that she nearly died of it. If she had suffered from it for a long time, or even from childhood, that might explain her struggle to find meaning in physical pain. Later generations have sometimes found that struggle excessive, even morbid. The *Oxford Companion to English Literature* dismisses her rather cursorily as 'not in fact the most appealing of the 14th century English prose mystics'.

Mother Julian's *Revelations of Divine Love*, though famous in her own lifetime, virtually disappeared from circulation during the four hundred years between the Reformation and its rediscovery in the early years of the twentieth century, becoming better known after T. S. Eliot's use of it in his poem. As with most deep influences, it was something Eliot half-knew already. He felt he had experienced for himself the intersection of the timeless with time. His biographer Lyndall Gordon wrote: 'while walking one day in Boston, he saw the streets suddenly shrink and divide. His everyday preoccupations, his past, all the claims of the future fell away and he was enfolded in a great silence. At the age of twenty-one Eliot had one of those experiences which, he said, many have had once or twice in their lives and been unable to put into words.'

W. B. Yeats seems to have had a similar experience while sitting alone in a teashop in London. It was snowing outside. 'I was blessed,' he wrote in his diary. 'And I could bless.' The moment passed, but he always hoped the feeling might return. In all his years of studying the occult, and dabbling with table-turning and spiritualism and the theories of Madame Blavatsky, there is no evidence that it did; he had to make do with being a great poet.

In one of Mother Julian's visions, Christ shows her 'a little thing, the size of a hazelnut, lying in the palm of my hand'. When she asks what it is, the answer comes, 'It is every thing that is made.' A little later she writes: 'To a soul that sees the Maker of all, all that is made seems very small.'

'I could be bounded in a nutshell and count myself a king of infinite space,' says Hamlet. 'Were it not that I have bad dreams.'

It is just permissible to wonder whether Shakespeare could have been familiar with Mother Julian's book. Although it went out of general circulation at the time of the Reformation, Catholics continued to copy and circulate various proscribed writings. There were Catholic schoolmasters in Stratford-on-Avon and Shakespeare's father was probably either a Catholic or a Church Catholic, that is to say one who went to church but was Catholic at home. There is a theory that during the 'hidden years' of Shakespeare's early life he was a strolling player with a group of Catholics, entertaining the North Country nobility who were of that persuasion. More sensationally, it has been suggested that he might have accompanied the Jesuit missionary Edmund Campion, a man of persuasive personality, on the 1580 journey to the north which ended with Campion's hanging in December 1581. There is evidence that through the Catholic connection in Stratford certain clever young men were recruited to be further educated in Catholic, and therefore European, culture at such great houses in the north as Hoghton Tower, the home of Richard Hoghton and his wife, who was the sister of a Catholic priest. Shakespeare's connection with all this is unlikely ever to be proved, and it hangs upon his having taken the name Shakeshaft (which was his grandfather's name) during his time in the north.

The other difficulty with the theory is that the plays show little sign of secret Catholicism, or indeed of any kind of underlying religious dogma. Certainly Shakespeare was not much in tune with the hermit mentality. The life of the exiled court in *As You Like It*

even perching upon their chins to take food from their lips. When they had young, the birds would teach them to come for their food in the same way, urging them forward with vigorous pecks when they showed signs of timidity.

Dom Louis' description was not at all too enthusiastic for a visitor from Bath who arrived in 1776. Captain Philip Thicknesse, usually hard to please, was so delighted by Montserrat that he tried to buy his own plot and become a hermit too. He was an irascible fellow and a tremendous scandalmonger, in which capacity he had caused great offence to Charles Wesley, the Archbishop of Canterbury, the Earl of Coventry, the Lord Chancellor and the entire House of Lords, which had been asked to adjudicate on his claim to be his first wife's legal heir. His two sons by his second marriage were taking him to law, and his debts were considerable. It seemed a good time to undertake a Grand Tour.

Captain Thicknesse travelled with his third wife, their two children, a dog, a parakeet and a monkey. The monkey wore a red jacket and a hard hat, and rode postilion on the back of the horse – 'a little touched in the wind' – which Thicknesse had acquired in Calais to pull his two-wheeled cabriolet. The parakeet liked to sit on Mrs Thicknesse's shoulder while she played upon her viol de gamba. More adventurous than most travellers on the Grand Tour, they crossed the frontier into Spain, and when they reached the mountains of Montserrat they were so enchanted that they spent several weeks there. Having failed to procure a Spanish hermitage, Captain Thicknesse built his own when he returned to England. He found a ruined cottage on the hills overlooking Bath, restored and improved it and called it St Catherine's Hermitage. Its remains could until recently be seen at the end of the garden of number 9 Lansdown Crescent. His quarrels and debts continuing to plague him, Captain Thicknesse sold his hermitage after a few years and moved to Kent.

Mrs Pobjoy, on the other hand, ended her days in her Bath hermitage. She was the great Beau Nash's last mistress, and after his death in 1761, whether through poverty or a broken heart, she moved into a hollow tree, and stayed there until she died. It seems a long way from Richard Rolle, in the troubled fourteenth century, tearing up his sister's dresses in a wood in order to fashion for himself the outward sign of his passionate desire to be alone with God, to Mrs Pobjoy, former plaything of a dandy in the more carefree eighteenth century, raising her voice in cheerful but discordant song, clasping her ragged finery round her in her hollow tree. If you go to Camaldoli, however, high up in the foothills of the Apennines, where the monks keep their traditional silence among the great trees of the Casentino forest, you may buy a postcard of a white-clad monk reading his holy book, seated at a small table within the encircling trunk of a huge hollow chestnut tree. It was not only the eighteenth-century creator of his New Elysium who saw in the hermitage and its associations something so deeply appealing that it asked to be played with.

'... most attacked by voices
of temptation ...'

PERILS OF THE SOLITARY LIFE

William Cowper — John Clare — Ivor Gurney —
Robert Burton — accidie — ecstasies — Eros —
Flaubert and the temptation of St Antony —
J. K. Huysmans

> The word in the desert
> Is most attacked by voices of temptation
> The crying shadow in the funeral dance
> The loud lament of the disconsolate chimaera

Despondency is the big beast that stalks the solitary. St Seraphim warned against it because he had suffered from it himself. The joyful good humour which his fellow-monks loved in him was hard-won. For some years – perhaps because he had turned down an offer to be an abbot and then, tempted by ambition, regretted his refusal, or perhaps because the dark night of the soul was always going to be part of his journey – he stood on a rock in his bare feet in all weathers and at all hours and prayed to be relieved of his torment.

Religious faith may or may not be a consolation to the despairing, increasing as it does the sense of sin while at the same time offering the mysterious notion of redemption. William Cowper the mild eighteenth-century poet was desperately religious and was not thereby saved from madness. There is no knowing, of course, that he might not have been madder sooner but for the straw of faith to which he clung. He had tended to melancholia since early youth. His mother died when he was six and he was sent away to school, and bullied there. Later on he was happy at Westminster, but when, having read for the Bar, he was offered a clerkship in the House of Lords, he sank into desperate despair and tried to commit suicide. He decided that his best hope was in solitude and prayer, and sought it in the quiet town of Huntingdon, but his gentle and domestic nature was too fragile for the hermit life. Finding refuge with the Evangelical Unwin family in Huntingdon, he moved with the calm and kind Mary Unwin, after her husband's death, to Olney in Buckinghamshire, to be near John Newton, the fanatically Evangelical curate of the place.

Cowper was devoted to Mary Unwin, but the thought of marriage brought on another collapse, in the course of which he lost his faith. John Newton, to his credit, had him to stay in his house for a year while Mary Unwin nursed him through the crisis, but it was nature rather than religion this time which helped his return to sanity. A neighbour gave him a tame hare, and soon he had three, and looking after them and watching them became his chief delight. He brooded less on his own life, finding theirs so different and so enchanting. The dire John Newton, after the village turned against him for trying to prevent them letting off fireworks on November the fifth, left for a London parish, and Cowper spent several contented years of domesticity with Mary Unwin, writing the poems for which he became renowned and delighting his friends with his letters. At Mary Unwin's death he collapsed again, and for five more years he lived in a state of intermittent terror. During that time he wrote one of his most heartfelt poems, 'The Castaway', remembering an incident he had read about long before in which a sailor had fallen from a ship and despite all the efforts of his fellows had drowned. The poet felt he had drowned too.

> No divine the storm allay'd,
> No light propitious shone;
> When, snatch'd from all effectual aid,
> We perished, each alone.
> But I beneath a rougher sea,
> And whelm'd in deeper gulphs than he.

John Clare, born in 1793, a few years before Cowper died, was
another poet who died melancholy mad. He spent twenty-two
years in a Northamptonshire asylum. He too turned to nature and
solitude in search of calm, and made minute observations of natural
phenomena, but was not saved thereby. His home ground was
always where he had wandered as a boy, and like other poets he
regretted what he lost when he grew up.

> A solitary crow & sometimes a pair fly with heavy wing just
> overhead now & then uttering a solitary croak to warn their
> tribes around that a man is approaching & then make a
> sudden wheel round at the sight of the stick in ones hand
> perhaps mistaking it for a gun ... the meadow lakes seen
> from the bank puts me in mind of school adventures &
> boyish rambles the very spots where I used to spend the
> whole Sundays in fishing while the bells kept chiming in
> vain – I cannot make out where all these feeling or fancies
> are gone too – The plot of meadows now don't look bigger
> than a large homestead & the ponds that used to seem so
> large are now no bigger than puddles & as for fish I scarcely
> have interest to walk round them to see if there is any ...
> time makes strange work with early fancys ... I sigh for
> what is lost and cannot help it.

Of all poets Clare is the one most passionately rooted in his
own landscape. He would have understood the hermit's vow of
stability. The wide flat landscape of the limestone heath which lay
beyond the small village of Helpston was in the deepest sense the
whole ground of his being. When well-meaning admirers moved
him to a cottage only three miles away from his village he pined
and faded and became so mentally distressed he had to be removed
to Northampton asylum. His was no pastoral idyll; the narrow-
minded villagers laughed at him for his reading of books and

muttering of verse, and their laughter was malicious and possibly a little fearful. He hid his books, disliked the fame which he acquired as a 'peasant-poet' because it increased his neighbours' distrust of him, and kept himself to himself until he lost his sense of self altogether; in the asylum he assumed among other identities that of Lord Byron. Even then the observations of his boyhood would return: 'When I was a boy', was the start of so many sentences. The landscape he remembered was the landscape before the new drive for efficiency in agriculture led to the Acts of Enclosure, which began to come into effect when he was a youth.

> Inclosure like a Buonaparte let not a thing remain
> It levelled every bush and tree and levelled every hill
> And hung the moles for traitors.

The changes could not efface the memories so deeply imprinted on his mind: 'When I was a boy I used to be very curious to watch the nightingale . . .'; 'When I was a boy there was a little spring of beautiful soft water which was never dry . . .'

Ivor Gurney, another solitary poet who loved his native countryside, must have sensed a like-mindedness in John Clare, because he set one of Clare's poems, 'Ploughman Singing', to music. Gurney's father was a tailor in Gloucester and none of his family shared his passion for music and poetry. He wandered as a lonely youth through the countryside and villages of west Gloucestershire, not far from Elgar's country. He fought at Passchendaele in 1917 and was badly gassed. He wrote one of his poems sheltering in the mausoleum at Caulaincourt, freezing cold and weak with hunger.

> Only the wanderer
> Knows England's graces
> Or can anew see clear
> Familiar faces
>
> And who knows joy as he
> That dwells in shadows?
> Do not forget me quite
> O Severn meadows

Gurney loved England, but England had made him fight a war which almost destroyed him. He was a talented musician but found it hard to get his work performed. Anger and frustration sometimes overcame him and made him very difficult to live with. In the end, becoming incoherent, he was confined to a lunatic asylum. That year, 1922, he wrote an essay called 'The Spring of Beauty', in which he tried to say what it was that he needed to express in music or verse. He wrote of those moments when his perception of natural beauty became visionary.

> These visions were more clearly seen after the excessive bodily and mental fatigue experienced on a route march, or in some hard fatigue in France or Flanders ... There it was one learnt that the brighter visions brought music, the fainter verse; or mere pleasurable emotion ...
>
> Of all significant things, the most striking, poignant, pas-sioning, is the sight of a great valley at the end of the day – such as the Severn valley which lies hushed and dark, infinitely full of meaning, while yet the far Welsh hills are touched with living and ecstatic gold ... The quietest and most comforting thing that is yet strongly suggestive – the sight which seems more than any to provoke the making of music to be performed on strings, is that of a hedge mounting over, rolling beyond the skyline of a little gracious hill. A hedge unclipped, untamed; covered by hawthorn perhaps, showing the fragile rose of June, or sombre within the bareness of winter; the season makes no difference.

Robert Burton's *Anatomy of Melancholy*, first published in 1621, investigates the subject at length and with an immense efflorescence of lists. He suffered from it himself, a lonely Oxford scholar whose face appears on a column in Christ Church Cathedral in Oxford, over a memorial inscribed, as he had requested, to Democritus Junior, Democritus having been a Greek philosopher famous for laughing at the follies of mankind. Burton found no comfort in solitude. His advice to the melancholy was simple: 'Be not solitary, be not idle.' But Aubrey in his *Brief Lives* wrote: ''tis whispered that, non obstante all his astrologie and his book of Melancholie, he ended his dayes . . . by hanging himselfe.'

Accidie, despair, the dark night of the soul, includes the sense that the condition will last for ever. St John of the Cross wrote of it: 'That which this anguished soul feels most deeply is the conviction that God has abandoned it, of which it has no doubt; that he has cast it away into darkness as an abominable thing.' This is the solipsism which is the opposite of the freedom from self the contemplative seeks. It comes as a kind of dreadful dullness and sloth, Coleridge's state of blankness before the beauties of nature – 'I see not feel,/How beautiful they are' – a dryness of spirit, so that Gerard Manley Hopkins, miserable in his Dublin convent, could cry, 'Mine, O thou lord of life, send my roots rain'. An anti-depressant drug dulls the dullness, is no more than a pain-killer; time does a better job. 'Who would have thought this wither'd branch,/Could have grown green again,' wrote George Herbert of one such return to life. But the winters of the heart feel as though they might last for ever, and sometimes they do.

After dryness can come delusion; rather than the *horror vastae solitudinis*, the hysteria of the crowd, the clannishness of the cult, the flight from self to silliness. Cowper was not alone in finding that the contact with wild nature brought him back to sanity; it kept his feet on the ground. The idea of the contented hermit who lives close to nature, cultivates his garden and his bees, is trusted by animals and loves all of creation, is some kind of archetype. We think we could be like that ourselves if somehow things were different, 'calmer far/Than in their sleep forgiven hermits are', forgetting of course that the condition of complete simplicity costs, as Eliot said, not less than everything. Hermits can achieve that state, some of the time or all of the time. There are also restless hermits, ecstatic hermits and madmen. There is hallucination and there is fraud. Too much physical darkness and emptiness result in sensory deprivation in which the brain, finding nothing solid to work on, malfunctions frantically among phantasmagoria. Extremes of asceticism can lead to chemical chaos and hallucination of every weird description. Richard Rolle, sometimes thought of as over-ecstatic, had learned wisdom:

> It behoves him then who would sing his love for God and rejoice fervently in such singing, to pass his days in solitude. Yet the abstinence in which he lives should not be excessive . . . I myself have eaten and drunk things that are considered delicacies . . . in order to sustain my being in the service of God . . . For his sake I conformed quite properly with those with whom I was living lest I should invent a sanctity where none existed; lest men should overpraise me where I was less worthy of praise.

The frequent visions which medieval hermits in particular apparently experienced were probably of a different order from the hallucinations of the extreme penitents; they were insights manifested in a language more familiar then than now, expected appearances half in and half out of dream. Many of those to whom they occurred were illiterate. They were used to churches whose walls were painted with biblical scenes as well as with dramatic reminders of death and judgment. They might have found it easy to say, 'I saw', or 'I heard a voice', where we might say, 'I suddenly realized', or 'I understood'. Ecstasy was and is another thing again, treated with much caution by spiritual advisers. The author of *The Cloud of Unknowing* has nothing good to say of those who strain to achieve a 'spurious warmth' which they believe to be the fire of love, coming from the Holy Ghost. 'I tell you truly that the devil has his contemplatives as God has his.'

Such feelings, he continues, consolations, sweetness, tears, must be independent of the imagination. 'The earthly and physical fancies of inventive imaginations are very fruitful of error.' He talks of 'counterfeit contemplation' as sending people mad.

> Some squint as though they were silly sheep that have been banged on the head, and were going soon to die. Some hang their heads on one side as if they had got a worm in their ear. Some squeak when they should speak, as if they had no spirit – the proper condition for a hypocrite! Some cry and whine, because they are in such an anxious hurry to say what they think – heretics are like this, and all who with presumptuous and ingenious minds maintain error.

Reassuringly, the author goes on to say that those who engage with proper humility in the true work of contemplation 'find that it has a good effect on the body as well as on the soul, for it makes them attractive in the eyes of all who see them. So much so that the ugliest person alive who becomes, by grace, a contemplative finds that he suddenly (and again by grace) is different, and that every good man he sees is glad and happy to have his friendship.'

In ecstasy Eros too can raise his brazen head. Here is a twelfth-century Carthusian praying:

> when God visited me in power, and I yearned with love so as almost to give up the ghost . . . Love and longing for the Beloved raised me in spirit into heaven . . . Then did I forget all pain and fear and deliberate thought of anything, and even of the Creator. And as men who fear the peril of fire do not cry, 'Fire hath come upon my house; come ye and help me', since in their strait and agony they can scarce speak a single word but cry 'Fire, Fire, Fire!' or, if their fear

be greater they cry 'Ah! Ah! Ah!' wishing to impart their peril in this single cry, so I, in my poor way. For first I oft commended my soul to God, saying: 'Into thy hands', either in words or (as I think rather) in spirit. But as the pain of love grew more powerful I could scarce have thought at all, forming within my spirit these words: 'Love! Love! Love!' And at last, ceasing from this, I deemed that I would wholly yield up my soul, singing, rather than crying, in spirit through joy, 'Ah! Ah! Ah!'

It is not at all to doubt the authenticity of what is so touchingly described to say that it could also be a description of a physical orgasm. That is not to say that it actually was a physical orgasm, because it was on a spiritual plane, but we are physical beings and recognize things physically – shortness of breath, unexpected feelings of heat, Richard Rolle's *Fire of Love*. Agape and Eros can be confused, or intertwined, or unexpectedly lead from one to the other, exposing all our vulnerability and giving much opportunity for error and illusion, self-deception and fraud. As Auden's poem says:

> Soul and body have no bounds,
> To lovers as they lie upon
> Her tolerant enchanted slope
> In their ordinary swoon,
> Grave the vision Venus sends
> Of supernatural sympathy,
> Universal love and hope;
> While an abstract insight wakes
> Among the glaciers and the rocks
> The hermit's carnal ecstasy.

Bernini's statue in the church of Santa Maria della Vittoria in Rome of St Theresa ecstatically receiving her famous dart of love, here held over her by a most beautiful angel, is erotic without being lascivious, but perfervid fantasies about monks and nuns, temptations and seductions, were always the familiar stock in trade of pornographers. Matthew Lewis, always known as 'Monk' Lewis after his most famous work, was a success in eighteenth-century London, as he had known he would be when he was writing his book. Coolly cashing in on the success of such romantic but decorous novels as Mrs Radcliffe's *The Mysteries of Udolpho*, he expanded the genre into full-blown Gothic horror, with blasphemy, bloodshed and incestuous rape. Reviewers castigated *The Monk* as corrupt and indecent. Invitations to fashionable London parties poured in. Even Byron called 'Monk' Lewis 'a jewel of a man', though he also admitted that he was often 'a damned bore'.

Absurd as well as salacious, *The Monk* seems nevertheless to have influenced Flaubert's *Temptation of St Antony*, in which St Antony profanely lusts after the Virgin Mary in almost the same words as those of Lewis's monk Ambrosio, though the passage is not included in the final version. Through various revisions, between the first version of 1848–49 and the last, of 1874, Flaubert's St Antony became less Flaubert without becoming more St Antony. Even the final, more restrained, version expresses a sadistic fantasy which reveals more about the author, and the sensibility of his time, than about the saint.

Flaubert saw the picture of the temptation of St Antony, then attributed to Pieter Brueghel the Younger but now supposed to be by Jan Mandyn, in the Balbi Palace at Genoa, which he visited with his family when they were all accompanying his delicate sister Caroline on her honeymoon. Flaubert was obsessed with its crowd of monsters and impossible beasts for years; it fed his eager interest in the exoticism of the Orient as well as his sado-masochistic fantasies. In his book, flagellation, tortures of various kinds, bruised and beaten prostitutes, orgies of blood-letting and mutilation, all take place in a highly coloured and barbaric Orient, in which the Queen of Sheba, personified as a certain kind of late-nineteenth-century Paris courtesan, is no more out of place than anyone else.

> Her gown of golden brocade, cut across at regular intervals
> by falbalas of pearl, jet, and sapphires, pinches her waist in

a tight bodice . . . Her wide sleeves, garnished with emeralds and birds' feathers, allow a bare view of her little round arm . . . her ring-laden hands are tipped with nails so sharp that her fingers finish almost like needles . . . On her left cheekbone she has a natural brown fleck; and she breathes with her mouth open, as if her corsets constricted her. In her progress she waves a green parasol with an ivory handle, hung round with silver-gilt bells; and twelve frizzy little negroes carry the long tail of her gown, held at the very end by a monkey who lifts it up from time to time.

She is accompanied by a bird, which drops from the sky on to her head. It has four wings, vulture's claws, an immense peacock's tail and a human face. As she leaves, the saint having with the utmost difficulty resisted her advances, the monkey lifts up the edge of her gown, and she hops away on one foot, 'letting out a sort of convulsive hiccup, not unlike a sob or a snigger'.

The powerful nightmare quality of Flaubert's Queen of Sheba excited contemporaries. Painters became entranced by the subject; the poet Verlaine in 1878 threatened to write an opera libretto. Cezanne went through a process of identification with the saint, and gradual subsequent detachment, not unlike Flaubert's own. His first treatment of the subject, painted about 1870, shows the monk in a dark wood confronted by four enormous nudes, one of them distinctly provocative and all of them alarming. He returned to the subject several times until in the much later water-colour, known as 'The Hermit', the scene is calmer, and includes the saint's hut, much as described by Flaubert. The painter's terrified eroticism has abated; as always, the hermitage conveys a gentler message than the hermit himself.

The Symbolist painter Odilon Redon explored the same subject in a mysterious and rather sinister series of lithographs. Anatole France's novel *Thais*, published in 1890, clearly also under the influence, has a monk reduced to almost total disintegration by the agonies of asceticism and lust, but the quintessential decadent solitary is Des Esseintes, protagonist of J. K. Huysmans' novel *À rebours* which was published in 1884 and translated into English in 1959 as *Against Nature*. The sophisticated Des Esseintes despises the world. Mankind is made up of fools and scoundrels, he believes. Friendship, art, literature, women, the so-called pleasures of the town, equally disgust him. 'Already he had begun dreaming of a refined Thebaid, a desert hermitage equipped with all modern conveniences, a snugly heated ark on dry land in which he might take refuge from the incessant deluge of human stupidity.'

In fact, the portrait of Des Esseintes is psychologically acute. He is a man who has chosen solitude out of scorn and hatred of the world and as a result is almost destroyed by the cruel circle of solipsism which closes round him. He buys an uninteresting little house in the suburbs of Paris and fits it out with every extravagance calculated to please the senses – exotic colours, luxurious silks, leather-lined walls with deep indigo mouldings, tiger-skins and blue fox furs on the floor, beautifully bound editions of the classics, poems by Baudelaire inscribed on vellum and hung on the walls. Two old servants sworn to do their work in silence bring him tiny exquisite meals. He invents toys for himself: an aquarium which he can fill with different coloured waters, ingenious tricks by which he can give himself the illusion that he is travelling the world without the bother of leaving his armchair. All is to be artifice, nothing natural. He experiments with the tastes of various liqueurs, likening them to music and inventing new harmonies. He buys a tortoise and has its shell gilded and decorated with precious stones. He gazes at it while dipping slices of hot buttered toast into his China tea, not realizing for some time that it has died.

Like the tortoise his fancies fail him. Plagued by uncontrollable unhappy memories, unable to escape his devouring self, he progresses from tedium to despair and then to acute hypochondria. His only slender hope, as he returns under doctors' orders to the Paris he detests more than ever, seems to lie in a rather sickly form of Catholicism, the Church as he imagines it to have been before the modern world poisoned religion as it poisoned everything else. Huysmans himself did indeed – though many years later – become a Roman Catholic. In the meantime his book became hugely influential. Oscar Wilde's Dorian Gray is a pale shadow of the exquisitely effete Des Esseintes.

Melancholy and morbid fantasy do assail the hermit. He remembers Ecclesiastes: 'Woe to him that is alone when he falleth; for he hath not another to help him up.' A solitary may take leave of his senses, misinterpret messages or invent them, diminish, despair, die. 'Be not solitary, be not idle,' remains then the best advice, until such time as the branch grows green again.

CHAPTER 11

'*'Tis ROUSSEAU,*
let thy bosom speak the rest ...'

EIGHTEENTH-CENTURY ROMANTICS

The Harcourts — the Man of Feeling —
the Hermitage Museum — William Kent —
Alexander Pope — the Badminton root house and other
garden hermitages — Gilbert White of Selborne
— ornamental hermits — antiquarianism —
William Stukeley — Sir John Soane — William Beckford

When Joseph Addison published his *Remarks on Several Parts of Italy* in 1706 he included a description of a hermitage which he had seen near Fribourg in Switzerland. 'It lies', he wrote, 'in the prettiest solitude imaginable, among woods and rocks.' He describes the dispositions which the hermit, who has lived there for twenty-five years, has made for his comfort and convenience – a 'pretty chapel', a kitchen, a cellar, two or three little fountains, a garden. He has made, says Addison, 'such a spot of ground of it as furnishes out a kind of luxury for a hermit'.

Fortunate age, in which to be a hermit is a luxury. The fear has gone out of solitude. Terror of God, like terror of the natural world, is being replaced by pleasurable awe and humble respect. It is time to play.

'As Sir George and Lady Harcourt were superintending the Labours of their Haymakers, rewarding the industry of some by smiles of approbation, & punishing the idleness of others by a cudgel,' begins the sixteen-year-old Jane Austen cheerfully, 'they perceived lying

closely concealed beneath the thick foliage of a Haycock, a beauti-
full little Girl of not more than 3 months old.'

Henry and Eliza was one of a number of happy and heartless
sketches Jane Austen wrote in her early years to amuse her family
and exercise her developing talent, grounded as it always was in
her acute sense of the ridiculous. The foundling Eliza achieves an
ill-deserved happy ending, unlike Emma of *Edgar and Emma* who,
when the young man she has her eye on fails to accompany his
family when they come to call, 'retiring to her own room, continued
in tears the remainder of her Life'. (Charlotte, in *Frederick and
Elfrida*, equally unfortunate, realizes her error in having engaged
herself to marry two different gentlemen in one evening and com-
mits suicide by flinging herself into 'a deep stream which ran thro'
her Aunt's pleasure Grounds in Portland Place'.)

Jane Austen took liberties with the Harcourt name because the
story was never intended for publication and the Harcourts had
aroused her amusement by the excesses of their enthusiasm for
Jean-Jaques Rousseau, whose works the Austen family found highly
ridiculous. Their serene common sense was no more impressed by
Goethe's *The Sorrows of Werther*, but that book, like Rousseau's
La nouvelle Héloïse, swept Europe, and the cult of sensibility became
all the rage.

In August 1789 the Harcourts staged a feast in the grounds of
Nuneham Court, their country seat. There were two pictures on
the lawn, one showing an idyllic cottage scene, with clean little
children playing peacefully on the doorstep while the housewife
plied her spinning wheel, and the other depicting a miserable and
dilapidated hovel, with dirty children neglected by a slatternly
housewife. The deferential villagers bedecked the first with flowers
and the second with nettles, urged on by their benevolent landlords,
who then presented awards for virtue and industry. Later on the
most deserving villagers were visited, and granted a red M for
Merit to put in their windows. All this was in imitation of the
scene in Rousseau's *Julie où La nouvelle Héloïse, Lettres de deux
amants habitants d'une petite ville au pied des Alpes*, in which Julie

presents similar prizes at a Fête de Vertu on the lawns of her Elysée at Wolmar.

Lord Harcourt may have been excessive in his admiration of Rousseau, but he was not alone. Rousseau's novel was published in England in 1760 and became immensely popular; George III gave the author a pension. The book's attitude to nature harmonized with ideas already current in England. The ideal of 'L'homme de la nature et de la Vérité' was very similar to the English 'Man of Feeling', and the description of Julie's Elysée agreed with the ideal of the cultivated wilderness. The Marquis de Girardin, inspired by the description of Julie's garden, made a garden at Ermenonville, where Rousseau had died and been buried on l'île des Peupliers. Many English people dutifully visited. How much Rousseau himself really cared for solitude is open to question, but he did have short periods in his life when being alone with nature seemed to him the only way in which he could be truly himself. His influence not only on the cult of sensibility but also on the growth of interest in a life lived in closeness with nature – always part of the hermit idea – was enormous.

Robert Heron, author of *Observations Made in a Journey Through the Western Islands of Scotland*, published in 1793, wrote: 'I am sometimes almost tempted to fancy, that men were intended for hermits and savages . . . No wonder that living and writing, as he did, in the midst of Paris, John James Rousseau should have been led to maintain, that man was happier, more dignified, more independent in the savage state, than in a condition of polished civility.'

The Man – and Woman – of Feeling did not much suffer from accidie; they had learnt how to transform it into a poetic melancholy which was positively pleasurable. Thomas Gray's 'Elegy in a Country Churchyard' conveys the sentiment, as do Edward Young's 'Night Thoughts', and Thomas Parnell's 'The Hermit', all in varying degrees melodious, charming or – in the case of the latter – unbearably sententious, and all tremendously popular.

Such feelings could be indulged, for a reasonable period, an afternoon perhaps or early evening, in a hermitage. Rustic buildings of a playful sort had been appearing in gardens and woods in England since the 1740s; the French taste for rustic cottages and Marie Antoinette's dairy came a little later.

The hermitage had in the meantime lost its strictly religious connotation, probably when it came to be seen as a place of retreat from the demands of formality for kings and their courtiers. Louis XIV built the Château de Marly as an escape from Versailles in the late seventeenth century. He called it his hermitage, and planned to spend a few periods of retreat there every year, with no more than a few attendants. In fact, a swarm of courtiers followed him, building was continuous, grandiose gardens were laid out, and life carried on with only a little less ceremony than at Versailles.

Peter the Great saw Marly soon after Louis XIV's death, and hurried home to build his own hermitage, in the park of Peterhof. He was particularly proud of the system of pulleys by which the dining-room table on the first floor could be supplied from below, and hauled up by unseen servants. Later, Catherine the Great commissioned a French architect to build her a hermitage in the garden of the Winter Palace at St Petersburg. When she ran out of space for her collection of paintings, she commissioned another building. Eventually the Small Hermitage, the Old Hermitage, and the New Hermitage became the immense State Hermitage Museum, which absorbed the whole palace, but Catherine's original idea had been to use her hermitage as a place for informal entertainments, complete with the same *tables volants* on pulleys which had so appealed to Peter the Great. 'There are two tables side by side laid for ten,' wrote a German visitor in 1774. 'Waiting is done by machine. There is no need for footmen behind chairs, and the Provost of police is distinctly at a disadvantage as he is unable to report to Her Majesty anything that is said at these dinners.'

The St Petersburg museum must be the biggest building to bear the name Hermitage. English architects were meanwhile exploring the opposite extreme. The first hermitage to feature in a picturesque garden was probably William Kent's at Richmond, built for Queen Caroline about 1735. It was an odd mixture, predominantly rustic

but with a Palladian pediment on the front. 'The stones of the
whole edifice appear as if rudely laid together, and the venerable
look of the whole is improved by the thickness of the solemn grove
behind it, and the little turret on top with a bell to which you may
ascend by a winding walk.' The interior was octagonal and formal,
with niches containing busts of famous thinkers. The hermitage
aroused a good deal of comment, some critical and none as adoring
as the following:

> Flow swiftly, Thames, and flowing still proclaim
> This building's beauty, and the builder's fame;
> Tell Indian seas they Naiads here have seen
> The sweetest grotto and the wisest Queen,
> Whose royal presence blest this humble seat;
> How small the mansion, and the guest now great!

The self-taught – and here no doubt self-interested – poet was
Stephen Duck, an agricultural labourer who subsequently became
the queen's assistant gardener and royal thatcher, and custodian
of the hermitage. In his retirement he became Rector of Byfleet.
It seems also that he ended his days by drowning himself in a trout
stream in 'a fit of despondency' in 1756. Perhaps he missed the
hermitage, where he could have poeticized his despondency to the
edification of the visitors. The hermitage has now vanished, but
Kent's similar building at Stowe still stands.

Kent's next extravaganza for the queen was Merlin's Cave, built
in 1735, and thatched. This time, rather than busts, there were
waxwork figures of Queen Elizabeth, Minerva and Merlin himself,
with attendants, which were shown to visitors by Stephen Duck.
The waxworks, which possibly set the later fashion for ornamental
hermits, whether waxen, live or stuffed, were the subject of general
ridicule. George II was not sympathetic. 'You *deserve* to be abused
for such childish, silly stuff,' he told the queen. In the 1770s Merlin's
Cave was abolished in the course of the landscaping of the Old
Park at Richmond by Capability Brown, who was criticized in his
turn in a poem by William Mason, for having 'marred with impious

hand each sweet design/ Of Stephen Duck and good Queen Caroline'.

It was Pope's response to landscape, especially landscape romantically embellished with ruins, that inspired Kent's first hermitages and endowed them with the spirit of melancholy and reflection with which they came to be associated. In Pope's 'Eloisa to Abelard', 'Black Melancholy' sits amidst

> A death-like sentence and a dread repose:
> Her gloomy presence saddens all the scene,
> Shades ev'ry flow'r, and darkens ev'ry green.

This was written as early as 1717; Pope's medievalism and Kent's Gothic buildings preceded by more than twenty years Horace Walpole's remodelling of his own house at Strawberry Hill. Nevertheless, it is Strawberry Hill which is generally thought to be the first example of that happy mixture of antiquarianism and fantasy which produced the frivolous charm of Georgian Gothic, soon to be dismissed with scorn by the serious Gothic Revivalists of the nineteenth century.

Pope is credited with being the first to use the word 'picturesque', though he meant it simply to refer to a landscape whose composition was like a picture, rather to carry all the significance it later acquired. Kent, Pope and Kent's great patron Lord Burlington, were three brilliant people who stimulated each other's genius. Their relationship was always good – there is much good-natured teasing in their correspondence. Kent liked to eat and drink, and grew very fat. Pope was a valetudinarian with a weak digestion. Pope's letter to Lady Burlington recommending Kent for a vacant living in the Church of England which was under her control sets the tone of the friendship:

> He is as learned, tho' not so courteous as Bishop W — x; as eloquent tho' not so courtly as G — t; as well-bred, tho' not so bookish, as H — re, and (to sum up all) has as good a taste as R — le, and as good a stomach as all the clergy put together. I think your Ladyship begins to find

the excellent person at whom I point (or rather to *smoke* him, for he is very hot and very fat,

> Of size they may be a pulpit fill,
> Tho' more inclining to sit still.)

And I presume to name him, and defy any objections, viz. Mr. William Kent.

Thomas Wright succeeded Kent as garden designer at Badminton in Gloucestershire. He built various garden buildings, including a hermit's hut, or root house, with thatch, knotted tree trunks and moss, which still stands. Wright proposed that such buildings should 'be naturally supposed the only Production of the Age before Building became a Science', but in fact they were not modelled on the primitive hut traditionally supposed to have been Adam's house in Paradise so much as on the caves of hermits, the difference being that stone was replaced by the irregular shapes of wood and root.

Work began on the Badminton hermitage in 1747. When it was first constructed it was in the middle of dark woods, and was intended to merge into its surroundings until the approaching wanderer came near enough to see that it was a building. Now the woods have gone, and the building sits squat and toadlike among the aristocratic oaks which, beautifully paced, grace the perfect parkland. The ingenious woodwork of the exterior has endured, but the interior, which was unexpectedly elaborate, with a Palladian room all furnished in wood and lined with moss, has deteriorated. Only a huge tree stump without a top marks the place of the original table, and the moss has long ago fallen off the walls. It is just possible to see from the shapes of the scattered paving stones that the floor was once laid out in some kind of pattern of a vaguely cabalistic kind. There is a feeling about the place such as to make one think perhaps its original inhabitant would have been a druid rather than a hermit. Druids were not quite as popular as hermits among the romantically-inclined builders of the eighteenth century, but there was certainly one at Hawkestone in Shropshire.

The outside wall at the back of the root house has a recess in which were once two chairs. They were later replaced by a bench, on which is written in nails, 'Here the lounger loiters, here the weary rest'. When I went there on a blustery December day some coloured cellophane had lodged in the corner of the bench. It seemed to have been left there not very long ago, wrapped round a bunch of flowers which had withered away to nothing. There was another skeleton bouquet, still held together by a yellow ribbon, and a card to someone's mother, telling her she was missed and hoping her pain had gone. A hermit might have felt obliged to direct the mourner to the nearby churchyard. Perhaps some remains of local tradition recalled instead the druid.

The little building has always appealed to those with a taste for the supernatural. Notes made by two young ladies of the family of the Duke of Beaufort, owner of Badminton, in 1865 seem to show some slightly heavy-handed playfulness on the part of a certain Revd Mr Payne, chaplain to the fourth duke at the time of the building of the hermitage, who used references to a play by Lord Lansdowne called *The British Enchantress* in order to bring in the figure of a fairy known as Urganda.

'Urganda here with her magic spell/ In words ambiguous mutters many a spell', was apparently inscribed in Latin over the outside door. Miss Louisa Somerset and Lady Frances Somerset continued:

> At the entrance on the floor (which is plank'd with oak slabs) are several problems of Euclid, described with brass nails . . . On the table is inscribed a Horoscope or Planetary System for telling fortunes with this motto '*Huic quid dicam, aut erit – aut non*' – in English, 'What I shall tell you will come to pass, or it will not' . . . Behind the seat is a drawing on wood with a red-hot poker (by Mr. Payne) representing a grove, in which Urganda is introduced with her attendant Delia . . . In the inside of the Cell (which is entirely composed of roots of trees, knotted oak etc.) are hung globes, mathematical instruments, skeletons of birds and beasts, ditto fantastic and odd representation of faces etc.

Several *lusus naturae*, likewise, of the timber are to be seen, such as a dog lying under the table, a man's head with periwig of bark etc.

Another clergyman, Canon J. E. Jackson, antiquary, writes to the eighth duchess, with whom he corresponded on such matters, that Urganda is 'the name of a potent Fairy in the Romance of Amades de Gaul ... In the Spanish romances relating to the descendants of "Amadis de Gaul" Urganda is invested with all the more serious terrors of a Medea.' Evidently more of a sorceress than a fairy, as the Canon sagely comments.

The eighteenth-century enthusiast for rustic follies could choose his own from books of designs, such as Batty Langley's *Gothic Architecture improved by Rules and Proportions in many Grand Designs* of 1742, or William Wrighte's *Grotesque Architecture or Rural Amusement: consisting of plans, elevations and sections for Huts, Retreats, Summer and Winter Hermitages, Terminaries, Chinese, Gothic and Natural Grottoes, Cascades, Baths, Mosques, Moresque Pavilions, Grotesque and Rustic Seats, Green Houses, etc. Many of which may be executed with Flints, Irregular Stones, Rude Branches, and Roots of Trees.* From these pattern books you might choose any number of retreats, hermit's cells or hermitages: Oriental, Winter, Summer, Augustine (of classical design), Rural (made all of trees). Some remain, but many of the flimsier ones must have disappeared, along with the creators whose pleasant fantasies they embodied, back into the landscape which inspired them.

There were also once two root house hermitages built by William Shenstone at the Leasowes in Warwickshire; one was set among willows overlooking a cascade, the other was adorned with lines from Spenser's *Faerie Queene*. It was the fashion to ornament the building with a quotation, inscribed in an appropriately simple manner. Shenstone wrote the verses on paper and pasted them on strips of deal – 'very cheap', he commented. At Hagley, not far from the Leasowes, Lord Lyttelton displayed lines from Milton's *Il Penseroso*: 'And may not at last my weary age/ Find out the

peaceful hermitage.' Dr Jeremiah Pierce used the same lines in the
entrance to the thatched hermitage in the Gothic style that he
caused to be built at Lilliput Castle, near Bath. Hermitage and
house have both disappeared – or in the case of the house, been
replaced – but Thomas Robins, another garden designer, did some
sketches of the hermitage in about 1760.

The fashion for garden hermitages spread to Ireland. There was
one at Glin Castle, near Limerick and the Earl of Orrery, who was
a friend of Pope and Swift, built 'at the expense of five pounds, a
root house, or hermitage' at Caledon, described by his neighbour
Mrs Delany as 'made of roots of trees, the floor is paved with
pebbles, there is a couch made of matting, and little wooden stools,
a table with a manuscript on it, a pair of spectacles, a leathern
bottle ... in short everything that you might imagine necessary
for a recluse'. The earl himself wrote to a friend in 1748: 'Thomson's
Castle of Indolence came to me last post. I have not read it yet.
Such a poem will certainly be very proper to my hermitage, which
is now in such beauty that I am impatient to see you there.' For
him, as for Henry Hoare, the hermit was his *alter ego*.

Henry Hoare's hermitage at Stourhead was not built until 1770, and it was Charles Hamilton who advised him as to where exactly it should be situated. Charles Hamilton began to create the landscape garden at Painshill, near Cobham in Surrey, in the 1740s. He was the ninth son of the sixth Earl of Abercorn and not well provided with funds. His garden became his obsession and his extravagance; by 1774 he was overwhelmed by debt and had to sell it. By then it was famous all over Europe; it is even possible that he had always intended to make its reputation, and his own, and then sell it to discharge his debts. The place was everything the taste of the time admired, influenced as it was by visits to Italy, the pictures of Claude, the work of William Kent and the books and poems which were beginning to circulate the picturesque ideal. There are no straight paths; all is curving and irregular, and the nineteen-acre artificial lake, with its islands and the splendid grotto which adjoins it, can nowhere be seen as one sheet of water but is composed as a succession of beautiful views. It all very nearly returned to wilderness some few years ago, but a local trust has restored most of it, and is about to start on the hermitage, which was chopped up for firewood during the 1940s. Sir John Parnell, who visited the hermitage in 1763, wrote:

> You come to the top of a little eminence where you strike into a wood of different firs, acacias, etc, and serpenting through it arrive at a hermitage formed to the front with the trunks of fir trees with their bark on, their branches making natural gothic windows. The first room is furnished with a little straw couch, an old table and a few old chairs; in the back room are a parcel of odd old things, and from it you command a pretty view of the country. It is built on the side of a steep hill, so has another cave under its back apartment where you come to after several windings.

This cave is mentioned by an earlier visitor as 'like a sandpit (and mistook for such lately by a fox)'.

Hermitages evocative of pleasing melancholy or agreeable horror appeared in countless picturesque sites in the second half of the eighteenth century as romantic irregularity began to replace the correct harmonies of classical taste. Not all the buildings won the approval of the critical tourist. The hermitage built for the Duke of Atholl at Dunkeld, not far from Perth, in 1757 was of neoclassical design and was thought to be unsuitable for the wild sublimity of the Highland landscape. When the fashion for the works of Ossian was at its height – supposedly the epics of an ancient Scottish bard, they were in fact composed by an ingenious eighteenth-century Scotsman named MacPherson – the hermitage had its name changed to Ossian's Hall, and boasted a supposed portrait of the wild-eyed bard. Wordsworth called the building an 'obtrusive Pile' and 'recoiled into the wilderness'. The scene remains highly picturesque. The tallest tree yet recorded in the British Isles is there, a Douglas fir 212 feet high.

Eighteenth-century taste managed to combine a love of solitary contemplation – or at any rate a love of the idea of solitary contemplation – with a lively appreciation of the joys of society. A hermitage was felt to be just the place for a picnic. Gilbert White, the clergyman-naturalist of Selborne in Kent, whose book *The Natural History of Selborne* has never been out of print since it was first published in 1788, had a cantaloupe picnic in 1751 at the thatched hermitage he had built half way up the path to the top of the hill, known as the Hanger, that overlooks the village. He grew the melons in his garden, and his brother Harry was the hermit, though how often he was in residence does not seem to be known. White refers to another picnic, in 1763: 'Drank tea 20 of us at the Hermitage: the Miss Batties & the Mulso family contributed much to our pleasures by their singing, & being dress'd as shepherds, shepherdesses. It was a most elegant evening; and all parties appear'd highly satisfy'd. The Hermit appear'd to great advantage.'

In the absence of an obliging brother, the question of who might inhabit a picturesque hermitage presented problems. Having toyed with the idea of being its first resident himself, the dilettante land-owner probably advertised. Conditions were often quite precise. Charles Hamilton wanted a hermit who would 'continue in the Hermitage seven years, where he would be provided with a Bible, optical glasses, a mat for his feet, a hassock for his pillow, an hour-glass for his timepiece, water for his beverage and food from the house. He must wear a camlet robe, and never, under any circumstances, must he cut his hair, beard or nails, stray beyond the limits of Mr. Hamilton's grounds, or exchange one word with the servant.' If he lasted the full seven years his fee would be 700 guineas; if he broke the rules or left earlier he got nothing. He lasted three weeks before he was spotted creeping out of the grounds to go down to the local pub.

The perfect hermit, not surprisingly, was hard to find. There was one at Burley-on-the-Hill in Leicestershire who may have lasted longer than most. He was known as Hermit Finch, Finch being the name of his employer. Superior children's nannies used to be known by the name of their employer, the title remaining even when the holder of the office changed; so it is possible that Hermit Finch was not one but a series. He – or they – enjoyed better conditions than most; the hermitage had not only a thatched roof but two fireplaces.

At least one hermit advertised his own services. In 1810 a notice appeared in a newspaper: 'A young man, who wishes to retire from the world and live as a hermit in some convenient spot in England is willing to engage with any nobleman or gentleman who may be desirous of having one. Any letter directed to S. Laurence (post paid), to be left at Mr. Ottons, no. 6 Coleman Lane, Plymouth, mentioning what gratuity will be given, and all other particulars, will be duly attended.'

One employer sought a hermit prepared to live underground, unseen and unshaven, but in 'a very commodious apartment, with cold bath, a chamber organ, as many books as the occupier pleases, and provisions served from the gentleman's own table'. He was to receive a pension for life of £50 a year, but the hermit who accepted the position left after four years.

Sir Richard Hill, of Hawkstone in Shropshire, secured the services of a certain Father Francis, whose thoughts on the subject of death and eternity were found suitably solemn by visitors already terrified by the approach through a dark tunnel along a precipitous path. He was venerable and bearded and described as ninety in successive editions of the guidebook over the years, and when death caught up with him in the end no subsequent applicant could match him. At one time his place was taken by an automaton, which apparently both moved and spoke. Sir Richard Colt Hoare of Stourhead, on one of the tours of the countryside which he undertook at the time of the Napoleonic wars, when travel abroad was difficult, was critical: 'The face is natural enough, the figure stiff and not well managed. The effect would be infinitely better if the door were placed at the angle of the walk and not opposite you. The passenger would then come upon St. Francis by surprise, whereas the ringing the bell and door opening into a building quite dark within renders the effect less natural.'

Hoare preferred the artificial druid in the grotto, where he nevertheless found the shellwork excessive and most unnatural. The problem of the Hawkstone hermit was eventually solved by the introduction of a stuffed hermit, posed carefully in a dimly-lit window and adorned with a goat's beard.

Horace Walpole, charmed by the Hagley hermitage, said that it reminded him of Sadeler's prints. Joannis and Raphael Sadeler's book of engravings of hermits, *Solitudo Sive Patrum Eremicolarum*, published in the early seventeenth century, was full of thatched and wooden hermitages, and must have been in circulation among amateurs of taste in the eighteenth century, when it would have appealed to the current passion for antiquarianism. Walpole himself soon saw the absurdity of the hermitage fashion, pronouncing it ridiculous to set aside a quarter of one's garden to be melancholy in (even odder, perhaps, to pay someone else to be sad for one), but he was a keen amateur antiquarian.

Antiquarianism was the fashionable fad among men of taste in the late eighteenth century. Walter Scott's *The Antiquary*, published in 1816, mocks the phenomenon, though with affection; it was said to have been Scott's own favourite novel. Jonathan Oldbuck, the eponymous hero, is erudite and opinionated, and his most frequent interlocutor in antiquarian discussions, Sir Arthur Wardour, is less learned but even more opinionated. There were many such contentious friends at the time, amateur antiquarians of great learning and enthusiasm. Sir Richard Colt Hoare made many expeditions in search of signs of ancient habitation, sometimes accompanied by his friend and correspondent the Revd Stephen Skinner. Skinner was the vicar of nearby Camerton, and his life was blighted by ungrateful children and the unregenerate habits of the mining families of the north Somerset coalfield, who drank and fornicated in complete disregard of their vicar's often splenetic animadversions. He left diaries, from which one gets the impression that his only hours of happiness were on his antiquarian excursions, or when he was occasionally asked to spend a few days at Stourhead. There he could discuss with like-minded men his theory that Camerton was the site of Camalodunum and must therefore be King Arthur's Camelot, or admire Sir Richard's new mausoleum, even then being built in the churchyard to the designs of the Bath architect Pinch. He could examine Sir Richard's library, or marvel at his collection of ancient arrow heads. It was a long way from the intractable burdens of his home life.

William Stukeley, the son of a Lincolnshire lawyer, was an earlier enthusiast for ancient British and Roman remains. When he went to London he met 'the whole sett of learned men & Vertuoso's, who at that time abounded, & by having recourse to their library's I arriv'd to a considerable degree of knowledge & equal reputation'. In 1725 he moved to Grantham, where he practised, not very successfully, as a doctor, and seems to have spent most of his time embellishing his house and garden with antiquities. 'I have adorned my study with heads, bas reliefs, bustos, urns, & drawings of Roman antiquitys, as my bedchamber adjoining with Aegyptian.' In 1727 he married. When his wife miscarried, he buried the embryo in his beloved garden, along with a horned owl which the Duchess of Ancaster had sent him and which had died.

> The embrio, being as big as a filberd, I buryd under the high altar in the chapel of my hermitage vineyard; for there I built a nich in a ragged wall overgrown with ivy, in which I placed my Roman altar, a brick from Verulam, and a waterpipe sent me by Lord Colrain from Marshland. Underneath is a camomile bed for greater ease of the bended knee, and there we enterred it, present my wife's mother, and aunt, with ceremonys proper to the occasion.

The architect Sir John Soane, an inveterate collector of antiquities, invented a monk called Padre Giovanni and created a cell for him in the basement of his house in Lincoln's Inn Fields. He seems to have projected on to him certain feelings of melancholy and disappointment of his own. This was a variation on the hermit theme of the period, and it would be interesting to know how effective it was as therapy. Soane was a mildly paranoid character, who in spite of his success as an architect felt he had been misunderstood by his contemporaries. But he does not seem to have spent much time in solitary meditation in the monk's apartment, preferring to take friends down there for some evening conversation and a glass of port. He wrote a detailed description of his 'Monk's Parlour and Yard' in his 1835 guidebook. They are still much as he described, the house being now a museum.

The monk had a cell and an oratory as well as a parlour in which were a small library, various relics and a 'Glass, remarkable for an inscription on it, taken out of a convent in Flanders during the French Revolution'. There were chests full of architectural drawings, and behind a statue of the monk there was a model of the

lantern-light in the roof of Westminster Hall. 'Various scriptural
subjects, represented on glass, are suited to the destination of the
place, and increase its sombre character.' Various architectural
pieces and more depictions of saints and martyrs 'impress the
spectator with reverence for the monk'. Padre Giovanni could gaze
out upon the ruins of a monastery, in which the spectator is invited
to wander. It is necessarily a very limited wander, since the monastery
ruins are confined to the area outside the basement of a medium-
sized London house, but space has been found for the tomb of the
monk. The pavement of this hallowed place, 'composed of the tops
and bottoms of broken bottles, and pebbles found amongst the gravel
dug out for the foundation of the monastery, and disposed in sym-
metry of design, furnishes an admirable lesson of simplicity and
economy, and shews the unremitting assiduity of the pious monk.
The stone structure, at the head of the monk's grave, contains the
remains of Fanny, the faithful companion, the delight, the solace of
his leisure hours.' Fanny was a dog. Soane's friend Barbara Hofland,
as poet from Harrogate, wrote a somewhat overwrought account of
the whole fantasy. 'But where did the good monk get so many
bottles wherewith to aid his innocent labours?' she asks coyly.

Barbara Hofland mentions *Vathek* in passing. William Beckford,
that book's author, was a pioneer of the Gothic novel. *Vathek*
is oriental fantasy, so perfervid that it seems about to become
pornographic, but never quite does. The protagonist, a tyrant, is
forced into exile in a tower with 11,000 stairs. 'I am resolved to
become a hermit,' he says, 'and consume the residue of my days
on this mountain in expiating my crimes.'

In a sense Beckford lived out his fantasy. He became an obsessive
builder of towers, and his behaviour caused society to ostracize
him. Born in 1760, the son of a rich sugar planter, William Beckford
was handsome and precociously clever. His father, Alderman
Beckford, who visited his plantations in Jamaica only once and
otherwise pursued his business interests in the City of London,
was also involved in politics, being a supporter of the Earl of
Chatham, whom he made godfather to his son.

Beckford referred to his father as the Comendatore and remembered him with awe, real or assumed. He died when Beckford was ten, leaving him, in Byron's words, 'England's richest son'. He read *The Arabian Nights* as a child, and was so excited that his tutor was told to take the book away from him, for fear it might endanger his health. When he was seventeen and travelling with the same tutor, the Revd Edmund Lettice, he visited the Grande Chartreuse, and was overwhelmed. 'It has possessed me to such a degree that at present I can neither think, speak, nor write on any other subject.' His imagination had already been exalted by the lofty mountain peaks he had seen in Switzerland, and by a night spent at the house of a village curé who entertained him with tales of apparitions, spectres, goblins and sorcerers. He had been reading the life of St Bruno, and was determined to see his monastery. Its sombre solitude was all that he had hoped for and it fed his fantasies about the abbey he later built at Fonthill.

Beckford began work on Fonthill Abbey in 1796. In the meantime the scandal had broken, and his indiscreet behaviour with the eleven-year-old William, or 'Kitty', son of Lord and Lady Courtney and later Earl of Devon, broke the rules of the society that had previously doted on him. He was never readmitted to the social world in which he had been born. His young wife, of whom he was genuinely fond, supported him loyally, but died in giving birth to their second daughter. Afterwards his mother and her advisers encouraged him to visit the source of his riches in Jamaica, hoping the scandal might die down, but he disliked sea voyages and stopped off in Lisbon instead, where he amused himself in visiting abbeys and gardens and teasing the respectable English community.

On his return the project for his own abbey occupied him day and night, and involved frequent quarrels with his dilatory and often drunken architect James Wyatt. His original idea had been for a 'ruined Convent' into which he could retreat from time to time from the more prosaic Fonthill Splendens, but the plans grew into a design for a vast abbey, with a central tower rising above a huge octagon and four wings stretching out from the tower in the form of a cross. Beckford's own bedroom was in contrast to the splendid public rooms. It was a simple cell containing little but a truckle bed. At the far end of the immense galleries in the north wing was a five-sided oratory containing an alabaster statue of St Antony of Padua, Beckford's favourite saint, surrounded by thirty-six silver candlesticks, with a silver-gilt lamp overhead, and five small lancet windows of bright stained glass.

The contrast between resplendent luxury and a kind of asceticism continued throughout all Beckford's buildings. He was nothing if not a poseur, but his expert knowledge of books, and of the pictures and objects which he collected, was genuine, and so was his love of nature. Animals and plants flourished within the twelve-mile circumference of the Barrier, a wall twelve feet high, surmounted by iron spikes, which he caused to be built round the Fonthill Abbey estate. His plantations of trees and shrubs, both at Fonthill and in the garden he made at Cintra during his time in Portugal, remain witnesses to his judgement better perhaps than some of the objects he spent such happy hours collecting, which show an early Victorian taste no longer so appealing to modern eyes. The Barrier wall was erected to keep out hunters of all kinds, including seekers for sensation, since Beckford's reputation flourished on rumour, and the occasional glimpse of a handsome catamite or a mysterious dwarf fed the scandal.

Beckford enjoyed the theatricality of religion and perhaps sometimes succeeded in genuinely frightening himself. He cultivated the thought of St Antony of Padua as his patron saint – he was Portuguese and of good family – but his fits of religiosity, like *Vathek* itself, are more reminiscent of Ronald Firbank than St John of the Cross. As for solitude, he did not care for too much of it. He hated to be alone for too long and wrote letters calling Fonthill his 'mournful hermitage', complaining of puritanical England and asking for handsome tightrope walkers to be sent down to amuse him.

When given the opportunity, Beckford was a splendid host. When Nelson and Lady Hamilton came to see the half-finished abbey he arranged a stupendous banquet for them, even though none of the neighbours would attend. The great trees of the avenue were hung with lanterns; hooded figures with flaming torches lit the way inside. The guests were given a conducted tour of the treasures of Beckford's collection, and after they had feasted, Lady Hamilton consented to assume some of her famous 'attitudes'. She represented Agrippina carrying the ashes of Germanicus in a golden urn; the company was reported to be much moved.

When the sugar trade went through a bad patch in the early nineteenth century, Beckford's still considerable wealth could not cover the costs of Fonthill. He sold it, and soon afterwards the great tower fell down. (When he discovered how badly it had been built he offered to reimburse the purchaser, who with equal

magnanimity refused the offer.) He ended his days in Bath, riding every morning up to the tower he had built on Lansdown Hill overlooking the city. There he sat alone with his books and his collection of pictures and objects of virtu, writing learned and witty and sometimes scurrilous letters, gazing at the view and enjoying the notion of the hermit as disenchanted worldling. But he was also the hermit as Ishmael, outcast from society; he remained a figure of scandal, in spite of the devotion of his two daughters, who both married well. Unlike the P. G. Wodehouse character whose idea of heaven was to have enough tobacco and be cut by the county, Beckford never ceased to resent the fact that the world to which he felt he belonged, by right of birth, wealth, taste and wit, refused to acknowledge him.

CHAPTER 12

'*The louder and more tumultuous*
our hearts . . .'

ROMANTIC EXPECTATIONS

Chateaubriand — William Bartram —
Alexander von Humboldt —
Coleridge — William and Dorothy Wordsworth —
Samuel Palmer — Theodore Powys

'Unceasingly restless, the people of Europe have found it necessary to construct places of solitude. The louder and more tumultuous our hearts, the more we are drawn to silence and calm.' So speaks the young René, hero of Chateaubriand's novel of the same name. Through René, according to Flaubert, Chateaubriand 'filled half a century with the noise of his suffering'.

Born in 1768 in St Malo, Chateaubriand spent a lonely youth at the nearby Château of Combourg, where his father seldom spoke, his mother was always ill and his clever neurotic sister was probably in love with him. He wandered in the woods, read Rousseau, and began to write. In 1791 he set sail for America, unhappy about the course which the French Revolution was taking and determined to find some kind of personal salvation in the untamed wilderness of the New World.

In the event he found America difficult to grasp. He travelled, but not as far as he implied in his books. He was shocked by the commercial harshness of the East Coast traders, and he failed to find the harmonious life of the noble savage which his reading of Rousseau had led him to expect. Nevertheless his two American novellas, *Atala* and *René*, which were both extracts from his immense work *The Genius of Christianity*, were enormously popular. Previous romances about a return to nature, which were not uncommon in the eighteenth century, were pretty versions of pastoral, such as Bernardin de Saint-Pierre's *Paul et Virginie*, also much admired. It is a charming and sentimental tale about two children brought up in a state of natural innocence on a Pacific island; their happiness as adults is destroyed because of a worldly Parisian aunt's determination to turn Virginie into a proper lady. Chateaubriand was different, in that he put forward the idea of the noble savage as offering a morally superior, and fundamentally aristocratic, concept of civilization. There is something slightly absurd in Chateaubriand's determination to identify himself with an Indian brave on the basis of shared aristocratic values. He was writing at a time when the failure of the French colony in Louisiana and the virtual annihilation of the Natchez people by the French was still a sore point in French memory. Chateaubriand saw himself as a romantic writer, but he was also the future French politician. Dreams of empire remained with him. Years later, when he was ambassador to England, he could write: 'Let us say, to the honour of our country and the glory of our religion, that the Indians were strongly attached to us ... The savage still loves us beneath the tree where we were his first guests.' His dream of an Eden on the Mississippi, where the noble savage and the French nobleman could be blood brothers, still haunted him.

Chateaubriand's ideas of America had been fed by travellers' tales. Europeans expected alligators, as well as armadillos, Indians, exotic plants and unknown dangers. The south offered more than the north in this respect. William Bartram, son of a self-taught botanist, spent several years exploring the south-east, and his *Travels Through North and South Carolina, Georgia, East and West Florida, the Cheroke Country, the Extensive Territories of the Muscogules or Creek Confederacy, and the Country of the Chactaws* was read with enthusiasm by European romantics, Chateaubriand among them.

Bartram's descriptions of fighting crocodiles are stirring: 'Behold him rushing forth from the flags and reeds. His enormous body swells. His plaited tail, brandished high, floats upon the lake. The waters like a cataract descend from his opening jaws. Clouds of smoke issue from his dilated nostrils. The Earth trembles with his thunder.'

The landscape through which he rides sounds indeed like the Elysian fields to which he compares it:

> [A] vast expanse of green meadows and strawberry fields; a meandering river gliding through, saluting in its various turnings the swelling, green, turfy knolls, embellished with parterres of flowers and fruitful strawberry beds; flocks of turkeys strolling about them; herds of deer prancing in the meads or bounding over the hills; companies of young, innocent Cherokee virgins, some busily gathering the rich fragrant fruit, others having already filled their baskets, lay reclined under the shade of floriferous and fragrant native bowers of Magnolia, Azalia, Philadelphus, perfumed Calycanthus, sweet Yellow Jessamine and cerulian Glycine frutescens.

Chateaubriand's travels were not quite so rewarding. He was in America for about six months, arriving in Baltimore and travelling to New York via Philadelphia. His account of his travels is vague but it seems that he sailed up the Hudson, and made an expedition to Niagara. Taking a precipitous path to see the Falls, in defiance of his guide, he slipped and broke his arm. When he had recovered, he travelled down the Ohio river as far as its junction with the Mississippi. In fact he only glimpsed the Mississippi itself because he turned back to Philadelphia, where he heard news of the dethronement of the French king and decided to return home to support him. Nevertheless, his lush descriptions of the river he called the Nile of the Americas appealed to a French public already entranced by the romance of the unexplored wilderness of America. His hero René became a prototype of the solitary adolescent with romantic leanings.

> Complete solitude, the spectacle of nature, soon plunged me into a state almost beyond description. Without kin, without friends, alone upon earth, still ignorant of love, I was yet overcome with a superabundance of life. At times I suddenly flushed, and I felt as it were streams of hot lava

flowing through my heart; at times I uttered involuntary cries, and the night was troubled equally by my dreams and my waking existence: I went down into the valley, I scaled the mountain top, summoning with all the power of my desires, the ideal object of a future passion; I clasped her imaginary form in the wind; her moaning voice came back to me in the stones of the river: her phantom was everywhere, in the stars of the sky, a very principle of life in the universe.

A less perfervid picture of the Americas came from the travels of Alexander von Humboldt, whose lectures were the excitement of the Paris season in 1804. He was a scientist, but his attitude to the wild nature which he observed so much more exactly than Chateaubriand was as romantic. He read *Paul et Virginie* aloud to his loyal travelling companion Aimé Bonpland, a doctor and botanist, during a thunderstorm on the Orinoco river.

Born in 1769 in Prussia, Humboldt inherited enough money from his mother to finance his travels. Influenced by Goethe and Rousseau, he wanted to dedicate his Spanish American works to the dramatist Friedrich Schiller, with whose views about the harmony of all nature he sympathized. He was a great scientist, the first to establish the basic principles of plant geography, but he also felt that all of nature was an interlocking system, a unity – 'everything is interaction'. Darwin called him 'the greatest naturalist in the world'. In fact, Darwin went on to eclipse Humboldt, and as a result Humboldt's view of the wholeness of nature went out of fashion. Perhaps Darwin would anyway have thought it cloudy German metaphysics.

Coleridge, of course, was interested in German metaphysics. He travelled in Germany with his friends William and Dorothy Wordsworth in 1798, but reading their several accounts of the voyage one feels that Coleridge, partly no doubt because he could speak the language, was much more in tune with what they were seeing and hearing on their travels than either William or Dorothy. The Wordsworths' feelings about nature were so grounded in an English landscape that they hardly needed other influences; they first knew inspiration together among the gentle hills of north Somerset, and after their retreat to the Lake District sublimity was Helvellyn, passion a Derwentwater storm, calm the homely cottage in Grasmere as evening drew in. All this they knew by heart; only William's philosophical temperament and belief in his own poetic destiny made him seek to systematize it. His intense feeling about nature differs from the overwhelming romanticism of Chateaubriand in the same way as the work of the great mystics differs from the vapourings of their sentimental adherents and it was something he was born with. In a note to the *Ode on the Intimations of Immortality* he wrote: 'I was often unable to think of external things as having external existence, and I communed with all that I saw as something not apart from, but inherent in, my own immaterial nature. Many times while going to school have I grasped at a wall or tree to recall myself from this abyss of idealism to the reality. At that time I was afraid of such processes.'

Putting it into words controlled the fear. Dorothy felt no such need to create. She lacked what Coleridge called the shaping spirit of the imagination. She wrote that Coleridge thought too highly of her capacities: 'I have not those powers which Coleridge thinks I have – I know it – my only merits are my devotedness to those I love and I hope a charity towards all mankind.' She was content to feed her brother's powerful intellect with the results of her observation, so much more acute than his. She was the more instinctive, he the more thoughtful. If her observation was better than his, the dimensions of his feeling, and his will to understand it, outstripped hers. Both of them sharpened their innate capacities on their long solitary walks. Bound by a love whose intricacies they did not question – though generations of students have done so ever since – they chose seclusion, not only in order for William to dedicate himself to his art but so that their life should express their faith in simplicity and closeness to nature. Seen as one unit, the brother and sister cease to be images of selfishness and sacrifice: the sister offered her talents to be subsumed in his greater genius, and by doing so made him a better poet. But the amount of housework she did would break any modern woman's heart.

They must have seemed so extraordinary when they were young. The image of the sage, grown sententious beneath the burden of his great task, surrounded by his devoted womenfolk and respectfully visited by the great of the world, prematurely old, for both he and his sister aged badly, looking sixty when in their forties, fearsomely reactionary in politics – partly as a result of the nervousness which followed the agonizing loss of two adored young children, as well as the debilitating effect of perpetual money worries – this image tends to block out the picture of the passionately strange young couple who set up house in Somerset in 1796.

The first house they were lent in those parts was at Racedown, on the Devon–Dorset border. It was the first time that the brother and sister had shared a home as adults; and it was there, in the orchard, that the two of them were standing – she tiny, animated, intense, he long and thin, ill-coordinated, with a formidable nose and an oddly impressive presence – when the young Coleridge came to call on them for the first time. In no doubt as to who these strange figures must be, Coleridge impulsively vaulted a gate, ran across a field and jumped a stream to join them. It was the beginning of the most intensely happy period in the complicated friendship between three remarkable beings.

The Wordsworths were so genuinely unconventional that they had no idea anyone might think them so. In fact William was suspected of being a French spy. Reported to the Home Office for roaming the country by night as well as by day, and living with 'only a woman who passes for his sister', he was watched by a detective named Walsh, who concluded that 'the inhabitants of Alfoxton House are a Sett of violent Democrats'. It was the time of the Napoleonic Wars and the Home Office was keeping an eye on possible subversive groups. Lord Sidmouth, the Home Secretary, had very few agents who reported directly to him, but local land-lords, postmasters and Justices of the Peace were expected to do their patriotic duty as observers and, where necessary, informers. Poets were naturally suspect. Shelley and his first wife were kept under close observation when they were at Lynmouth in Devon in 1812. Lord Sidmouth may have been slightly surprised to read of the messages in bottles, and the fleets of miniature sailing boats loaded with seditious pamphlets, which the teenaged revolution-aries launched into the sea from the remote North Devon rocks; they even once set off a fire balloon.

Wordsworth and Coleridge were passionate idealists, believing that the French Revolution had changed mankind's prospects for ever. What was remarkable was that, when disillusionment set in, two young men of such intellectual ability should turn away from the hope of political action and take refuge in the idea of becoming philosopher-poets in seclusion. Coleridge had had this idea even before he met Wordsworth, and had defended it against friends who accused him of wanting to become a monk. 'Can he be deemed monastic who is married, and employed in raising his children? – who *personally* preaches the truth to his friends and neighbours, and who endeavours to instruct tho' Absent by the Press?' Perhaps if they had lived in modern times they would both have been prophets of the ecological movement, but their minds were so much of their own time that it is hard to imagine. One might say that they had a view of man as a spiritual being which was lost some time between their time and ours.

The philosophy which Wordsworth developed on his long walks, alone or with his sister (for one can have solitude *à deux*, in the same way as one can have *folie à deux*), was not pantheistic, but nor was it the orthodox Christianity of his time. Perhaps in its faith in the union of Mind and Nature in the whole of Being it has more in common with Buddhism; but then there is always 'the still, sad music of humanity'.

Therefore I am still
A lover of the meadows and the woods,
And mountains; and of all that we behold
From this green earth; of all the mighty world
Of eye, and ear – both what they half create,
And what perceive; well pleased to recognize
In nature and the language of the sense
The anchor of my purest thought, the nurse,
The guide, the guardian of my heart, and soul
Of all my moral being.

Tintern Abbey was also Wordsworth's deepest expression of his devotion to his sister:

For thou art with me, here, upon the banks
Of this fair river . . .
Therefore let the moon
Shine on thee in thy solitary walk;
And let the misty mountain winds be free
To blow against thee: and in after years,
When these wild ecstasies shall be matured
Into a sober pleasure, when thy mind
Shall be a mansion for all lovely forms,
Thy memory be as a dwelling-place
For all sweet sounds and harmonies; Oh then,
If solitude, or fear, or pain, or grief,
Should be thy portion, with what healing thoughts
Of tender joy wilt thou remember me.

Dorothy's true originality lay in the intensity of her spontaneous response to natural sights and sounds and associations. Her friend de Quincey wrote that she was the 'most natural (that is to say the wildest) person I have known'. How much she had been alone as a child is not known; she was taken away from home when her mother died and brought up by kindly relations among whom she found friends of her own age, but there must have been times of loneliness. Her journals are full of tiny masterpieces of natural description, as visionary in their transfigurative power as the

landscapes Samuel Palmer was to paint not so very long afterwards.

> Walked with Coleridge. A very clear afternoon. We lay side-
> long along the turf, and gazed on the landscape until it
> melted into more than natural loveliness. The sea very uni-
> form, of a pale greyish blue, only one distant bay, bright
> and blue as a sky . . . A winter prospect shows every cottage,
> every farm, and the forms of distant trees, such as in sum-
> mer have no distinguishing mark. On our return, Jupiter
> and Venus before us. While the twilight still overpowered
> the light of the moon, we were reminded that she was
> shining bright above our heads, by our faint shadows going
> before us.

It was Dorothy who saw the wild daffodils by the lake and heard
the story of little Alice Fell, who ran crying after her torn cloak
when it was caught in the wheel of a post-chaise, Dorothy who
heard the thrush and remembered how she would never catch a
butterfly as a child for fear of rubbing away the dust on its wings
so that it would not be able to fly. All these things her brother
turned into poems. Her journals are full of accounts of what she
saw on her immensely long walks, the beggars and wayfarers she
encountered, the landscapes she gazed at when she paused for rest:
'As I lay down on the grass, I observed the glittering silver line on
the ridge of the backs of the sheep, owing to their situation respect-
ing the sun, which made them look beautiful, but with something
of strangeness, like animals of another kind, as if belonging to a
more splendid world.'

This was the world Samuel Palmer saw, and painted in his early
tiny masterpieces. He was born in 1805. His father was an unworldly
and unsuccessful bookseller and both parents were deeply religious
Baptists. One evening when he was three years old his devout and
poetry-loving nurse Mary Ward held him up to the window to
watch the rising moon. She recited some lines by the then popular
poet Alexander Young which the child never forgot:

Fond man, the vision of a moment made,
Dream of a dream, and shadow of a shade.

In his old age Palmer wrote: 'I never forgot those shadows, and am often trying to paint them.'

From his happy, cherished, childhood, the boy was sent away to be a boarder at Merchant Taylor's school in London. Shocked to find that the world was not the gentle place he had thought it, he was desperately unhappy until after several months he was allowed to leave. At about the same time his mother died, and he suffered periods of depression ever after. The great influence of his life was William Blake, whose visionary fervour, both in his life and in his art, confirmed Palmer's own instinct, and inspired much of his early work. These watercolours and drawings, often very small, are of natural scenes transfigured by the painter's eye, that 'visionary gleam' which Coleridge so bitterly lamented when he lost it. Yet the vision is not quite Coleridge's, or Wordsworth's; it is somehow simpler, without Coleridge's anxiety or Wordsworth's fearful awe. There is often a shepherd with his flock, or reapers returning in the evening beneath a harvest moon, or an orchard whose trees are laden with apples. His loving parents brought him up on Virgil and the Psalms, and both are there in his early works.

Palmer's vision of nature – which faded under the strains of a not particularly happy marriage and the necessity of supporting his much-loved children, two of whom died young – was far too true to itself ever to seem sentimental; but it was blissful. It was the world of men which seemed to him alarming, and likely (for this was at the beginning of the Industrial Revolution) to do untold damage both to nature and to itself.

A later writer who had a similarly immediate apprehension of nature, though his vision was darker, was Theodore Powys. All the Powys brothers seem to have been aware of the dark side of nature, as well as of the darkness in themselves. They were the extraordinary children of a late-nineteenth-century Anglican clergyman. The best known now is probably the novelist and lecturer John Cowper

Powys, who died in 1963, but there were five other bothers and five sisters, all remarkable. Their childhood and the closeness of their family relationships were enormously important to all of them all their lives.

'Do you ever think about your childhood?' someone asked Theodore. 'I think of nothing else,' he answered.

Theodore struck contemporaries as the most genuinely strange. Unhappy at school as a small boy, he did not follow his brothers to Sherborne, the public school not far from the family vicarage at Montacute, but went instead to a small preparatory school at Aldeburgh at the unusually late age of fourteen and left it a few years later to become a farmer in Suffolk. Abandoning that career soon afterwards, he moved to Dorset, married a village girl and lived there in extreme simplicity. His short novels, such as *Mr. Weston's Good Wine* and *Mr. Tasker's Pigs*, were utterly original, farcical yet realistic about country life, sometimes gleefully horrid, always God-haunted. He felt himself to be on such intimate terms with God that when, on one of his solitary walks, he heard his brothers calling in mock fearsome tones from behind a hedge he answered, 'Yes, God?' without surprise.

Like Palmer, Theodore Powys was fundamentally a solitary; the core of his being, and the source of his creative imagination, lay in his childhood solitary acquaintance with nature. All the Powys brothers were physically formidable, large and rather fiercely handsome. John Cowper Powys owned himself much plagued by sadistic thoughts, and in Theodore's novels too the earthy realities of rural life are often sinister or frightening. Sons of the vicarage, their glimmerings of morbid imagination added guilt to their creative impulses. Theodore's personal God was always a terrible one. 'His love is a terrible love – terrible and deep, hard for a man to bear; I have lived in it, I know it.'

For all that, there is something reminiscent of Samuel Palmer in the way Theodore Powys saw the natural world. 'I see the awful Majesty of the Creator come into our own Grange mead,' he wrote. 'And lie down amid a joyous crowd of buttercups and red clover.'

CHAPTER 13

'In Wildness is
the preservation of the world . . .'

AMERICAN CONSERVATIONISTS

Emerson and Wordsworth —
Miss Mary Moody Emerson —
Henry David Thoreau — John Muir

Ralph Waldo Emerson called on Wordsworth in 1833, on his first visit to England. By that time Wordsworth was becoming a national monument. Everybody who was anybody and a great number of people who were nobody wrote to him and visited him. He seems never to have turned anyone away, though he must sometimes have been exhausted – or bored. Emerson seems to have found him rather sententious – a failing of which he himself was not entirely free. They probably irritated each other. Emerson described Wordsworth as 'narrow and very English ... off his own beat, his opinions had no value'. He told Emerson that America 'needed a civil war to teach the necessity of knitting social ties', and that Americans were 'too much given to making of money and secondly to politics'. Emerson seems to have let this pass, but they could not agree over Carlyle, whom Wordsworth pronounced to be inter-mittently insane. Emerson at the time felt unbounded admiration for Carlyle, though later, after Carlyle had dismissed Emerson's opinions as 'moonshiny', he became slightly more critical.

Emerson and Wordsworth went for a walk together, and Words-worth, perhaps sensing that he had not quite lived up to expec-tations, suddenly recited some sonnets.

'This recitation was so unlooked for and surprising – he, the old Wordsworth standing apart, and reciting to me in a garden walk, like a schoolboy declaiming – that I at first was near to laugh; but recollecting myself, that had come thus far to see a poet, and he was chanting poems to me, I saw that he was right and I was wrong and gladly gave myself up to hear.' The sight and sound of Wordsworth declaiming his own verse was evidently deeply impressive. He never lost his North Country intonation, and the painter and diarist Benjamin Haydon describes him reading to Mary Wordsworth, 'moaning out the burthen of the line, like a distant echo'. Hazlitt wrote: 'His manner of reading his own poetry is particularly imposing; and in his favourite passages his eye beams with preternatural lustre, and the meaning labours slowly up from his swelling breast ... His language may not be intelligible; but his manner is not to be mistaken. It is clear that he is either mad or inspired.'

This time, the performance seems not to have been enough quite to redeem the whole occasion. There was an even less successful visit in 1848, when Emerson called with the novelist Harriet Martineau to see the nearly eighty-year-old Wordsworth. He was asleep on the sofa; 'a little short and surly as an old man is, suddenly waked before the end of his nap'. Harriet Martineau was so annoyed by Wordsworth's reactionary views that she left, and Wordsworth went grumbling on about the French Revolution and – once again – Carlyle, whom he called 'a pest to the English tongue'. Emerson described the great poet as 'a bitter old Englishman ... whose conversation is always simple and not usually distinguished by anything forcible ... Occasionally, his face lights up and he says something good but I thought I could easily supply such table talk as this without the cost of journeys.'

Perhaps writers should be known only through their works. Wordsworth's influence, not only on Emerson but through him on Thoreau and Walt Whitman, was immeasurable. As much as anything it was the reverence for nature which he learned from Wordsworth that underlay the Transcendentalist movement which Emerson developed from the remnants of the Unitarian faith in which he had been brought up but had abandoned. Transcendentalism was more or less Wordsworth with added vague mysticism, somehow derived from the philosophy of Kant and mediated by Coleridge.

Emerson was born in Boston, the son of a Unitarian minister who died when Emerson was eight. His aunt, Miss Mary Moody Emerson, who was responsible for his upbringing after his father died, sometimes spoke of her whole life as having been spent in her own inner hermitage. She was four feet three inches tall and wore her short hair tucked into a sort of mobcap. She was fiercely independent and fiercely religious. Unconventional in her behaviour – she often took her teeth out in company 'to give herself more ease' – she was uncompromising in the puritanism of her religious outlook. 'What has done the most injury to men and women since the allegory of Adam?' she asked Emerson as a young man, and answered herself firmly, 'Sexual influence.' She called herself an Aryan, on the grounds that she did not believe that Christ was of the same substance as God. She slept in a bed made in the form of a coffin, and was gratified to notice the shadow of the nearby church making the shape of a coffin on her wall.

Emerson, raised by this eccentric embodiment of the New England conscience and tested by early sorrows, including the madness of two of his brothers and the early death of his first wife, developed a resilient optimism which seemed to elevate him above his fellows. His second wife found such serenity hard to live with, and periodically retreated into melancholy and ill health. 'It's a very striking and curious spectacle', said Thomas Carlyle once to the American scholar Charles Eliot Norton, 'to behold a man so confidently cheerful as Emerson.'

Emerson always saw the love of nature as being closely associated with solitude. He wrote in his first book *Nature*: 'in this pleasing contrite wood life which God allows me, let me record day by day my honest thoughts, and the record ought to have the interest to a philosopher which the life of a gymnosophist or stylite had.' But the man who did make such a record, and who also had a manual dexterity which Emerson conspicuously lacked, was his disciple Henry David Thoreau – 'my brave Henry' as Emerson called him.

Thoreau was born in 1817, in Concord, Massachusetts, where Emerson came to settle. He lived with Emerson and his family for two years as a young man after he had given up being a school-master, and was drawn into the Transcendentalist circle. He was short, dark and hirsute, with a piercing gaze. Emerson wrote, 'I admire [his] perennial threatening attitude, jut as we like to go under an overhanging precipice', and described him as 'not to be subdued, always manly and able, but rarely tender, as if he did not feel himself except in opposition'. His attitude to life was less penitential than that of some of his associates: when he was dying of consumption and a devout aunt asked him if he had made his peace with God, he answered firmly that he was not aware of there having been a quarrel.

It was another member of the group, Ellery Channing, who first suggested that Thoreau might build a hut beside Walden Pond; Channing had thought of doing something of the kind himself, though only for use as a refuge in which to write poetry. Emerson owned some property along the north shore of Walden. Thoreau liked building and had done some work on a new house for his parents not far away. He began by cutting down some of the white pines, then he bought an abandoned shanty for its well-weathered boards and shingles, and set to work.

He claimed that the total cost of the cabin was $28.12. This figure has been doubted by some who have tried to build their own versions of the cabin. Others have meanly claimed that no one who could leave so many bent nails as the site has subsequently revealed could have managed to build the place on his own. But he is a great man in American literature, and his reputation grows as concerns for the ecological soundness of the planet increase. His plea for 'little oases of wildness in the desert of our civilization' is more relevant now than it was in his own day.

He wrote:

> I went to the woods because I wished to live deliberately,
> to front only the essential facts of life, and see if I could
> not learn what it had to teach, and not, when I came to
> die, discover that I had not lived . . . I wanted to live deep

and suck out all the marrow of life, to live so sturdily and
Spartan-like as to put to rout all that was not life, to cut
the broad swath and shave close, to drive life into a corner,
and reduce it to its lowest terms, and if it were sublime, to
know it by experience.

He cleared two acres of bramble patch for a vegetable garden,
and passed his time in carpentry, gardening and writing. His hut
was simply furnished and he was proud of the fact that his only
mirror was no bigger than a penny postcard.

Thoreau was quite a sociable hermit, saying that he had three
chairs in his house, one for solitude, two for friendship, three for
society. His most constant visitors were two other members of the
Transcendentalist circle. Ellery Channing was his near contemporary, a contributor to *The Dial*, the literary organ of the movement;
he wrote many poems in a style characterized by Thoreau as 'sub-
lime-slipshod'. Bronson Alcott was an enthusiastic and penurious
educationalist, whose daughter Louisa contributed to the comfort
of his declining years by the huge success of her novel, *Little
Women*, and its sequels. Ellery Channing stayed in the hut sometimes, sleeping on the floor beside Thoreau's bed, and helping to
make the fireplace and the chimney. There was always too the
pleasant walk along the shores of the pond to dinner with the
Emersons.

Thoreaus hared Emerson's Transcendentalist view of the natural
world 'as a means and a symbol', but in spite of many fine passages
of rhetoric, his writings show a clearer perception of the reality of
nature than is revealed by Emerson's more gnomic pronouncements about 'nature as the incarnation of thought'.

In his adventurous wanderings about the wilder parts of
America, Thoreau was quite certain as to his preference for nature
tended by the hand of man. When he first went to Maine, and
climbed the mountain Ktaadin, he found the unpeopled woods
awe-inspiring rather than entirely lovable. 'Nature was here something savage and awful, though beautiful . . . This was that Earth

of which we have heard, made out of Chaos and Old Night.'

After an eloquent attack on the wilful destruction of trees by the logging companies, he admits to feeling relief on getting back from the forests of Maine to the tamer landscape of Massachusetts, where a civilized man can enjoy nature humanized into woods and fields, swamps and village commons. The pioneers have been there first, he says, 'like John the Baptists; eaten the wild honey, it may be, but the locusts also'. But the civilized man needs sometimes to follow the logger and the Native American into the recesses of the wilderness, for the good of his soul.

Thoreau's hut is no longer to be seen, but the pile of stones left as homage by visitors to its site continues to grow. *Walden; or Life in the Woods* was published in 1854. Thoreau was by then known as the man who had been briefly sent to prison for refusing to pay taxes to a state which supported slavery and the war against Mexico. The rest of his short life, however, was spent as an amateur naturalist, seeking to understand more deeply what he felt he had glimpsed during his two years living by Walden Pond: 'We are surrounded by a rich and fertile mystery. May we not probe it, pry into it, employ ourselves about it – a little?' His many notebooks from this period are still being patiently transcribed and published, his handwriting being exceptionally difficult to decipher. He died of tuberculosis in 1862 at the age of forty-two.

In May 1871, at the age of seventy, Emerson went to California to see the giant redwoods. He was with a party of admirers, travelling by train, wagon and horseback, with lectures in his baggage for delivery should they be requested. They called on Brigham Young in Salt Lake City, though the women in the party refused to see him, since he was reputed to have sixteen wives. Emerson thought Mormonism an 'after-clap of Puritanism' and was not much impressed by its leader, who for his part had never heard of Emerson. From San Francisco they set off for the four-day journey to Yosemite, with Emerson in benign mood, discoursing at length upon Goethe, Coleridge, Byron and Swedenborg. When he came to the woods, however, he bowed before the force of another man's obsession and let John Muir do the talking.

Muir was working in a sawmill at the time, and had made himself a cabin high up at one end of it. Emerson climbed the ladder into the little room to see Muir's notes and sketches, and came back every day of his stay in the valley to talk and listen. Muir suggested that Emerson might camp out with him in the Mariposa Grove, but the great man's entourage was alarmed for his health. ('You would have made him perfectly comfortable,' wrote Theodore Roosevelt firmly to Muir years later, 'and he ought to have had the experience.')

As the dark cloud of the nineteenth century which Ruskin had so fearfully envisioned came to haunt the dreams of more and more of his contemporaries, moves to save what there was of unpolluted nature gathered pace in various parts of the Western world. England's Open Space movement developed into the National Trust, and its pioneers were effective as well as far-sighted and high-minded. But the vast spaces of the American wilderness, ripe for exploitation in the fine old pioneering American spirit exemplified by the exterminators of the buffalo and the native population, called forth something more like an Old Testament prophet. If St Antony is the prototype of the Christian hermit, John Muir must be the apotheosis of the solitary whose god is Nature. Called by a sense of vocation which he did not claim to understand, he spent years alone in the wilderness before reluctantly returning to the world to call for the protection of what he had come to see as sacred.

A Scot from Dunbar on the Firth of Forth, he had been brought to America in 1849 at the age of six by his father, a fanatical Presbyterian, recently converted to an extreme sect known as the Disciples of Christ. Daniel Muir beat his sons regularly to instil into them the need for repentance and the virtue of wretchedness.

On the boat to America he came across fellow religionists going to Wisconsin and abandoned his original idea of going to California in order to settle near them, buying eighty acres of uncultivated land and setting up as a farmer.

Whether in Scotland or Wisconsin, nature was John Muir's refuge from his father's wrath, but he was an obedient son who for years worked long hours on the farm, and pursued his studies of natural phenomena, as well as his interest in making things, only in his spare time. One of his inventions was a clockwork contraption which could be timed to tip him out of bed in the morning. A friend persuaded him to show some of his inventions at the State Fair in nearby Madison, much to his father's disapproval. His stall was a success, largely because of all the children who queued up to be thrown out of the clockwork bed, and it attracted the attention of the wife of a university professor.

Jeanne Carr was twelve years older than the intense young inventor; she became his patroness, and probably loved him as he probably loved her. Certainly she became his confidante, and much of what is known of his hermit years comes from his correspondence with her. Wandering in obedience to what seemed to him the only necessity he understood – the need to know the natural world and in the course of acquiring that knowledge to come to his true self – he spent two years in Canada, avoiding the possibility of being drafted to fight in a Civil War which seemed to him a tragic mistake. Then came his years in the Californian forests and the Sierra Nevada. His passion was as insistent as a holy hermit's who wishes to live with God as a spouse; he wanted truly to know the mountains in all their moods.

Muir admired Thoreau – Emerson thought of him as Thoreau's true successor and always hoped he would enter into public life as Thoreau had refused to do – but he would not have agreed that a humanized landscape was to be preferred to the mountains. Nor had he much sympathy with Romantic poets who wrote of mountain gloom and horror. His experiences in the mountains were often ecstatic, but he also devoted hours to minute observations of plants, ants, water ouzels and the weather. He lived on such earnings as he could find in sawmills and machine shops and whenever he could he disappeared on long treks on a mustang called Brownie, taking not much more than a blanket roll and the bread and tea on which he mostly subsisted. He became a skilful climber. One man who walked with him was astonished to see Muir '*slide* up that mountain. I had been with mountain climbers before, but never one like him. A deep lope over the smoother slopes, a sure instinct for the easiest way into a rocky fortress, an instant and unerring attack, a serpent-like glide up the steep; eye, hand and foot all connected dynamically; with no appearance of weight to his body.' It was as if he had acquired the lightness of being of the shaman.

Eventually he was prevailed upon, largely through the influence of Jeanne Carr, whose emotional support had been his mainstay during his hermit years, to come down from the mountains with his message that they should be saved – as far as possible inviolate, or as he put it 'unblighted, unredeemed'. He gave his first public lecture in January 1876 in Sacramento. The following month he published his first article on forest preservation.

Even though in the succeeding years John Muir married and had two daughters and became a successful fruit farmer as well as a renowned preservationist and a powerful influence on the president and the legislators, he never lost his feeling for the wild. He went back on many occasions when the world was too much for him, or to save his health, confident always that a spell in the mountains would put him right. Nor did he ever lose his sacramental attitude to nature, despite the practicalities of daily involvement in controversy. In this he was inspiring to many, sometimes infuriating to others. Like the true hermit he instinctively was, he always said his going to the wilderness 'was no solemn abjuration of the world. I only went out for a walk, and finally concluded to stay out till sundown, for going out, I found, was really going in.'

———

CHAPTER 14

'I stood amazed . . .'

THE CONTINUING TRADITION

Some contemporary Christian hermits

'She has hermits in her garden,' someone said.

So I went to try and find them. The garden turned out to be a wood which had grown up in a disused quarry, and the hermits had gone. The owner had sold the wood. She was not prepared to say that it had been the only way to get rid of the hermits, but she did admit that most of them had been more in the nature of drop-outs than genuine hermits – like those who used to be called 'plastic hippies' in the 1960s, the ones who went home after the weekend to jobs and schools and the conveniences of the despised System.

'Wait, though,' she said, 'I will take you to see a real hermit.'

We walked through the garden of a convent in Godalming. It was also a nursing home; the respectable families of the Surrey commuter belt had had their babies there, and some of them in due course died there. Through a door in the wall, usually kept locked, we came to another part of the garden. Behind some trees at the end of it there was a small shack, the hermitage of Sister John Francis.

Some hermits who have been monks and nuns wear the habits of their orders all the time, some seem not to find this necessary. Sister John Francis wears only the most minimal of nun-like head-dresses, and is otherwise neat in skirt and blouse, unintimidating and unintimidated; sharply alert but fortunately benevolent. She joined the Poor Clares in York at the age of eighteen. Over the years her feeling for solitude became stronger and stronger. In the meantime she was responsible for making Church vestments, and organizing their delivery on time and to order; then she was appointed novice mistress. In 1971 she asked permission to become a hermit, and was told she must wait for at least five years. It took ten. She had to overcome the resistance of her own abbess, who probably found her an extremely competent novice mistress and did not want to lose her. She had to accept that she must give up her membership of the order of Poor Clares and take a different vow as a hermit, but she found support from her bishop and from three hermit-monks from Ampleforth Abbey in Yorkshire. In association with these three she lived for a trial period in the woods somewhere near Liverpool, where the physical conditions were hard and her happiness intense. Even when she had secured the necessary permissions she still had to find somewhere to live – possibilities came and went until at last she found the haven where I met her.

She told me that the 'freelance' hermit's life had not been recognized by the Catholic Church after the reorganization of the monasteries in the thirteenth century; only in 1983 had canon law allowed it once more. She felt that the increasing busyness – and even worldliness, in the sense that life inside is increasingly like life outside – of much monastic life might account for an increase in the number of monk and nuns, particularly nuns, who want to become hermits. 'The spirit's not got time to move,' she said. Later she wrote to me: 'I – and others I know – need solitude for the silence and "space" to communicate with God – without ceasing, if possible.' She had originally joined a contemplative order so that she could devote her life to prayer, and found herself so busy that she was not able to find enough time to pray. Like all the religious hermits I met, she had had a long struggle not only to get the necessary permissions, but, having done so, to find herself a hermitage. She was able, patiently, to see the waiting as part of her 'formation'. She had found her refuge in the corner of a convent garden. Part of every day she works at copying documents. Beyond her hut is a grassy field where the roe deer come in the evening and sit in the grass, quite still, with their heads raised towards the west.

The hermit life in religion declined after the Reformation. The religious orders of monk and nuns were abolished. In Catholic countries the religious orders became much stricter and more centralized. Institutions under threat become more authoritarian, in order to keep control of events; independent thought becomes disloyalty, likely to lead to dissidence, which is heresy. The counter-reformation made life difficult for those religious who were outside the institutionalized Church, or whose independence of thought made them a danger to conformity. St Theresa of Avila had to exercise a great deal of skill and charm to keep the authorities of the Spanish Church on her side, and her fellow mystic and friend St John of the Cross was imprisoned by them. Her own order of Carmelites endured, as did the Carthusians and the Cistercians of the stricter kind, but less recognized hermits – and in particular hermits who came from a lay background – were not encouraged.

The Rule of St Benedict had always allowed for the possibility of a few monks going out from the community to solitude, and presumably this practice from time to time quietly continued, but only in the twentieth century did the need for more general recognition of the solitary life re-emerge. There may be all sorts of reasons for this. The need grew after the Second World War. It could be seen as a reaction to the horrors that war exposed, or to the speed and violence of a hectic technological age; or it could be a need that had never gone away. All the hermits I met spoke of a necessity, an absence of alternative.

I was surprised, having thought the energies of the established churches were all towards the other end of the religious spectrum. I was also disconcerted, as people always have been by hermits. Needing simply to be confronted by someone to whom the phenomenon was not unusual, to whom it seemed a perfectly sane and normal part of life, I went to see the spiritual adviser of several hermits, who was also a priest and a medieval historian. After that I understood the tradition a little better – understood, perhaps I should say, that there *was* a tradition.

In 1975 there was a meeting, at St Davids in Pembrokeshire, to discuss the Christian solitary life. Roman Catholics, Orthodox and Anglicans took part. The meeting acknowledged the continuing tradition of the solitary life in the Christian East and its rediscovery in the churches of the West. Solitaries looking for their own deserts took heart.

The meeting reflected among other things the way of thought of the contemplative nuns known as the Sisters of the Love of God at Fairacres in Oxford. They are an Anglican order set up in 1906 and influenced by the Oxford Movement, in which contemplative prayer was given greater importance than it had been in other sections of the Church. One has only to read Mrs Humphrey Ward's novel *Robert Elsmere* to see how much earnest agonizing the conflict between faith and works caused in the 1880s.

An irregular sort of trail presented itself to me. It took me from Godalming to Berwickshire, from North Wales to Florence. Slowly – because I was on unfamiliar ground – I learned a little about the life of the contemplative, and found it to be as it has always been. Hermits live as best they can on nothing much; they have to find a hermitage, and some means of subsistence. Their way of life being simple and in varying degrees ascetic, their needs are few; where they can, they grow their own vegetables, sometimes they keep bees. They are doorkeepers, calligraphers, gardeners, embroiderers of vestments, painters of icons, translators, carpenters. As they have always been.

I sat in a famous abbey and was told that there was nothing interesting about being a hermit, hundreds of people live alone, you spend your time fetching damp logs and trying to stop the fire from smoking; don't romanticize it, she said. She had spent seven years somewhere in Wales, there was a yew tree so old she thought Merlin might have sat under it. She was there because she had walked into the Sahara desert and had sat down and said to herself, here I will meet Yahweh, the fierce God of the Old Testament, but what had powerfully but quietly come was not Yahweh, and she had responded with her seven years of solitude. There was, she said, no alternative.

Ampleforth is a few miles from the ruins of the Carthusian monastery of Mount Grace. Rievaulx Abbey is not far away, nor is Fountains, both fine ruined witnesses to the power of the medieval monasteries. Ampleforth overlooks a wide valley, with the Yorkshire moors not far behind to the north. The English Catholic monastic orders moved to the Continent when Henry VIII proclaimed the dissolution of the monasteries. When they were allowed back into England in the nineteenth century the Benedictines in particular saw their duties as pastoral and educational, to administer to the English Catholics, often as parish priests, and to organize schools. This tradition has lasted. Father Aidan, whom I went to see at Ampleforth, had been at the school as a boy, become a monk, trained as a teacher at Oxford, been ordained as a priest after ten years and done further theological studies after that. Then he had taught in the school, and been a house master and novice master.

When he first suggested becoming a hermit, the attitude was simply, we don't have hermits – 'as it might have been, we don't keep bees', he said. He did not give up hope. His abbot seemed to be gradually coming round to the idea but then Father Basil Hume became abbot and the process of persuasion had to start again; Father Basil was cautious, and besides he wanted a house master. As a house master, prime time had to be given to the boys. Eventually, Father Aidan found a derelict cottage, the landlord gave him a licence to occupy, and Father Basil gave his permission. From 1969 to 1975 Father Aidan lived as a hermit on the Yorkshire moors, twelve miles from Ampleforth – too far, as his abbot had put it, for hermit-hunting boys on a Sunday afternoon.

Had he, after all, kept bees, I wondered. He had indeed, starting as a complete amateur, and had supplied his community with cutcomb honey. He had grown all sorts of vegetables too – 'always very neat' – and had fruit trees and bushes. His moorland surroundings were a source of great pleasure – he watched adders and stoats (which turned white in the winter), noted the date of arrival of the curlews (2 March), listened to the rare sound of the rodding woodcock, saw dippers, nuthatches, nesting redstarts, fishing herons. In silence and calm, he said, you noticed every wingbeat. Eventually he was called back to the monastery for other duties, and when I met him had been back in solitude for only a year – this time closer to the monastery, down in the valley among the trees.

We talked in the guest room. He had come out to meet me with friendly smiles, wearing the ordinary black Benedictine habit, and had ushered me along the passage with every sign of goodwill and slight nervousness; he said apologetically that the abbot had asked him to insist on seeing anything I might write, did I mind? I didn't mind; institutions have to protect themselves, and I had no wish to trap my courteous interlocutor into heresy. But the institutional atmosphere hung over us at first. Ampleforth Abbey is a big boarding school. I had a strange feeling that I was my own mother and that this kindly concerned schoolmaster might lean forward to say, Isabel doesn't seem to be fitting in very well, we are wondering whether this is really the right school for her? But I was talking to the hermit not the schoolmaster. His desire had been to live with God as a spouse. Thus he needed to be a hermit, but he was not determinedly reclusive – a Carthusian monk would be more so. He felt that the revision of Canon Law which had come about in 1983 and which allowed for the possibility of hermit life had been in response to demand from the bishops because of lay people who were wanting to pursue the solitary life and needed a framework, rather than at that time to meet the needs of professed monks and nuns. He was able to live as remotely as he did because he was a priest and could celebrate mass by himself. He was sympathetic to women priests who were only just beginning to be allowed to do the same. The disciplined and reasonably ascetic life suited his purpose, was his vocation. He would not recommend it lightly.

If one of the boys he had taught had wanted to be a hermit, Father Aidan would have counselled caution – and perhaps a trial period in a Carthusian monastery. He looked worried at the thought of this imaginary boy. When I asked him if he had suffered like St Antony from terrible temptations, he said he thought his hadn't been as bad. He had been in love two or three times, and that was difficult, because you were so concerned about what happened to the other person afterwards. He thought his worst failing was worry, disproportionate anxiety. There had been proposals that the abbey should build an underground sports complex for the school. Their space is limited and the buildings are on a steep hill; architects had come up with an exciting and extraordinarily expensive scheme. Father Aidan had suffered tortures of anxiety: did he want to be a monk in an institution which had an exciting and extraordinarily expensive sports complex? In the event the scheme was not pursued.

We went into the chapel for the noonday prayers; a young monk read to us about Northumbrian kings. Back in the guest room, Father Aidan entertained us to lunch, hospitably rueful about the quality of the food. The guest master brought us a jug of beer; it would have been better in the old days, said Father Aidan, something had happened to the brewery in Malton. He collected up the remains of the cheese into the knapsack he had brought for the purpose and when he had waved us goodbye set off down the hill towards the trees. He would be down there in the evening with his God, prayers said, the dogs of anxiety kenneled and quiet.

The hermit's daily life is not necessarily as regularized as that of a monk or nun. Sister Maximilian, whom I went to see in the beautiful North Tyne valley, to the north of the Roman wall, had written (and then sung) her own ceremony of committal as a hermit; but she wanted to emphasize her obedience. The Divine Office was the centre of her life, she said; she spent six hours a day chanting it, and she would make no decision about her way of life without reference to her spiritual adviser.

The sparsely populated country in this part of Northumberland is wooded where the valleys are, and marshy and sheep-grazed on the high hills. Generations come and go with the joys and sorrows flesh is heir to – births, deaths, marriages, bankruptcies, lunacies, divorces – but families seem somehow to stay put, the hermit's virtue of stability unthinkingly observed in a hard land whose hold is strong. Many seemed somehow never to have bothered to change their religion at the Reformation, escaping attention here in the hills; one family still painted their gates blue, the colour of the King over the Water; most seemed to have been at school at Catholic Ampleforth in Yorkshire with the old friend who was with us and with whom we had asked ourselves to stay. 'Sensible enough not to get involved in the Fifteen', he said of one family whose woods we passed. He meant that they had kept quiet during the Jacobite rebellions, unobtrusively holding on to their land as well as their faith. Round a corner, backed by high woods and a semi-circle of hills, was another estate and a perfectly enormous house. The owner's son-in-law had met a homeless hermit. 'Oh, they'll find room for you,' he'd said. They had, at once. I had come to see the hermit through the intercession of another friend.

'I'll take you up,' said John Charlton, the owner, setting off into the vastness within, walking with a stick. 'You'll like the lift.' I sat obediently in a structure rather like one of those booths you go into to take your own passport photograph. 'You can telephone New York if you like.' He indicated a shelf of instruments as we rose slowly towards the ceiling. He had had some trouble, had thought he would have to be in a wheelchair so had installed a lift which would allow for one. It would probably have allowed for a bed, had that been called for. On the floor above Sister Maximilian, a slight figure in a white habit, waited, had been downstairs, seen the others, come up again. I followed her up more stairs and into a large light sparsely furnished room, a former night nursery and temporary hermitage.

She had had to move, she told me. She had been in a cottage on some kind of repairing lease which had foundered; was it the cost of building work or the intrusive cows? Obviously, the problems of finding yourself a hermitage are acute, particularly if you are female and not built for heavy building work. Sister Maximilian's father had recently died and that meant that, through her uncle, she would have enough money to buy the bungalow she had found further north, in the middle of a Scottish moor. It was extremely basic, she said, but it had a small concrete building next to it, housing at the moment a number of pedigree terriers, which she hoped to turn into her chapel. But money bothered her – you can't, you really can't, serve God and Mammon, she said – I imagined some correct solicitor, explaining to her about her inheritance, confronted by a sudden burst of flame from the unarmed opponent across the desk.

A hermit, possessing nothing, she felt, could feel solidarity with the poor, could know also what it was like to count your money to see whether you could afford a loaf of bread, to be without a roof over your head, to sleep in the street. For it was not that you didn't care for the world; it was God's world. You were in love with God, so you were in love with his world. You were not rejecting it, only spreading your prayers for it more widely. She had been at prayer with her sister nuns in the convent when it was as if a voice had said, How would you like to be alone with me? So she had begun her quest to be a hermit. The moment had been as if someone she had been in love with all her life had asked her to marry him.

Sister Maximilian was forty-two, and had recently taken a vow as a diocesan hermit. She had been a Benedictine in Kent, had found the bishop there unwilling even to consider her request, and had had a long search to find a more sympathetic hearing. Her grandparents had died at Auschwitz, but that was not the main reason for her having become a nun in the first place – 'although I feel Jewish, certainly'. She had taken the name Sister Maximilian in memory of Maximilian Maria Kolbe, a priest who had been sent to Auschwitz for harbouring Jews and who had persuaded the German guards to let him die in the place of a man who had cried out, What is to become of my wife and children? Aware so strongly of evil, did she feel herself called to the combat in the desert like a soldier in the special services? She would rather emphasize penance, saw spiritual pride as a danger. Dangers and temptations were not the obvious ones: you recognized those and set yourself to overcome them. Living in solitude, with no one else to blame for your short-comings, there were temptations worse than carnal ones, but you could not long deceive yourself if you were alone with God. In the monastery there were too many prayers, too little prayer. She felt that French nineteenth-century monasticism had brought in an emphasis on words and work to the exclusion of silence and contemplation (she was speaking presumably of the Benedictine Order). She kept herself by meticulous heraldic painting and calligraphy, corresponded with other hermits – one in a high-rise flat in nearby Newcastle – had been doing a post-graduate degree at Oxford when she decided to become a nun; her parents had been upset. Like other hermits I met, she spoke affectionately of St Seraphim of Sarov, for whom the true purpose of life was 'the acquisition of the Holy Spirit'.

A month or so later, in November 1999, Sister Maximilian moved into her own remote hermitage over the Scottish border. We went to see her there some months later. Her white bungalow bore witness to her developing capacity as builder, decorator and vegetable gardener. She gave us some excellent spinach soup. In the corner was a pretty painted clavichord. It needed repair, but she did not yet trust herself to keep her love of music subservient to her present obligations. Perhaps one day she will, and the little instrument will come to life again, no longer a symbol of necessary sacrifice. In the meantime Sister Maximilian supports herself by her heraldic painting. The next day she was off down the motorway on her motorbike for a four-day calligraphy course somewhere in Wiltshire.

Not all hermits travel. For some the first principle remains the *fuga mundi*, the flight from the world. In 1965 the General Chapter of the Cistercian Order decided that an abbot should be able to give one of his monks permission to live as a solitary on the estates of the monastery. Father Theodore wrote to me in 1999:

> I availed myself of this immediately . . . For me it is simply a question of solitude: apart from that, I live much the same life as others live in community – prayer, reading, work. That is really all that there is to be said. From the beginning (I had had thirteen years of previous training and experience of Cistercian life in community) I found great joy, complete satisfaction and contentment in my solitary life, and it has continued to be so throughout the decades. Now, in my seventieth year, I hope to continue to the end so living.

Brother Patrick had said: 'Bring wellingtons, there are gates to open and it's muddy.' There was also a stream to cross, after the fields and the gates, and on the other side of the stream the path led up to a small stone cottage and a wide view of hills, over which the late autumn sunlight moved according to the movement of the clouds. Brother Patrick had to bend his head to come out of the door, a tall black-habited Greek Orthodox monk with a long red beard, in happy occupation of twenty acres of Welsh border wilderness. He is making a lake, has planted trees, has a neat vegetable garden down the hill which leads into a miniature valley with a stream running through it. On the stream, raised up on stone piles, he has built an even smaller hermitage of wood, from whose window you can look along the stream and through the trees. The building is beautifully designed and expertly made, extraordinarily satisfying. 'You love the purpose of the building, you love the materials . . .' It sounds easy.

Brother Patrick was born in England but spent his childhood and youth in New Zealand, coming back to England as an adult. He had met two Greek Orthodox monks and wanted to become a monk too. They suggested that he should travel first, so he went to monasteries in America and England, and acquired as his spiritual adviser a well-known Orthodox monk and academic, who suggested that he might work in a parish for a few years, which he did in Bath. After a year learning Greek at a Greek university he spent two years under obedience to a monk in North Wales and was then sent to Mount Athos for two years. He came back to England to live alone.

Brother Patrick was a sculptor before he became a monk, and his manual skills were developed during his time in the monastery on Mount Athos. His present hermitage, built originally to house a shepherd, had become a cow byre with a hayloft above it and a pigsty next door. It is now a simple but warm cottage, furnished in the main with wooden furniture which he made himself. His front door is made from coffin oak; he has made a pebble mosaic for the doorstep. The former pigsty is a chapel, its interior filled with the glowing colours of the frescoes which cover the walls. Brother Patrick is a skilled painter of icons, and his work supports his way of life; he has commissions enough to keep him busy for a long time to come. It was the painting of icons that led him to become a monk, rather than the other way round. The Greek Orthodox understanding of icons as a door into the spiritual life, a means of union between spirit and matter and between the soul and God, answered his own desire for closer union with God. Now he sees every human being as an icon, and believes that however overlaid by sin and error the icon of God is still there somewhere. He glows with enthusiasm, with desire that one should understand the beauty of his faith, that man is made in God's likeness, that we are part of the natural world, that in our search for scientific knowledge we have forgotten to celebrate our unity with each other and with God.

People seek out Brother Patrick, undaunted by the muddy path and the gates and the stream. He returns to his monastery on Mount Athos from time to time, but his is the age-old problem of the hermit who leaves the world only to find that the world follows him. He is a rasophore monk, wearing the rason, or monastic habit; in the Orthodox tradition no vows are taken at this stage, which means that there is more than one way still open to him.

I spoke to the spiritual adviser of another hermit with the same problem. She is a Benedictine nun, and her adviser is a monk from a monastery some way away from where she lives. She wrote several books, most of them 'under obedience', that is to say as tasks given to her by her superiors. This led to so much correspondence and activity that she had not enough time for solitude. In order to become a hermit, she had to have three permissions: those of her abbess, the Benedictine Council and the president-general of the Benedictines. She found a small cottage, where she works on translations of St Augustine, using the Internet for reference. Twice a week she keeps a night vigil. Her adviser goes to see her every month, walks, talks and eats with her. Modestly, he says he learns more from her than she does from him. He is always impressed by what he calls her joyfulness.

The prayer of most religious hermits, though not all, is contemplative prayer, which is apophatic prayer, or the way of negation, such as is referred to in the fourteenth-century *Cloud of Unknowing*, and the work of the sixteenth-century St John of the Cross, as well as in much of Zen Buddhism and Hinduism – and indeed it is expressed in the poetry of Rilke, among others. It requires solitude, in the same way as, for most poets, writing a poem requires solitude, because only in solitude can the chatter of the mind be stilled and full attention given to the matter in hand. For religious people the matter in hand is the Matter of God, which is one of the most interesting subjects in the world; but it is not one about which I am competent to write. I thought about it, though, sitting in the wood in front of the ornamental hermit's cell in the dead of winter, with the tall trees bare and only the sound of the wind in their topmost branches mingling with the usual stream below. I came to no conclusions, but was reminded that the dead of winter is a beautiful time of year.

I went for three days to a small convent of Anglican contemplative nuns on the Welsh borders, to look through their library. There were thirteen nuns, two of whom were young and one or two of whom were very old. One of the younger nuns had done her previous training with Buddhists; one of the older ones had received the last rites a few months earlier, but that had turned out to be premature. She had a special seat in the plain stone chapel, with a very bright light behind it so that she could read. The order is a silent one, and the silence feels like a benediction, perhaps because of the unseen others with whom it is shared. There is speech when it is necessary, and there are meetings and discussions to which people come from outside; there are also associates who come for short or longer visits. There is complete silence for most of the morning and after six o'clock in the evening. Once or twice a slip of paper slid under my door with helpful suggestions about the books I might need.

I became much attached to the kitchen scene, and found myself taking longer and longer to pass through to the small pantry where the guests do their washing-up. At certain times of the day the nuns are gently moving to and fro, washing up and putting things away, in peaceful silence and what seems like complete concentration. Once I saw a large and stately nun standing at one side of the kitchen, holding in her hand a red plastic tray with a cup on it. Serenely solemn, she rose into the air and disappeared through the ceiling. I had not realized that there was an open-sided lift just there. A painting by Stanley Spencer would have made the scene as uplifting as I felt it to be. The two nuns nearest to me saw my pleasure, and shared it.

In the chapel the young novice, Emma, sang the responses in a clear and tuneful treble. The old nuns quavered, but when it was their turn to read a passage, or to say the prayers, they did so plainly and well, the frail voices becoming immediately authoritative, as little boats whose sails are trembling suddenly steady when the familiar wind blows their way. Keep me as the apple of an eye, they said, hide me under the shadow of your wings.

I sat in a cabin in a field not far from the sea. Sheep-cropped grass filled half the view from the window; the rest was the sea beyond the cliff's edge and the blue-grey sky into which the sea merged. The sister sat straight-backed beside the window and talked of quantum physics, multi-worlds, how she had come to want to do nothing but explore the void. She had been a medical student until it had seemed to her that the spiritual being was more interesting than the physical one, and gradually this interest had become all-absorbing. She was an Anglican, and had been in a community of Anglican contemplative nuns. She had worked very hard running a retreat house in Chester and had become ill, and despairing, and felt she had been between life and death. Afterwards her need for solitude increased and she thought a great deal about something one of the nuns of the Fairacres Convent had said about the solitary being able to stand at the intersection between the love of God and suffering humanity. Walking on the cliffs one day she found an abandoned cabin which had been used as a holiday hut and persuaded the farmer who owned the field to allow her to repair and live in it. She had been there for eighteen years when I went to see her.

'What's a hermit, then?' said the farmer. 'People come and see her all the time. They bring her their troubles. When she has troubles, she brings them to me.'

Like the Charltons when they were giving shelter to Sister Maximilian, he was proud of his hermit. She shared the vicissitudes of farming life and the cycle of the seasons. She watched the dolphins below on their migrations and noticed the first lesser celandines and the first swallows. The lesser celandines were coming out earlier, she said, but the swallows kept to their old timetable, apparently unaffected by global warming. She had been in Vienna before the war, had been brought to England to escape the Nazis, being half-Jewish. She had thought she had forgotten all that, because she had been only five years old when she had left and she had been protected by a loving family, but in solitude some of it had come back to her. You go deeper and deeper into yourself, she said, but you are beyond ego. Her faith was connected with humanity and the human race, without that it would have no meaning. It is a journey of the mind, she said. You cannot name it. It is not this. It is not that. It is like this, but it is not this. It is like that, but it is not that. But it is love, she said; almost as an afterthought.

She was glad of her position as an outsider. The hermit's calling is anti-institutional. It is also ecumenical. Those in the institutional churches who approve of it say that it is at the heart of the church and not separated from it, but there are others who look on it as dangerous and potentially disorderly. If as the result of some great change the Christian Church should one day need to remake itself from the beginning, I'd say I have seen the hands which hold its kernel, like a hazel nut, or a monstrance saved in the sand, or an icon from the wall of a ruined chapel. But the hermit who went to meet Yahweh in the desert would say that that was romanticizing.

CHAPTER 15

'. . . a wish not to be seen . . .'

RECLUSIVE MISANTHROPES

Scopophobia — Howard Hughes —
the Duke of Portland – Calke Abbey – Stephen Tennant —
the hermit of Epping – Rodinsky's Room
— the Prisoner of Chillon

It seems our wood once had a rather superior entrance gate. One pillar alone was standing, but we found the other in pieces nearby and re-erected it, not without some difficulty because the stones were very heavy. Ian eventually constructed a pulley by which to raise the pediment to its proper place; the system was first used by the Phoenicians, he said.

Ian lives in a village on the outskirts of the Mendip Hills. There were tramps and gypsies and wandering knife-grinders in his childhood. He was told not to talk to the tramp who was often near the bus-stop when he was on his way to school, but he liked him so he did talk to him. Then there was a man who lived for very many years in an old cottage in the middle of a field. He was said to be the son of a respectable family who had banished him, no one knew why. He was seldom seen. Everyone knew he was there, but he was left alone. There used to be an old woman who drove goats through the village; she was a bit funny and lived alone. It was part of life in those days. I suppose there are villages where it is still part of life, and other villages where the social workers and the commuters and the general sanitization has done away with the eccentrics. You would find them now in the inner cities; it is probably sentimental to think things were any easier for them in the country.

Near Ian's village, there is a small wood in which a young man lives. He blackens his face with oil, and walks quite peaceably away when anyone approaches. Every two weeks someone from the social services comes for him, and drives him away in a taxi, but the next day he is back in the wood. His mother was the daughter of a local farmer, so he is not a stranger; he is just the young man who blackens his face and lives in the wood. Perhaps he suffers from scopophobia, the fear of being looked at.

The recluse who retreats from being seen, and from the horror of having to see himself being seen, may be suffering from no more than extreme timidity. Many shy people will cross the road rather than speak to an approaching acquaintance, whom in another mood they might be glad to see. A rather grand friend of mine was averse to being recognized while doing his shopping in the local supermarket – but that may have been something to do with etiquette. On the other hand, if allowed to run unchecked this kind of reluctance can develop into an advanced neurosis. Howard Hughes became so averse to being seen that no one knew what he looked like and a man called Clifford Irving was able to impersonate him, thus depriving him of many thousands of dollars.

Born in 1905, Hughes did not become a recluse until his mid-fifties. He died in 1976. He inherited an oil-well drilling equipment company from his father when he was young. Tall, not un-handsome, mad about aeroplanes and film stars, he seemed at first like a fairly average young American millionaire. He made a few films, and learnt to fly. Flying became his great enthusiasm; he set records, built the largest flying-boat in the world, and put together an enormously successful airline company, TWA. Power attracted him, and he intrigued with government officials, to whom he paid bribes for contracts. These circles led him into involvement with the CIA, which fed his incipient paranoia and made him more and more secretive. He surrounded himself with a palace guard of subservient underlings, and set up an organization called Rose-mount Enterprises which claimed large fees from any newspaper that mentioned his name. No one was allowed to take his photograph. He became increasingly demanding and dictatorial to work for and quite impossible to be married to.

His wife was a Hollywood star called Jean Peters. Hughes insisted on her giving up her career for the fourteen years during which they were married. For most of that time they lived in separate bungalows in the Beverly Hills Hotel, communicating by letter or telephone. Hughes lived in perpetual twilight, behind drawn curtains, surrounded by dust and crumbs because he could not bear anyone to come into the room to clean it, although at the same time he was paranoid about germs. On one occasion his wife forced an entrance with a vacuum cleaner, but it was so dark that she could only see where to clean with a member of Hughes's staff crawling along the floor ahead of her with a torch. Hughes was careful never to touch anything which had not first been disinfected, and would not allow anyone other than himself to touch his cupboard handles or the knobs on the television set, for fear of contamination. He would not cut his toenails, and they became so long that they rattled when he turned over in bed. For a time his wife used to insert pieces of paper between his toes to reduce the noise, but before long he would only see her for twenty minutes a day before dinner, and in the last ten years of their marriage they seldom met at all. He still proclaimed that he had always loved her. After they were divorced and she had remarried, he bought houses on either side of the new marital home, and two houses opposite, so that she could be kept under observation. He was apparently obsessed with the thought that she might be kidnapped and that he, rather than the new husband, would be expected to pay the ransom.

After his divorce and after he had sacked his devious but sane business manager Noah Dietrich, Howard Hughes became almost unapproachable. At the time of his death the Internal Revenue Service was trying to investigate his affairs. He died, in a state of complete self-neglect, on an aeroplane; his desperate attendants were trying to get him to hospital in Houston. He left vast areas of land, companies, hotels, more than 200 million dollars in notes, and no will.

The nineteenth-century Duke of Portland must always have been a scopophobe, one who cannot bear to be seen. His servants were dismissed if they were caught looking at him. When he was ill he would consult the doctor only through a closed door. When he went to London from his country house, Welbeck Abbey in Nottinghamshire, he was driven to the local station in his coach with the blinds drawn. The coach, with the duke still inside it, was then loaded on to a railcar at the back of the London train and met at the other end by a coachman with a fresh pair of horses who took him to his town house in Cavendish Square. He caused to be built fifteen miles of tunnels, so that he could drive to the station without being seen; the tunnels were gas-lit and lined with glazed white bricks. There was also an underground ballroom, though there is no evidence that he ever gave a ball there. There was a billiard room as well, and an underground railway to carry food from the kitchen to the dining-room, a hundred and fifty yards away.

The kindest explanation of the duke's underground activities is that he undertook all the building in order to provide work for local labourers at a time of agricultural depression. He employed over ten thousand men, and gave each of them a donkey and an umbrella as a bonus.

The Harpur-Crewe family of Calke Abbey in Derbyshire were more or less hereditary hermits, at least from the days of the eighteenth-century Sir Henry Harpur, known as the 'Isolated Baronet'. His descendant in the early years of the twentieth century, Sir Vauncey Harpur-Crewe, was more interested in birds and butterflies than in his daughters, with whom he communicated only by letter, although they lived in the same house. He left a vast collection of stuffed birds, still to be seen in the house, which now belongs to the National Trust. The last member of the family to live in the house was one of the most reclusive. He died setting traps for moles in the park, and when, as a result of death duties, the house came to the National Trust, the rooms were found to have been almost unchanged for the last hundred years, except that nothing had ever been thrown away. The family's preference for the hermit life seems to have been congenital rather than a matter of principle; they do not seem to have been a lively lot, but were probably contented enough in their own way.

Accidental hermits are not usually contented. Some are widows or widowers, some are neglected, unloved or paralytically shy, some have given their lives to an institution or a business and find they have nothing to think about when they retire, some hate the world only because the world seems to hate them. Alone through chance rather than choice, they fail to see anything in solitude to enjoy, and escape it by whatever means they can. Some let it take them over, passively allowing their world to diminish as if there were no other way to be alone than to fall in upon yourself like an unused building. Past success is no comfort. The poet Siegfried Sassoon was more or less a recluse for the last few years of his life, and not far away (within easy visiting distance but they did not visit) Stephen Tennant, object of the poet's former passion, was even more withdrawn from the world. Neither was happy. Both had known other ways and could still at times regret them.

The writer V. S. Naipaul rented a cottage for some years in the grounds of Stephen Tennant's house not far from Salisbury. During the time that he lived there he glimpsed his landlord only twice. *The Enigma of Arrival*, half novel, half-prolonged autobiographical meditation, uses the reclusive figure as a metaphor of loss, lost beauty, lost empire, lost place in the world. 'Here in the valley there now lived only my landlord, elderly, a bachelor, with people to look after him. Certain physical disabilities had now been added to the malaise of which I had no precise knowledge, but interpreted as something like accidie, the monk's torpor or disease of the middle ages – which was how his great security, his excessive worldly blessings, had taken him. The accidie had turned him into a recluse, accessible only to his intimate friends.'

Naipaul had seen faded photographs of parties once held in the grounds, glamorous young people from the fast set of the 1920s posed in fancy dress, the host the most extravagantly dressed and made up, camp at its gayest. Now the untended gardens dripped in the rain and the host, once renowned for his beauty, had grown fat; glimpsed back view sitting on a chair in the garden, he exposed a shining plump knee.

Naipaul saw him only on one other occasion, being driven in his car along a lane, between beech trees, waving 'a little low wave ... I invested that wave with his shyness, the shyness of his illness, the shyness that went at the same time with a great vanity, the shyness that wasn't so much a wish not to be seen as a wish to be applauded on sight, to be recognised on sight as someone stupendous and of great interest.'

Not a scopophobe, in other words, so much as a narcissist. Not surprisingly, Tennant had periods of serious depression during his years of seclusion, but a few friends remained, and though he was sometimes unwilling to see them or strangely nervous when he did, at other times he would be wildly excited. Cecil Beaton lived not far away and would often bring over visitors. Christopher Isherwood and his friend Don Bachardy were delighted by the performance Tennant produced for them in the summer of 1961. Cecil Beaton drove them over to Wilsford, the fine house in the Queen Anne style which the Edwardian architect Dettmar Blow had built for Stephen Tennant's mother, and found it full of 'still lives (on floors & chairs) consisting of lengths of material, pyjama tops, shells, bears, lots of soap (with carnation-pictured lids), with huge Italian straw hats ... littering the staircase ... The sketch books & diaries & pictures are displayed on the floor with a fan, a glove, a mask – a straw tray.'

Beaton went upstairs and found Tennant 'lying like a porpoise in one of the many bedrooms he inhabits ... fat & appallingly painted with a bang of greasy dyed hair over his forehead ... His finger nails were not very clean.' He insisted on seeing his visitors and entertained them with his enthusiastic admiration, and a flood of talk about California and his favourite American writer, Willa Cather. He took them out into the garden, and became, in Cecil Beaton's account, 'as he used to be, a simple boy who loved his nannies, insects, nature ... like Peter Pan among the trees'. But then Beaton's immaculate taste was appalled by the orchard: 'a mess of statues – some even painted pink and gold; iron heron, wire archways, potted palms, stone bordered beds that might have been part of Bournemouth's Municipal Gardens. Christopher, accustomed to the vulgarity of Hollywood, could yet not believe such things were possible.'

The visit ended with photographs, much enjoyed by the recluse. 'Oh, show my legs, please!' he cried.

The Hermit of Epping may not have been born a scopophobe; he was probably reduced to the condition by a cruel father. Raleigh Trevelyan wrote about him in *A Hermit Observed*, first published in 1960.

The house in which Trevelyan lived as a child had once belonged to the family of the hermit, Jimmy Mason, whose hut was hidden away in a corner of the orchard. Trevelyan found Jimmy's diary, written between 1895 and 1897, hidden in the attic. Over a period of years he transcribed the diary and gradually became fascinated by the picture, albeit one-sided, that it gave of a whole village at a particular point in its history. Jimmy's hut had started as a retreat from his strict and sometimes violent father, but as the boy grew up he became more and more reclusive and finally moved into the hut altogether. He died there in 1942 at the age of eighty-four.

In spite of the detail in Trevelyan's book, and the picture it gives of a small village in the early part of this century, the dramas and superstitions, the suppressed feuds and secret suspicions which lay beneath its life of outward calm, the mystery of the hermit is never quite resolved. He was protected by his brother Tommy, who lived at the gate of the orchard in the far corner of which, behind the vegetables and the beehives, Jimmy lived, and from which he would sometimes emerge when no one was about to stick apples or sweets or notes on the hawthorn hedge for the girls who passed and to whom it seems he never spoke: Lucie, Lillie, Fanny Bell. He was said to have had two religious experiences – 'something so strange come down from heaven' – and to have sometimes suspected that he was being poisoned. In 1927 there were some rather sensational newspaper articles about 'The Hermit of Great Canfield' who had renounced the world after being jilted by the girl he loved. Fanny Bell revisited him after a gap of fifty years for a tearful reunion and a photocall.

It seems more likely to have been the fear of his father that made Jimmy into a hermit. The Rector of Great Canfield, who knew him, said: 'He was a gentle, lovable old man, so shy he could hardly bear to look at other people. He kept bees, grew his few plants, and read his Bible. That was his whole life.'

There is a tendency to mythologize the solitary, whose story often turns out to be simpler than at first supposed. He is expected to provide a fable, or at very least a symbol. In the Spitalfields area of London there is a synagogue, no longer used, in which there lived at one time a man called Rodinsky. Spitalfields is one of the many parts of London which were once separate entities with histories of their own, and which became absorbed in the spreading metropolis; it was the centre of the East End Jewish community. The immigrants in that area now are mostly from Bangladesh, except for those more prosperous residents who have moved into the Georgian houses and formed the Spitalfields Historic Buildings Trust. These new enthusiasts became interested in Rodinsky. He had disappeared, leaving his room above the synagogue untidily filled with his few belongings and his many books and papers. An article about him appeared in the *London Review of Books*. He became some kind of icon, representing the loss of tradition within the Jewish community, and the possible threat to cultural continuity from the gentrification of a particular area. He was written about in evocative terms by Ian Sinclair, whose explorations in some of the more obscure areas of London were well known.

Later, Sinclair wrote a book with a Jewish artist called Rachel Lichtenstein whose own grandparents had settled in East London after their escape from Poland in the 1930s. She had become obsessed with the story of the vanished hermit Rodinsky, whose past had so much in common with her own, and in the end she elucidated it. In the 1960s he had been confined in an asylum called the Longrove, which was, so she was told, 'the kind of place that was full of cabbalistic geniuses and religious scholars wrapped up in the world of metaphysics. In that period there were many mistakes made . . . there were very serious communication problems.' Rachel Lichtenstein found Rodinsky's grave, and said the Kaddish over it, which is the Jewish prayer for the dead.

Rodinsky would have done quite well somewhere down in someone's woods; it would have suited the situation if he had disappeared, leaving only his few mysterious traces. Like the hermit in Tom Stoppard's play *Arcadia*, the puzzle of his identity would only have enlarged his potential significance. He could have been part of the dance to the music of time which is Stoppard's intricate theme, the figure in the landscape which represents the impossibility of ever knowing for sure what really happened anywhere.

Any Solitary could become a scopophobe; that is one of the dangers to be averted. Byron's Prisoner of Chillon, finally freed from the cell in which he had been confined, had no wish to leave it:

> These heavy walls to me had grown
> A hermitage – and all my own!
> And half I felt as they were come
> To tear me from a second home.

He had become diminished, like a battery chicken.

CHAPTER 16

'I think I need this hill . . .'

THE DESIRE AND PURSUIT OF SOLITUDE

John Carter — A Time to Keep Silence —
Thomas Merton and Rilke — Richard Jefferies —
Thomas Traherne — Mr Disney Roebuck and his hermitage

Not much is known about Mr Henry Disney Roebuck, who built the hermit's cell in our wood. He was certainly no hermit himself. It seems he was left money by an uncle in Yorkshire and married as his second wife a rich Bath widow. He decided to build himself a house outside that city and chose a design by an architect of the time (1775 was the year) for *A Gothic Mansion to be Erected on an Eminence that Commands an Extensive Prospect*. The architect was a rather furious fellow called John Carter, and the design was to be found in a magazine he edited called *The Builders Magazine*.

Carter was a passionate Gothicist, and believed that most of the restorations of the time – especially those undertaken by his late employer, James Wyatt – were inaccurate and disrespectful, and his criticisms of them were often intemperate. Evidently a musician as well as a scholar, he wrote an opera called *St Oswald's Cell*, 'based on the habits of former times', but nothing seems to be known of it now. Curiously enough, he must have approved of Horace Walpole's Gothic house at Strawberry Hill, with its pretty mixture of the genuine and the playful, because he did some water-colours of the interiors. He probably never saw the interiors of the house Mr Roebuck built, because it seems that local builders adapted the design and made the inside of it more or less what they were used to, with leafy plasterwork rather than the awesome vaults John Carter might have preferred.

Mr Disney Roebuck did not spend all his time in his new house.

He had other properties, including a considerable estate in Kent. In due course he and his wife were divorced – unusually for those days – and he lived alone on a yacht off the coast of Kent, not far from Deal. Perhaps he did have some inclination for solitude after all. It seems more likely, though, that his impulse in laying out his little wood with walks and a folly and a hermitage was simply to be up to date. Fashion dictated that eighteenth-century pleasure grounds should make space for contemplation as well as conviviality.

Before he went off to end his days as a solitary yachtsman, Mr Disney Roebuck sold his house to an anaesthetist, a pioneer in the science of obstetrics called Benjamin Pugh, who died in 1797. The property then went to a family called Conolly, illegitimately descended from the grand Conollys of Castletown in Ireland. They were proud of the connection and caused the Conolly coat of arms to be displayed on doors and windows wherever space could be found. The last of them, a widow, was of Neapolitan descent and an extremely devout Roman Catholic. Perhaps she made her way across the muddy English field to mutter her lonely foreign prayers in the hermit's cell. It seems more likely that she forgot all about it, for soon after her death it seems to have disappeared. It vanished under the damp earth in the years of the wood's decay.

When Patrick Leigh Fermor visited several different monasteries in the 1950s, he described in his subsequent book, *A Time to Keep Silence*, his discovery of his own capacity for solitude: 'in the seclusion of a cell . . . the troubled waters of the mind grow still and clear, and much that is hidden away and all that clouds it floats to the surface and can be skimmed away; and after a time one reaches a state of peace that is unthought of in the ordinary world.'

This is Wordsworth's 'calm existence that is mine/ When I am worthy of myself'. It is a condition of extreme wakefulness. Leigh Fermor found that on his initial visit to the Abbey of St Wandrille in France he spent the first few days in a state of disorientation and great need for sleep. Once this need had been assuaged, he found that 'night shrank to five hours of light, dreamless and perfect sleep, followed by awakenings full of energy and limpid freshness'.

It is this attentiveness which is the reward of the diligent hermit. Even a brief period of solitude, undertaken perhaps for some entirely practical reason, such as the need to get something finished – a book, a thought, a hedge – tends to clear the mind and improve concentration. Religious hermits concentrate on God and on their chosen duty of prayer for the whole world, poets pursue that truth which they believe to be there although it may be just beyond their reach. Scientists know this too; they pursue a particular theory when they believe that it is out there to be found.

If the reality the contemplative apprehends turns out not to be 'out there' so much as already within, that is surely Eliot's 'the end of all our exploring/Will be to arrive where we started/And know the place for the first time'. The exploration is not the same for the religious hermit as for the poet, because the poet has to come back with news. The hermit's venture into the interior can go beyond words.

The American monk Thomas Merton, who died in 1968, having spent the last few years of his life in increasing solitude within his monastery, wrote of this difference in his diary. He was reading Rilke, a German poet hard to grasp in translation, whose intense investigations of consciousness struck him as similar to his own.

In the *Duino Elegies*, Rilke wrote

> Never, not for a single day, do we have
> before us that pure space into which flowers
> endlessly open. Always there is World
> and never Nowhere without the No; that pure
> unseparated element which one breathes
> without desire and endlessly knows. A child
> may wander there for hours, through the timeless
> stillness, may get lost in it and be
> shaken back. Or someone dies and is it.

Rilke, who lived from 1875 to 1926, was writing at a time when reality seemed to be collapsing round him (he was born in Czechoslovakia, when that country was still part of the Austrian Empire). Much of his most lyrical poetry is a passionate attempt to return to the pure consciousness of the very young child who cannot tell the difference between itself and the world around it; this search fascinated and at the same time threatened him. His life's work was an attempt to lose himself in the essence of being without also losing the ego which produced the poems. He felt it extremely important to protect his poetic ego from too many outside demands; luckily a succession of charming and interesting and rich women were prepared to help him do so.

Merton wrote, on 29 November 1965:

> This morning I really opened the door of Rilke's *Duino Elegies* and walked in . . . For one thing I got the *sound* of the German really going, and got the feel of the First Elegy as a whole . . . I think I need this hill, this silence, this frost, to really understand this great poem, to live in it – as I have also lived in *Four Quartets* . . . the *Duino Elegies* and *Four Quartets* talk about my life itself, my own self, my own destiny, my Christianity.

A few days later he wrote: 'My solitude is not like Rilke's, ordered to a poetic explosion . . . What is it then? What has been so far only a theological conception, or an image, has to be sought and loved. "Union with God!" So mysterious that in the end man would perhaps do anything to evade it, once he realises it means the *end* of his own Ego-self-realization, once and for all.'

During the last years of his life Merton became increasingly interested in Eastern religion, particularly Zen Buddhism, in which he found much in common with the Christian mystical tradition, and about which he wrote one of his best books, *Zen and the Birds of Appetite*. It was on a journey to the East that he died, at the age of fifty-four, accidentally electrocuted by a faulty fan in the cottage where he was staying at a conference centre.

Merton had become enthusiastic about photography in the months before his death. A friend who was a professional photographer had noticed his interest and given him a camera. It became one of Merton's greatest pleasures and a means of recording the increasing attentiveness to natural phenomena which he was developing in his solitude. He photographed natural forms – trees, roots, branches – as well as corners of his hermitage, an old bench, a watering can. The intense appreciation of his natural surroundings was something he came to see he needed to be alone for, just as Ruskin did when he wrote: 'I could only feel this perfectly when I was alone; and then it would often make me shiver from head to foot with the joy and fear of it.'

The joy and fear are difficult to convey in prose, and few have achieved it. Richard Jefferies tried, in *The Story of My Heart*, published in 1883. Jefferies was a secular solitary. He said he had no religion, although much of his writing seems more or less pantheistic. He found it extremely difficult to express the strength and power of his feelings when he was alone with nature, or the depth of his longing to give voice to them. Ivor Gurney had music for such feelings, and poetry for his less intense apprehensions, but Jefferies had only a workmanlike prose, and a wonderfully observant eye for the small particulars of natural life.

He was born in 1848, a farmer's son. His boyhood at Coate Farm, not far from Swindon, is the source of *Bevis, the Story of a Boy*, a children's book which he published in 1882. By that time he was becoming known as a writer on natural history and rural life; his first book, *The Gamekeeper at Home*, was a collection of articles that had first appeared in the *Pall Mall Gazette*. His country writings had some success, and because he wrote to support his wife and children he continued to produce them, but he felt he could have done more as a writer. *The Story of My Heart*, which was published in 1883, was not what people expected of him and its pantheistic tone was thought improper.

> I was utterly alone with the sun and the earth. Lying down on the grass, I spoke in my soul to the earth, the sun, the air, and the distant sea far beyond sight. I went there every morning, I could not exactly define why . . . Later on I began to have daily pilgrimages to think these things. There was a feeling that I must go somewhere, and be alone . . . After the sensuous enjoyment always came the thought, the desire: that I might be like this; that I might have the inner meaning of the sun, the light, the earth, the trees and grass, translated into some growth of excellence in myself, both of body and of mind; greater perfection of physique, greater perfection of mind and soul; that I might be higher in myself.

Jefferies was a middle-aged man when he wrote this, and in some ways he expresses his feelings more completely when he writes in the person of his idealized boyhood self. The smell of the mud on the marshy edge of a pond is not inexpressible, nor is the activity of a flock of small birds feeding on hawthorn berries in winter; these things can be described precisely. Bevis and his friend Mark hollow out a cave on their island, and extend it by building a hut on to the front of it, a perfect hermitage, its method of construction exactly detailed.

Had he been born in the seventeenth century, as was Thomas Traherne, Jefferies might have found the English language better adapted to his needs: 'so is there in us a World of Lov to somwhat, tho we know not what in the World that should be. There are Invisible Ways of Conveyance by which some Great Thing doth touch our Souls, and by which we tend to it. Do you not feel yourself Drawn with the Expectation and Desir of some Great Thing?' Jefferies could not have read Thomas Traherne, because no one had read him in Jefferies' time. Until the chance discovery of two manuscripts on two separate London book-barrows in 1897, very little was known of the man who was vicar of the small village of Credenhill in Herefordshire from 1657 until his death in 1674. Those manuscripts were published in 1908 as *Centuries of Meditations*. Other manuscripts have been slowly emerging. One was recovered from a burning rubbish heap in Lancashire, one was found in a Washington library, another among theological manuscripts in the library of Lambeth Palace. An anonymous contemporary of Traherne's wrote, in a preface to one of his works, that he spent 'most of his time when at home, in digesting his notions . . . into writing', and Traherne himself expressed his pleasure at finding that his soul was 'so Prone to Imployment', so there is no reason to suppose that there may not be more discoveries to be made.

'One great Discouragement to Felicity,' he wrote, 'or rather to great Souls in the Persuit of Felicity, is the Solitariness of the Way that ledeth to her Temple. A man that Studies Happiness must sit alone like a Sparrow upon the Hous Top, and like a Pelican in the Wilderness.'

This happiness is not the unlooked-for solitude of the abandoned, or the bereaved, or the disgruntled. It is the elected silence of someone who choses to look within himself for that capacity with which we are all born, diminished though it may become through neglect, to lose ourselves utterly in what we see, or hear, or do, as a child does, engrossed in a world of play. Then looking sees beyond appearances and listening hears the perfection of silence. So are the doors of perception cleansed.

Traherne was born in 1637, the son of a Herefordshire shoemaker – possibly quite a successful shoemaker, for Aubrey says he employed two apprentices. Perhaps he had enough money to send his son to Brasenose College in Oxford at fifteen or sixteen, or perhaps by that time Thomas and his brother Philip were orphans, in the care of Philip Traherne, a successful innkeeper who was twice Mayor of Hereford. Thomas Traherne was appointed to the living at Credenhill in 1657, but seems not to have been ordained until 1660, by which time the Restoration of the monarchy under Charles II meant the return of the Anglican faith. He acquired a patroness in the person of Mrs Susanna Hopton, a devout lady who had a circle of friends interested in religion, and through whose good offices he was appointed chaplain to Sir Orlando Bridgeman, the Lord Keeper of the Privy Seal, a position which he held until the latter's fall from power in 1672. It seems that he enjoyed the world into which his position took him. It was not only nature that he loved, but art and talk as well. Perhaps it was to remind himself that he wrote, 'A little colour in the face, a gay Coat, a fine Horse, a Palace and a Coach, an Exchequer full of Gold . . .'Tis better starve than eat such empty fruit'.

In the most visionary of his writings it is clear that he speaks from direct experience, an experience which goes back again and again to the world of childhood.

The corn was orient and immortal wheat. Which never should be reaped, nor was ever sown. I thought it had stood from everlasting to everlasting. The Dust and Stones of the Street were as Precious as Gold. The gates were at first the End of the World, the Green Trees when I saw them first through one of the Gates Transported and Ravished me; their Sweetnes and unusual Beauty made my Heart to leap, and almost mad with Extasie, they were such strange and Wonderfull Things . . . Boys and Girls Tumbling in the Street, and Playing, were moving Jewels. I knew not that they were Born or should Die. But all things abided eternally as they were in their Proper Places. Eternity was Manifest in the Light of the Day, and som thing infinit Behind evry thing appeared: which talked with my Expectation and moved my Desire.

Unlike Coleridge, Clare and Gurney, Traherne seems to have been able to hold on to that childhood vision, or rather to recover it in adulthood after a period of doubt, caused by his exposure to 'corrupt Custom': 'I knew by Intuition those things which since my Apostasie, I Collected again, by the Highest Reason.' This is recollection in maturity, as described by Wordsworth on his second visit to Tintern. Traherne trusted in reason, as well as in the direct apprehension of God. Believing that the 'child's eye' is man's natural inheritance, he thought the proper aim should be to become a child again with all the consciousness of an adult.

Traherne continued to combine his duties as chaplain to the Lord Keeper with those of rector of Credenhill until Sir Orlando Bridgeman fell from power. Bridgeman died in 1674. Thomas Traherne died three months later, aged thirty-seven.

Traherne must have possessed within himself both those qualities which the eighteenth-century idea of the hermitage expresses: the capacity for devout contemplation and the love of conversation with his friends. It seems he sometimes talked too much. The anonymous preface to one of his works describes him as 'a man of cheerful and sprightly temper . . . very affable and pleasant in his conversation', but there is a slight suggestion that some people might have found him too much of an enthusiast, even a bit of a bore: 'He was so full of [these things] when abroad, that those who would converse with him, were forced to endure some discourse upon these subjects, whether they had any sense of Religion, or not. And therefore to such he might be sometimes thought troublesome, but his company was very acceptable to all such as had any inclinations to Vertue, and Religion.'

He himself wrote, somewhat ruefully: 'Profound Inspection, Reservation and Silence; are my Desires. O that I could attain them: too much openness and proneness to speak are my Disease. Too easy and complying a nature. Speaking too much and too Long in the Best Things . . . Here I am Censured for speaking in the singular number, and saying I.'

The eighteenth-century builders of hermitages were playing with ideas of paradise, drawing together what they had absorbed from their studies of the classics and their travels in Italy, what they read in their libraries and looked at in the paintings of Poussin and Claude, making ideal worlds and walking about in them, in the knowledge that the real world was not like that and that these delightful creations would probably bankrupt them, as quite often happened. In that sociable age, the merits of solitude were appreciated, but it was not felt that contemplation need necessarily exclude conviviality. The eighteenth-century amateur hermit – who of course for the most part was the proprietor himself, or some member of his family, pausing on an afternoon walk – was often also a serious amateur scientist, or archaeologist, or for that matter theologian. No one could complain, for instance, of the acuteness of Gilbert White's solitary observations, nor of the seriousness of his application to his chosen study. Here he is on 18 April 1768:

I make no doubt but there are three species of the willow-wrens: two I know perfectly; but have not been able yet to procure the third. No two birds can differ more in their notes, and that constantly, than those two that I am acquainted with; for the one has a joyous, easy, laughing note; the other a harsh loud chirp. The former is every way larger, and three-quarters of an inch longer, and weighs two drams and a half; while the latter weighs but two; so the songster is one-fifth heavier than the chirper. The chirper (being the first summer-bird of passage that is heard, the wryneck sometimes excepted) begins his two notes in the middle of March, and continues them through the spring and summer till the end of August, as appears by my journals. The legs of the larger of these two are flesh-coloured; of the less, black.

On 29 January 1774, he is thinking about the bird whose return after the winter is the one that always most delights him:

All the summer long is the swallow a most instructive pattern of unwearied industry and affection; for, from morning to night, while there is a family to be supported, she spends the whole day in skimming close to the ground, and exerting the most sudden turns and quick evolutions. Avenues, and long walks under hedges, and pasture-fields and mown meadows where cattle graze, are her delight, especially if there are trees interspersed; because in such spots insects most abound. When a fly is taken a smart snap from her bill is heard, resembling the noise at the shutting of a watch-case; but the motion of the mandibles are too quick for the eye.

Nevertheless, he builds his hermitage most sociably by the path leading up to the hill overlooking the village, so that anyone walking up to see the evening view from the top may pause there; and when he is in a cheerful mood he dresses up his brother Harry in a hermit's smock and invites his neighbours to a picnic, with melons from his garden.

*   *   *

So I like to think that Mr Disney Roebuck, not wishing to be a spiritual commando, not aspiring at all to be a saint, might have paused by his newly erected hermit's cell not just to congratulate himself on keeping up with the fashion set by his grander neighbours, but to sit still for a little and give his attention to the sound of solitude before continuing on his way to his commodious tea-room.

SOURCES

There are a great number of books on the subject of hermits and solitaries. In the following notes I have mentioned those from which I have quoted as well as those most likely to interest a reader wanting to go further into matters I had only touched upon.

INTRODUCTION

Sir Henry Hoare's letter to his granddaughter Harriet is quoted in Kenneth Woodbridge, *Landscape and Antiquity: Aspects of English Culture at Stourhead 1718–1838* (1970).

John Ruskin, *Modern Painters*, Vol. III (1856).

G. M. Trevelyan, *The Call and Claims of Natural Beauty* (1931).

CHAPTER 1 *'Going to see the hermit, finding him gone . . .'*

The chapter title comes from Jai Dao's poem 'On Looking in Vain for the Hermit'.

The poem by Li Bai is translated by Vikram Seth in *Three Chinese Poets* (1992).

As I have mentioned in the text, Bill Porter's *Road to Heaven: Encounters with Chinese Hermits* (1993) told me about present-day hermits in China and John Crook and James Low's *The Yogins of Ladakh* (1977) is an immensely informative and expert study.

Two Views of Mind by Christopher deCharms (1998) examines the differences and similarities between Buddhist and Western scientific theories of perception.

Cave in the Snow by Vicki Mackenzie (1988) tells the story of Tenzin Palmo.

I went to see the model temple in the Victoria and Albert Museum because it is mentioned in Peter Levi's *The Frontiers of Paradise: A*

Study of Monks and Monasteries (1987), a book I returned to many times, always with pleasure.

Madame Blavatsky has been extensively written about, most recently in Peter Washington's *Madame Blavatsky's Baboon* (1993). There is an account of her time in Simla in Edward J. Buck's *Simla Past and Present* (1904).

Krishnamurti (1990) is a condensation by Mary Lutyens from her earlier two-volume biography.

Kipling's story 'The Miracle of Purun Bhagut' comes from the second *Jungle Book* (1985). Swami Abhishiktananda's *The Secret of Arunachala* (1979) is a delightful account of his hermit experiences on that holy mountain. There is also *Swami Abhishiktananda: His Life Told through His Letters*, edited by James Stuart (1990).

Somerset Maugham's description of his visit to the Maharshi comes in a collection of essays called *Points of View* (1936).

CHAPTER 2   *'Cedar, and pine, and fir, and branching palm . . .'*

The chapter title comes from Milton's description of the Garden of Eden in *Paradise Lost*, Book IV.

The irreverent quotations from Edward Lear come from his letters to Chichester Fortescue, October 1856 and January 1857, quoted in *Edward Lear in the Levant*, compiled and edited by Susan Hyman (1988).

Peter Frances, *Hermits: the Insights of Solitude* (1996) was helpful on Russian hermits, and indeed on the whole subject. So too were John B. Dunlop's *Staretz Amvrosy; Model for Dostoevsky's Staretz Zossima* (1972) and V. Zander's *St. Seraphim of Sarov* (1975).

Tolstoy, *A Confession and Other Religious Writings* is translated by Jane Kentish (1987).

Ian Hamilton's life of J. D. Salinger was published in 1988.

The story of Agafia Lykov is told in *Lost in the Taiga* by Vasily Peskov (1994).

CHAPTER 3 '*. . . sighing once again to take part in its pleasures and allurements . . .*'

The chapter title comes from George Frederick Ruxton, *Life in the Far West* (1849), quoted more fully in the text.

Letters of Pliny the Younger, translated by E. T. Merrill (1903).

Mircea Eliade, *Bengal Nights* (1994); *Shamanism* (1964); Autobiography Vol. I (1981).

Maitreyi Devi, *It Does Not Die* (1994).

On the American frontier, Roderick Nash's *Wilderness and the American Mind* (1969) and R. A. Billington, *The American Frontiersman* (1954) were interesting.

Jon Krakauer's *Into the Wild* (1996) tells the story of Chris McCandless.

CHAPTER 4 '*. . . then would I wander far off, and remain in the wilderness . . .*'

The chapter title is taken from Psalm 55.

Among the many books on the hermits of the desert are:

Peter Anson, *The Call of the Desert* (1964).
D. J. Chitty, *The Desert a City* (1966).
Caroline White (ed. and trans.), *Early Christian Lives* (1988).

Eugene F. Rice, Jr, *Saint Jerome in the Renaissance* (1985).
J. N. D. Kelly, *Jerome, His Life, Writings and Controversies* (1975).

The quotation from Edward Gibbon's *Decline and Fall of the Roman Empire* comes from chapter 37.

Peter Brown, *The Rise and Function of the Holy Man in Late Antiquity* – this brilliant essay, first published in 1971, started trails which are still being followed, not only by the author himself but by the whole army of his students and admirers in universities all over the world.

Helen Waddell, *Beasts and Saints*, ed. and introduced by Esther de Waal (1995).
D. H. Farmer (ed.), *The Age of Bede* (1965).

Julia Butterfly Hill, *The Legacy of Luna* (2000).

Karen Armstrong's *A History of God* (1992) is full of thought-provoking matter on this whole subject.

CHAPTER 5   *'The act of departure is the bravest and most beautiful of all . . .'*

The chapter title comes from Isabelle Eberhardt.

Anne Freemantle, *Desert Calling* (1950) is a biography of Charles de Foucauld.
Jean-François Six, *Charles de Foucauld* (1982) includes photographs of the stark Hoggar mountains as well as of the hermit himself.
Lesley Blanch, *The Wilder Shores of Love* (1954).
Isabelle Eberhardt, *The Oblivion Seekers* (1975).

Frank Hamel, *Lady Hester Stanhope* (1913).
Alexander Kinglake, *Eothen* (1906).

The Epic of Gilgamesh, trans. N. K. Sandars (1972).

CHAPTER 6   *'A clear pool to wash away sins . . .'*

The chapter title comes from a ninth-century Irish hermit's song, translated by Kuno Meyer and quoted in Meyer (ed.), *Selections from Ancient Irish Poetry* (1911).

William Plomer (ed.), *Kilvert's Diary 1870–1879: Selections from the Diary of the Rev. Francis Kilvert* (1944).

Ian Bradley, *The Celtic Way* (1993).
Esther de Waal, *The World Made Whole* (1991).
Thomas Cahill, *How the Irish Saved Civilization* (1995).

Geoffrey Moorhouse, *Sun Dancing* (1997), is a part historical, part fictional account of the hermitage of Skellig St Michael.

J. Saward, *Perfect Fools. Folly for Christ's Sake in Catholic and Orthodox Spirituality* (1980).

CHAPTER 7   *'. . . going forth well-armed . . .'*

The chapter title comes from the Rule of St Benedict, quoted more fully in the text.

Annabel Davis-Goff, *Walled Gardens: Scenes from an Anglo-Irish Childhood* (1989), describes among other things the author's search for the cave in which her regicide ancestor was concealed.

Lobsang Jivaka, *Life of Milarepa* (1962).

Among the many books on medieval hermits, the following are important:

Henrietta Leyser, *Hermits and the New Monasticism* (1984).
Sir Samuel Dill, *Roman Society in Gaul in the Merovingian Age* (1926).
W. J. Sheils (ed.), *Monks, Hermits and the Ascetic Tradition* (1985).
C. H. Lawrence, *Medieval Monasticism* (1984).
Roberta Gilchrist, *Contemplation and Action: the Other Monasticism* (1995).
Fiona Maddocks, *Hildegard of Bingen* (2001).

CHAPTER 8 '*. . . no beast but one kat . . .*'

The chapter title comes from *The Ancrene Riwle* (Anon. c.1200–25).

R. M. Clay, *The Hermits and Anchorites of England* (1904).
Francis Darwin, *The English Mediaeval Recluse* (1944).
Georges Duby, *Women of the Twelfth Century. Vol. 3: Eve and the Church* (1988).

M. Mayr-Harting, 'Functions of a Twelfth-century Recluse', *Bulletin of Historical Literature* (1975).

The article by Richard Cobb appeared in *The Times Literary Supplement* in December 1981.

CHAPTER 9 '*I could be bounded in a nutshell . . .*'

The chapter title is from Shakespeare's *Hamlet*.

The following are available in modern translations from Penguin Classics:
Julian of Norwich, *Revelations of Divine Love*.
Richard Rolle, *The Fire of Love*.
The Cloud of Unknowing and other works.
Walter Hilton, *The Ladder of Perfection*.

I have quoted from Lyndall Gordon, *Eliot's Early Years* (1977) and from Helen Gardner's *The Composition of the Four Quartets* (1978). Richard Wilson's article, 'Shakespeare and the Jesuits' appeared in *The Times Literary Supplement* in December 1997.

CHAPTER 10 '*. . . most attacked by voices of temptation . . .*'

The chapter title is from T. S. Eliot's 'Four Quartets'.
On William Cowper: David Cecil, *The Stricken Deer* (1929).

Mario Praz, *The Romantic Agony* (1933).

Flaubert's *The Temptation of St. Anthony*, trans. Kitty Mrosovsky (1980), is available as a Penguin Classic. Its effect on artists is elucidated in Jean Seznec, 'The Temptation of Saint Anthony in Art', *Magazine of Art*, vol. XL (1947) and Theodore Reff, 'Cezanne, Flaubert, Saint Anthony and the Queen of Sheba', *Art Bulletin*, vol. XLIV (1962).

J. K. Huysman, *A rebours* (1884), English trans., *Against Nature* (1959).

Ivor Gurney, *The Spring of Beauty* (1922).

CHAPTER 11   *''Tis ROUSSEAU, let thy bosom speak the rest . . .'*

The chapter title is from an inscription by Sir Brooke Boothby for a statue of Rousseau in the Harcourts' garden; it is quoted in Mavis Batey's excellent *Jane Austin and the English Landscape* (1996).

Also useful were:
Barbara Jones, *Follies and Grottoes* (1953).
Eileen Harris, 'Hunting for Hermits', *Country Life* (May 1988).
Michael I. Wilson: *William Kent* (1984).

The quotations from the Somersets about the root house at Badminton come from the Badminton archives and are quoted by permission of the Duke of Beaufort and his archivist, Mrs Margaret Richards.

Gilbert White, *Invitation to Selborne* (1788).

Marjorie Hope Nicolson, *Mountain Gloom and Mountain Glory* (1959).
Malcolm Andrews, *The Search for the Picturesque Landscape* (1989).
M. W. Thompson (ed.), *The Journeys of Sir Richard Colt Hoare* (1983).

Boyd Alexander (ed. and trans.), *Life at Fonthill 1807–1822, from the Correspondence of William Beckford* (1957).
Lewis Melville, *The Life and Letters of William Beckford* (1910).

CHAPTER 12 *'The louder and more tumultuous our hearts . . .'*

The chapter title is from Chateaubriand's novel *René*.
George Painter, *Chateaubriand*, vol. 1 (1977).

Paul Gittings and Jo Manton, *Dorothy Wordsworth* (1985).

David Cecil, *Visionary and Dreamer* (1969) – on Samuel Palmer.

Belinda Humphrey (ed.), *Recollections of the Powys Brothers* (1980).

CHAPTER 13 *'In Wildness is the preservation of the world . . .'*

The chapter heading is from Henry David Thoreau.

Carlos Baker, *Emerson Among the Eccentrics* (1996).

H. D. Thoreau, *Walden* (1854); *In the Maine Woods* (1892).

Frederick Turner, *John Muir* (1997).

CHAPTER 14 *'I stood amazed . . .'*

The chapter title comes from George Herbert's poem *The Holdfast*.
"'But to have nought is ours, not to confess/That we have nought.' I
stood amazed at this."

A. M. Allchin (ed.), *Solitude and Communion: Papers on the Hermit
Life* (1977).

Eve Baker, *Paths in Solitude* (1995). The author is Correspondent for
the Fellowship of Solitaries, founded in 1990.

CHAPTER 15 *'. . . a wish not to be seen . . .'*

The chapter title comes from V. S. Naipaul's speculations about the
character of the recluse in his novel *The Enigma of Arrival* (1987),
which is quoted in the text.

James Phelan, *Howard Hughes, The Hidden Years* (1977).

Cecil Beaton's diaries: 1955–1963 *The Restless Years* (1976).
Rachel Lichtenstein and Iain Sinclair, *Rodinsky's Room* (1999).
John Timpson: *English Eccentrics* (1991)
Patrick Wright, 'Rodinsky's Palace', *London Review of Books*, 24
October 1987.

CHAPTER 16 *'I think I need this hill . . .'*

The chapter title comes from Thomas Merton's diaries, in a passage quoted more fully in the text.

Patrick Hart and Jonathan Montaldo (eds), *The Intimate Merton, His Life from His Journals* (2000).

Thomas Merton: *Zen and the Birds of Appetite* (1968).

Rilke's *Duino Elegies* (1923) can be found in various translations, including Stephen Mitchell's translation in *The Collected Poetry of Rainer Maria Rilke* (1980).

Thomas Traherne, *Centuries, Poems and Thanksgivings*, ed. H. M. Margoliouth (1958).

Various articles on the Traherne discoveries have appeared in *The Times Literary Supplement*.

Gilbert White, *The Natural History of Selborne* (1788).

Richard Jefferies, *The Story of My Heart* (1883).

INDEX